The Anchor Course
Exploring Christianity Together

Tom Goodman

© 2006
Tom Goodman
All rights reserved

Unless otherwise noted, Scripture quotations are from the Holy Bible, *New International Version*, copyright © 1973, 1978, 1984 by International Bible Society. Scriptures marked (CEV) are from the *Contemporary English Version*, copyright © 1995 by American Bible Society. Scriptures marked (NLT) are from the Holy Bible. *New Living Translation*, copyright © 1996 by Tyndale Charitable Trust. Scriptures marked NASB are from the *New American Standard Bible* Copyright © 1960, 1962, 1963, 1968, 1971, 1972, 1973, 1975, 1977, 1995 by The Lockman Foundation. Scriptures marked (LB) are from *The Living Bible*, copyright © 1979 by Tyndale House Publishers. Scriptures marked (Msg) are from *The Message* Copyright © 1993, 1994, 1995, 1996, 2000, 2001, 2002 by Eugene H. Peterson. Scriptures marked (NCV) are from the Holy Bible, *New Century Version*, copyright © 1991 by Word Bibles. Scriptures marked (TEV) are from *Today's English Version* (also called *Good News Translation*), copyright © 1992 from the American Bible Society. Scriptures marked (NKJV) are from the Holy Bible, *New King James Version*, copyright © 1982 by Thomas Nelson, Inc. Scriptures marked (Phillips) are from the *New Testament in Modern English* by J.B. Phillips, copyright © 1958 by Macmillan. Scriptures marked (HCSB) are from the *Holman Christian Standard Bible*, copyright © 1999, 2000, 2002, 2003 by Holman Bible Publishers. Scriptures marked (ESV) are from the Holy Bible, *English Standard Version*, copyright © 2001 by Crossway Bibles.

Library of Congress Control Number: 2006906541

ISBN: 978-1-84728-143-2

Printed in the United States of America

Contents

Introduction i

Part One: I Believe

The Benefits of Believing 3
The Barriers to Believing 13
Trust the Bible 21
Use the Bible 31

Part Two: I Believe in God

Don't Ignore the Evidence for God 43
Clear Up Your Misunderstandings of God 51

Part Three: I Believe in Jesus

Jesus is Everything It Means to Be God 61
What If God Was One of Us? 69
What Does the Resurrection Prove? 77
The Return of the King 87

Part Four: I Believe in the Holy Spirit

The Hound of Heaven 99
You Can Live Strong 107
Great is the Mystery of Our Faith 113

Part Five: I Believe in the Church

Don't Go It Alone 123
Lost in Translation 133
Life Together 143

Part Six: I Believe in Forgiveness

Beauty and the Beast 155
Why the Cross Matters 165
God Can 175

Part Seven: I Believe in Eternal Life

Waiting for Reveille 185
What Is Heaven Like? 195
You Don't Have to Go 205

Part Eight: Amen

The "Ready Aim-Aim-Aim-Aim Syndrome 215
Alrightokuhuhamen 225
Your Mount Everest 235

Discussion Questions 247
Use these questions in a small-group study

For Further Reading 255
Appreciation 259
Notes 261

www.anchorcourse.org

Introduction

He was friendly, but blunt. "My friend gave me this because I was asking him a lot of questions about Jesus," he said, holding up a copy of the Gospel of John. "You expect a lot when the first thing I'm supposed to believe is that Jesus turned water into wine."

That was my introduction to Terry, a Canadian businessman with a practical mind who had begun to explore the Christian faith. He was referring to a Bible story of Jesus transforming pots of water into wine at a first-century wedding feast.

Terry and I began to meet at his house, along with his wife, Susan, and a few others who wanted to understand what Christ-followers believed. One evening a week, we would sit in his family room or around the magnificent kitchen table he had built, and we would discuss my Christian faith. As the weekly meetings progressed, clearly what the group was looking for was more than the *rationale* for the things I believed; they wanted the *relevance*. Fifteen proofs that the resurrection really happened, for example, wouldn't be enough. The "so what" question had to be answered: what difference did my belief in the resurrection make in my life?

Terry and Susan became believers through those evening chats, and even though we no longer live in the same community, we still keep up with each other.

The book you're holding is the result of my conversations with Terry's family and friends. I'm hoping that those who believe and those who are still spiritual explorers will benefit from my thoughts. More than that, this book was designed to bring believers and explorers *together* for the kind of conversations that took place at Terry's house.

Better Together

In her time, she was popular culture's most famous atheist. Life magazine once called her the most hated woman in America, and she seemed to relish the regard. Yet a poignant plea interrupted the diary entries of Madalyn Murray O'Hair:

> "Somebody,
> somewhere,
> love me."

Behind her public hostility to anything related to religion was a thirsty soul. In her diary, she privately longed for a real connection to someone. She wanted to be appreciated, cherished, and understood—in a word, *loved*.

Too bad that most of the believers she mocked easily confirmed her hostile prejudices. The angry faces and protest signs that met her at public appearances and the hate mail she received at home did nothing to change her mind about those who embraced the faith she ridiculed.

Thankfully, the chasm between those who are curious about Christ and those who believe in him is rarely so wide. Among those who have not expressed a commitment to Christ, very few would identify with either the atheism or the antagonism of O'Hair. And, unlike the Christians O'Hair encountered, few Christ-followers have ever acted so rudely to those who don't embrace the faith.

But the alternative too many believers and seekers have chosen isn't helpful either. In many cases, those who believe in Christ and those who are curious about him have chosen to simply coexist. In our office break rooms and at our family reunions and on the sidelines of our kids' soccer games we do nothing more with each other than share space. We chat—if we talk at all—about the newspaper headlines or the progress of our college team or the prospects for a break in the weather we're having. It's as if we're afraid to let our conversation cross into the territory of belief. Some of us are fearful that the peaceful coexistence would come to an end if people of faith actually talked about what they believed or if explorers asked honest questions about why anyone would believe that.

As a result of this concern, most believers and spiritual explorers make assumptions *about* each other instead of having conversations *with* each other. This book is written so that the kind of conversations I had at Terry's house can happen in your world, too. I want this book to kindle conversations between seekers who want to *explore* the Christian faith and believers who want to *explain* it. Even if you found this book while browsing alone in a bookstore or a library, I hope you won't read it alone. It's designed to bring together those who are curious about Christ and those who believe in him.

The Basics

A conversation about the Christian faith needs to cover some basic convictions. We need to talk together about what Christ-followers believe about God and his relationship to us. We need to talk about the life and death and resurrection and return of Jesus. We need to talk about Christ's vision for his church, especially since believers have been so imperfect at making that vision a reality. We need to talk about heaven and hell. We need to talk about the meaning of the cross, which stands as the most recognizable symbol of the Christian faith.

To cover all these bases, this book is organized around an ancient statement of faith recited by millions around the world and down through the centuries. It's known as the Apostles' Creed. The words transcend denominational differences and cultural distinctions to summarize what believers have always embraced:

> *I believe in God the Father Almighty,*
> *Maker of heaven and earth;*
> *And in Jesus Christ his only Son our Lord;*
> *who was conceived by the Holy Spirit,*
> *born of the Virgin Mary,*
> *suffered under Pontius Pilate,*
> *was crucified, dead, and buried.*
> *The third day he rose again from the dead.*
> *He ascended into heaven,*
> *and sits at the right hand of God the Father Almighty.*
> *From there he shall come to judge the living and the dead.*
> *I believe in the Holy Spirit;*
> *the one holy church;*[1]
> *the communion of saints;*
> *the forgiveness of sins;*
> *the resurrection of the body;*
> *and the life everlasting.*
> *Amen.*

Here we have a summary of what was taught by those Christ chose as his apostles. In fact, this is why it is called the *Apostles' Creed*. They did not write it, despite the old legend that the Apostles each contributed a point. Few ever took that legend seriously; instead, the Creed dates back to at least the early third century and it was used as a confession that new believers recited before baptism. So, we call it the Apostles' Creed because it summarizes what we find in the Apostles' writings—the Bible. Every line in the Creed is either an echo or an actual quote of Scripture.

According to the Bible, one of the characteristics of the first believers was that "they devoted themselves to the apostles' teaching" (Acts 2:42). So, the best way to discuss Christian faith with each other is to organize it around what the apostles taught. In this book, the points of the Creed will serve as touchstones for conversations over the basics of what Christ-followers believe. We'll cover eight topics in the order that we find them in the ancient Creed:

- **"I Believe"**—We'll look at the benefits and the barriers to belief, and the role the Bible plays in Christian faith.
- **"I Believe in God"**—We'll look at the evidence for God and the three most important things to know about who he is.
- **"I Believe in Jesus"**—We'll look at the claims Jesus made about himself and his promise to return.
- **"I Believe in the Holy Spirit"**—We'll look at the active role God plays in our world today.
- **"I Believe in the Church"**—We'll look at Christ's vision for the gathering of believers he called his church. Neither our spiritual search nor our spiritual growth should take place on our own.
- **"I Believe in the Forgiveness of Sins"**—We'll look at the way our sins have separated us from God, and we'll look at how God commissioned the death of Jesus on the cross to remove the record of our sins.
- **"I Believe in Eternal Life"**—We'll look at what Christ-followers believe about the resurrection, heaven and hell.
- **"Amen"**—The word "amen" is a Hebrew word that means, "it is so . . . this is true . . . I buy that." We'll look at the things that make people hesitate at the edge of Christian commitment, and the steps you need to take when you're ready to cross the line into faith.

We'll devote a few chapters to each of these topics. If you decide to use this book to discuss the Christian faith with others, I've provided some discussion questions at the end of the book.

Making Me

The late singer-songwriter, Rich Mullins, set the Apostles Creed to music in his award-winning song, *Creed*. He occasionally broke into the flow of the ancient lines to sing, "I did not make it . . . it is making me."[2]

I like that line. In the end, this book is about what makes us. Whether we're committed to Christ or just curious about him, we all operate out of a set of assumptions about the way the world is, such as:

> "If I do good things, then good things will happen to me."
> "The only person you can count on is yourself."
> "Life is a dressing room for eternity."
> "God likes me."
> "God hates me."

We make our decisions and respond to circumstances out of the assumptions we hold. As Mullins sang, what we believe makes us what we are. This book, and your conversations with others about this book, will give you a chance to examine the beliefs that drive your life.

Now, I confess I'm not neutral in my hopes of where such an inspection will lead you, whether you are a believer or a spiritual explorer. If you are exploring Christianity, I hope your experience with this book will help you trade in your way of looking at the world for the way Jesus looked at things. On the other hand, if you are already committed to Christ, I hope your time in this book will help you operate more consistently out of the beliefs you hold. I have yet to meet a believer who was a "finished product." Mullins said the Creed was *making* him, and that implies a work still underway. Even as believers, we need reminders of the freedom of living in God's grace, the power of living by God's Spirit, the encouragement of living with God's people, and the hope of living for God's eternal kingdom.

In short, God isn't finished with any of us yet—whether we are believers or spiritual explorers. I hope this book will be part of *beginning* or *building* a relationship with God.

Be sure to check out my website at www.anchorcourse.org. There you will find more information about *The Anchor Course*, as well as additional articles and links for further study of the topics covered in this book.

Part One: "I Believe"

*I believe
in God the Father Almighty,
Maker of heaven and earth;
And in Jesus Christ his only Son our Lord;
who was conceived by the Holy Spirit,
born of the Virgin Mary,
suffered under Pontius Pilate,
was crucified, dead, and buried.
The third day he rose again from the dead.
He ascended into heaven,
and sits at the right hand of God the Father Almighty.
From there he shall come
to judge the living and the dead.
I believe in the Holy Spirit;
the one holy church;
the communion of saints;
the forgiveness of sins;
the resurrection of the body;
and the life everlasting.
Amen.*

Chapter 1
The Benefits of Believing

"I'm the sort of character who's got to have an anchor.
I want to be around immovable objects."
Bono, in response to a question about his Christian faith[1]

"We take hold of the hope offered to us. . . .
We have this hope as
an anchor for the soul,
firm and secure."
Hebrews 6:18-19

In Judith Guest's novel *Ordinary People*, Calvin Jarrett is a middle-aged attorney going through mid-life crisis. Unsure of who he's supposed to be and what he really wants out of life, he listens carefully whenever he overhears someone say, "I'm the kind of man who—" and they fill in that blank to describe themselves. At parties, in bars, or in casual conversation, the phrase always catches his attention because he hopes to hear some wisdom he can apply to himself. Finally he admits to himself, "I'm the kind of man who—hasn't the least idea what kind of man I am."[2]

Calvin Jarrett was looking for a way to define himself. That's what *The Anchor Course* is all about. Defining who we are starts by clarifying what we believe. That's why the most revolutionary words you can say are the first two words of the Apostles' Creed, "I believe." That's a translation of the Latin word *credo*, from which we get our English word "creed." It means, "I put my trust in this, I let these things shape the way I deal with life."

With the lines of the Creed, believers continue to recite the things that define them: "I believe in God the Father Almighty. I believe in Jesus. I believe in the Holy Spirit. I believe in the church. I believe in the forgiveness of sins. I believe in the life everlasting."

How does someone get to the point that she can say, *"Credo*, I believe these things, my life is defined by these convictions"? You begin to consider a search for something to believe only when the motivation is strong enough. What are the advantages to Christian belief?

You Can Find Meaning for Your Life

After the Thanksgiving meal, my wife and her mother and sister often spread out a thousand pieces of a jigsaw puzzle on a tabletop and talk as they put the pieces together. I can't be persuaded to join them in this challenge, but I've occasionally looked over their shoulder on my way to the kitchen for another slice of pie. Of course, most of the effort in putting together jigsaw puzzles involves trying to find the pieces in the pile that fit the gaps in the incomplete picture. Often four or five pieces will be held up to a gap before the correct piece is found.

It's true when trying to find meaning, too. Life remains an unsolved puzzle until we enter into a relationship with God as Jesus revealed him, but first we'll often hold up several incorrect puzzle pieces to the God-shaped gap. We'll try to fill the gap with personal *accomplishments*, public *recognition*, physical *pleasure*, or even inspiring *sacrifice*. Over time, however, we find out that the various options simply cannot satisfy for long. The sense of fulfillment from these things fades, and once again we become aware of the gap in our unsolved puzzle.

Sometimes we are slow to recognize this. We know that our accomplishments, recognition, pleasure or sacrifice has failed to satisfy us so far, but we assume that it's simply because we haven't experienced enough of them. That's why we need to listen carefully to those who have reached a phenomenal level in these things as they call back to the rest of us, saying, "This puzzle piece doesn't fit the gap!"

For example, there's Thom Yorke, frontman of the band Radiohead, who once explained why he was still in the recording studio after earning more money than he would ever need: "It's filling the hole. That's all anyone does." When asked if it was filling the hole in his life, he replied, "It's still there." Lee Iaccoca said the same thing. In his autobiography, the business titan said, "Here I am in the twilight years of my life, still wondering what it's all about. I can tell you this, fame and fortune is for the birds." Bob Geldof raised millions of dollars for famine relief in his worldwide effort known as Live Aid, but found the fulfillment fleeting. In the end he considered it nothing more than a rocket that briefly lit the sky and faded. In fact, his autobiography is entitled, *Is That It?* "I am unfulfilled as a human being," he said in an interview. Then, thumping his chest he continued, "Otherwise, why are these large holes here?" [3]

We hear the same world-weary sigh in a long poem in the Bible called *Ecclesiastes*. The poet simply identified himself as "the Teacher," but the popular conclusion is that the poet is Solomon, the ancient Jewish king famous for his astonishing wealth, insightful wisdom, impressive national projects, and multi-cultural harem. We don't have to wait long to hear his conclusion from all of these things: "Meaningless, meaningless!" he says right at the start, "Everything is meaningless" (Ecclesiastes 1:2).

He then proceeds to chronicle all that failed to fill the gap in his puzzle:

> *Wisdom*: "I worked hard to distinguish wisdom from foolishness. But now I realize that even this was like chasing the wind. . . . I saw that wise and foolish people share the same fate. Both of them die. Just as the fool will die, so will I. So of what value is all my wisdom? Then I said to myself, 'This is all so meaningless!' (1:17; 2:13-15 NLT)

Pleasure: "I said to myself, 'Come now, let's give pleasure a try. Let's look for the 'good things' in life.' But I found that this, too, was meaningless. 'It is silly to be laughing all the time,' I said. 'What good does it do to seek only pleasure?'" (2:1-2 NLT)

Accomplishments: "I also tried to find meaning by building huge homes for myself and by planting beautiful vineyards. I made gardens and parks, filling them with all kinds of fruit trees. I built reservoirs to collect the water to irrigate my many flourishing groves. . . . I collected great sums of silver and gold, the treasure of many kings and provinces. . . . I had everything a man could desire! So I became greater than any of the kings who ruled in Jerusalem before me. . . . I even found great pleasure in hard work, an additional reward for all my labors. But as I looked at everything I had worked so hard to accomplish, it was all so meaningless. It was like chasing the wind. There was nothing really worthwhile anywhere." (2:4-11 NLT)

Wealth: "Those who love money will never have enough. How absurd to think that wealth brings true happiness!" (5:10 NLT)

His entire poem describes the futility in his efforts to find meaning. While many people simply find the poem depressing, what would *really* be depressing is to dismiss his observations and then spend half a century or more in pursuit of these very things only to come to the same conclusion!

The key to understanding this sobering poem is in a little phrase that shows up twenty-seven times. Over and over again, Solomon speaks of the futility of everything "under the sun." That phrase refers to things that are confined to the relatively few years of earthly life. Solomon's poem is meant to clear the table of all the things that cannot ultimately satisfy so that we will finally consider the option that is outside of life as we know it: a relationship with God. This solution to the meaning of life is "above the sun," so to speak, and, like Solomon, I believe it's the only thing that fits the gap in our unfinished puzzle.

You Will Find Someone to Thank

Whenever I lead small-group studies for seekers, as I talk about the need to find a way to fill the gap in life's unfinished puzzle, most people nod in solemn agreement. For many in attendance, life has become frustrating without knowing what it's all for. But I vividly remember one young woman in one of my study groups. As others shared their desire to find something that would give meaning to life, she said, "I have a different reason to be part of this study. I just had a baby and my life is filled with so much joy. I want to know who to thank."

> *"I just had a baby and my life is filled with so much joy. I want to know who to thank."*

What a profound statement! This young woman recognized that much of the wonder and joy in her life could not be attributed to anything she had earned. Perhaps for the first time in her life, she felt an overwhelming sense of what could only be described as *gratitude*, and for her that implied a Giver. It led her on a search for someone to thank.

We can be like pigs that came upon apples on the ground: we can enjoy the sweet things of life without ever looking up to see where they came from. That is, too many of us react to the good things that happen to us with a sense of entitlement instead of a sense of wonder and humble gratitude.

It's true that a lot of people experience unfair pain and disappointment, and later in the book we'll look at how believers reconcile that with Jesus' teaching that God is both good and great. But we are not looking at *all* the facts if we simply point to the undeserved heartbreaks of life and conclude that an attentive God doesn't exist. We have to take into account the undeserved joys of life, too. When we do, like the young woman with her new baby, we will ask, "I want to know if there's someone to thank for all this."

David, the beloved poet-king of the Old Testament, had someone to thank. In one of his poems, overwhelmed with a sense of wonder and gratitude, he said to himself,

> "Bless the Lord, O my soul,
> And forget none of His benefits."
> (Psalms 103:2 NASB)

You Can Make Sense of the World

I'm sure you've read the conclusions of those who try to understand the world without the benefit of belief. For example, as of this writing William Provine of Cornell University does not believe that a personal God created the world and is guiding human history forward toward a purposeful conclusion. He has spoken at many college campuses across the U.S., often flashing the following list on an overhead projector to hammer home his understanding of a world that came about by chance: "No life after death; no ultimate foundation for ethics; no ultimate meaning for life; no free will."[4]

He's not the only one who has laid out such stark but obvious conclusions from unbelief. The Nobel-winning physicist Steven Weinberg said, "The more the universe seems comprehensible, the more it also seems pointless."[5] Jacques Monod said, "Man at last knows that he is alone in the unfeeling immensity of the universe, out of which he emerged only by chance."[6] Here in the twenty-first century, many around us seem to be returning to the view of life held by the ancient pagans of northern Europe. The Nordic tribes had huge meeting halls with doors on either end, and they viewed life much like a bird that would chance to pass through the meeting hall: from darkness we dart briefly into light and warmth, only to flutter out the other side into inky blackness once again.

Of course, several who teach such things still maintain that our lives have worth and meaning. But the effort reminds me of a scene from, of all things, a Teenage Mutant Ninja Turtles movie. When my boys were little, I rented *The Secret of the Ooze*, and we watched the Ninja Turtles discover the truth about their origin.

A scientist tells them that their existence came about through a chance encounter with some radioactive ooze that had been illegally dumped in the sewer. Before, the turtles had been common house pets, but when they were washed down the drain into the same sewer where the ooze had been disposed, they mutated into wise-cracking teenage Ninja Turtles. They found out they were simply the result of chance. Sound familiar?

Moments after the turtles hear the story, Splinter, the Zen Master who serves as the mentor for the turtles, notices Donatelo, one of the four turtles. He's off in a corner with his head down:

> Splinter: "What troubles you, my son?"
>
> Donatelo: "I just always thought there'd be more to it. To the ooze. To . . . you know . . . us. I always thought there'd be something that—I thought we'd find out we were special."
>
> Splinter: "Do not confuse the specter of your origin with your present worth, my sons."
>
> Donatelo: "I don't believe [the scientist]! There's just got to be more to it!"
>
> Splinter: "Perhaps the search for a beginning rarely has so easy an end."

Donatelo represents a lot of people who are troubled by a scientist's news that their existence is not, in fact, "special," and frankly the wise mentor's reassurances ring hollow. "People need purpose," a student said in a newspaper article about the rising religious interest on college campuses. "Nobody just wants to be on a piece of rock without a reason to be there."[7]

Christian belief helps us make sense of our world. We can "read" the experiences of life with greater clarity when we see them through the "eyeglasses" of the Bible's teaching on things like . . .

... the creation of the universe
... the creation of people in God's very image
... the impact of human rebellion on creation
... the attentive Fatherhood of God
... the loving sacrifice of Christ
... the convicting presence of God's Spirit
... Christ's promise to return to set everything right
... a time of ultimate judgment over every action

The Bible presents human history as an epic adventure, and you and I have our own roles to play in this story. As we will see throughout this book, Christian convictions have huge implications for how we understand ourselves and our place in the world.

You Can Make the Right Choices

Christian belief brings us into a kingdom with a King we want to please, and that gives us a frame of reference for deciding what is right and wrong.

Lee Strobel, former legal editor for the *Chicago Tribune*, is the author of the bestselling book, *The Case for Christ*. Reflecting on what life was like before he came to Christian belief, he now acknowledges that he had a simple reason to stay in atheism: It gave him a reason to ignore certain things in his life that really needed to be fixed. It was necessary for him that God *not* exist so that Strobel didn't have to think too much about things like his heavy drinking and the way he was treating his colleagues or his wife.

Of course, I have friends who live decent lives without any commitment to Christian belief. They keep their marriage vows, stick to their commitments, treat others with tolerance instead of prejudice, and give to charities.

The question is *why*.

Now, stay with me here: I'm not saying that unbelief always inevitably leads to immoral living. Instead, I'm asking for the *rea-*

son behind moral choices. Without the framework that belief provides, is there a *reason* to say that one way of life is "better" than another?

For example, many of us have been deeply inspired by J. Robertson McQuilkin's periodic articles across the last twenty years about his experiences with a wife affected by Alzheimer's disease. But take his difficult choice to *stay* with his wife and contrast it with a man who sat in my office explaining why he was *abandoning* his stroke-afflicted wife for a woman who could meet his personal needs. If we have been cast up from natural evolutionary forces for a few years of material existence before becoming decaying compost six feet under, what compelling reason did I have to tell him that his choice was objectively, inherently wrong and Dr. McQuilkin's choice was right?

Sure, if we act in ways that people consider honorable it makes us feel good, and nice things are said about us at our funeral. But what happens when the things we do don't make us "feel good" anymore, or when we begin to circulate with people who have a different idea of what is right than the people we used to know? Does our definition of what is right change, and would it matter if it did?

By contrast, believers are convinced that we live in the presence of a King we were created to please. That conviction gives us a framework to decide which choices are "better" than others.

The Right Start

The most significant words in the Creed are the words, "I believe," and this book is about getting to the point that those words are your own. As believers have come to that conclusion, we have found meaning for our lives, we have found someone to thank for life's undeserved joys, we have found a way to make sense of the world, and we have found a reason to make the right moral choices.

Chapter 2
The Barriers to Believing

In the last chapter, we looked at the benefits of believing, but to get to the point that you can say, "I believe," these benefits are not the only factors to consider. As you read through the explanation of Christian faith found in this book, be aware of the barriers to belief that may keep you from a thorough and fair consideration of Christianity.

You May Have Unanswered Questions

In the blockbuster, *The Passion of the Christ*, Mel Gibson presented Jesus as believers understand him. He was human and yet somehow more than *simply* human. He was treated horribly and yet claimed that his personal suffering and death would make the world new. He died from his tortures and yet rose up from the dead. The film provoked many questions from viewers. Why do Christians claim that Jesus was the divine Son of God? Why do Christians say that the horrible suffering and death of this man was what it took for God to forgive our sin? How can any reasonable person believe that a dead man returned to life and walked out of his tomb? Are the biblical passages where we find these claims reliable? Whether people raise these questions after watching a film or while discussing faith with a believing friend, people want reasonable answers as they think seriously about the Christian faith.

A couple of missionaries from a cult knocked on my door, and we talked about their beliefs. They gave me their book and urged me to read it and then simply look for "a warm feeling in my heart" as proof that the book was true. This was no answer for me—that I should let my feelings dictate the whole consideration of their faith claims.

Neither Jesus nor those he appointed to teach ever urged people to suspend all questions, put their minds away, and simply look to their hearts to know the truth. Instead, they said, "Test everything that is said to be sure it is true, and if it is, then accept it" (1 Thessalonians 5:21 LB). I like that Bible verse because it tells me to test every claim to truth. I shouldn't believe something simply because a friend or a persuasive leader tells me it is so. Every claim to truth should be tested.

I also like that verse because it tells me that if we find something to be true, we must accept it. Some fail the challenge from the first half of that verse: they don't test anything. Others fail the challenge from the second half of that verse: they don't accept the truth. Either they reject what they are asked to test without further thought, or they become the eternal seekers—always studying but never concluding, always traveling but never arriving, always gathering facts but too timid to render a verdict. This verse says we have to come to a point where we act on what we've discovered. Ultimately, not to decide is a decision itself.

You May Have Unrealistic Expectations

As I've talked with people about faith, I've found that some people want all their questions answered before they will believe. While it is right to want answers to your questions, there is a difference between having *all* questions settled and having *enough* questions settled. A jury, for example, is expected to determine whether a murder suspect is guilty, not why the suspect chose one weapon instead of another. Scientists adopt and defend theories based upon how well the ideas answer key questions, not based upon how well they answer *every* question.

Someone considering the Christian claims should ask at least three essential questions: Is the Bible a reliable source for finding truth? Does the biblical teaching do a good job of explaining why life is the way it is? Are the believers we know better off because of their faith? You may need a few more questions answered in addition to these, but it's unreasonable to demand that *every* question be cleared up before you can make a decision. Had I suspended my decision to marry until I could learn every detail about Diane, I would have never asked her to marry me—and I would have missed out on the joy of discovering life with her.

Another unrealistic expectation I've encountered is the anticipation of a problem-free life. Often people want something that will immediately make all their problems go away. They start to consider the Christian faith because life is no longer working. They are struggling with addiction, they're in trouble with the law, they're frustrated with a rebellious teenager, they're worried about a doctor's prognosis, or they're heartbroken over the condition of their marriage. Such situations lead many to ask questions of a spiritual nature. For some, that examination leads to faith. For others, if their crisis isn't resolved in the way they wanted, they abandon all consideration of the Christian faith.

Such an unreasonable expectation fails to take seriously what the Bible says about life after the ancient "Fall." The opening chapters of the Bible tell us that God placed Adam and Eve in a perfect world but their rebellion against him changed the way humans have had to experience earthly life.

In Chapter 10, we'll examine God's promise to restore his creation to the perfect state he intended. But until God's promise is fulfilled, Jesus never assured us that following him would make us immune from problems that have come from the Fall. Like everyone else, believers still experience injustice from *fallen people*, the pain of a *fallen natural world*, and consequences from the bad choices of our *fallen selves*. But believers know God will sustain them and grow their character even as they deal with these things.

Unfortunately, some people don't see their fallen selves as a problem, and this leads to yet another unrealistic expectation: that faith will not have to impact behavior. People with this mindset are like the man in the following poem:

> I would like to buy $3 worth of God, please.
> Not enough to explode my soul or disturb my sleep,
> but just enough to equal a cup of warm milk
> or a snooze in the sunshine.
>
> . . .
>
> I want ecstasy not transformation;
> I want the warmth of the womb, not a new birth.
> I want about a pound of the eternal in a paper sack.
> I would like to buy $3 worth of God, please.[1]

Christianity attracts people because of its *comforting* words about God's forgiveness, its *cheering* words about God's love, and its *captivating* words about God's heaven. It's the *convicting* words about God's expectations which some don't like—especially where it impacts their own attitudes and behavior. But the Christian faith is not a cafeteria where we choose what portions we prefer and ignore the rest. That's why Jesus actually told us to count the cost of following him before deciding to do so (Luke 14:25-35). It's interesting that Jesus chose to say this at the time that huge crowds were following him. He knew that a number of those who were checking out his message had unrealistic expectations of what he would do for them and what he expected from them.

You May Have Misunderstandings

For some, their barrier to belief has no basis in reality. They have drawn conclusions about the faith based on some misunderstanding of the faith.

Sadly, sometimes these misunderstandings come from Christians themselves. For example, while it is true that God has expectations that impact our behavior, some Christians have the wrong idea of the behavior that God finds important. For example, I once lived near a church where all the men were expected to wear long-sleeved shirts. Coats or ties were optional, but no man would have dared to attend the church in short sleeves. If that was a seeker's only exposure to the faith, he might accept or reject Christianity based upon whether he was willing to wear long-sleeved shirts for the rest of his life! Some churches have expectations that simply have no basis in the Bible, and some seekers have abandoned any consideration of the faith over issues that really aren't important.

Not all misunderstandings come from Christians themselves, though. Numbers of seekers have failed to give Christianity any serious consideration because family, friends, teachers, celebrities, or other people they trust have given them faulty information about what Christians really teach. They haven't checked things out for themselves.

For example, I've read the writings of some environmentalists who keep alive the long-held myth that the abuse of natural resources all comes down to what Christians have supposedly taught about our relationship to the earth.[2] I've talked to others who believe that missionary outreach has harmed indigenous cultures around the world. One person told me she could not accept the Bible as her source for truth because it "endorses slavery." None of these things are true.

It reminds me of an incident from the life of Paul (Acts 19:23-41). Paul was one of the most influential teachers of the early church, and he traveled to many Roman cities to deliver the claims of Christ. In Ephesus, however, a silversmith named Demetrius grew concerned. He felt that Paul's message would threaten the profitable silver trade that was built around Ephesian temple practices dedicated to the goddess Artemis. He provoked a huge crowd that nearly resulted in a violent riot. The Bible says, "The people were all shouting, some one thing and some another. Everything was in confusion. In fact, most of them didn't even know why they were there" (verse 32 NLT). The mayor of Ephesus finally calmed down the crowd and dispersed them after pointing out that none of the claims being made against Paul was, in fact, true. They were on the verge of a riot against Paul based on a misunderstanding passed from person to person in that alarmed crowd.

You May Have Fears

I can think of at least three fears that keep people from considering the Christian claims.

Some fear *the loss of life*. In some Islamic cultures, for example, a conversion to Christianity is punishable by death.[3] Even when converts are not threatened with death, many have suffered persecution, loss of income, confiscation of property, or slavery. It's hard for people in modern nations to conceive of this happening, but these threats are real to millions of people. No doubt the fear of these things has kept many from daring to even ask questions about Christ.

For others, they don't fear the loss of life but *the loss of love*. Some people know that their families will cut all ties with them if they commit to Christ. Families from some religious communities even hold a funeral ceremony for a still-living son or daughter who converts to Christianity. Even if reaction isn't this extreme, the potential of a family's disapproval has hindered many people from giving serious consideration to Christian claims. This doesn't just come from religious families. Some people who were raised in homes where religion was not discussed know that their family would not understand or appreciate their interest in Christianity.

Another fear that keeps some people from Christian commitment is the possible *loss of respect* from their peers. Parents of teens worry about what "peer pressure" will lead their children into, but we never really get away from peer pressure, even in adulthood. For example, occasionally a sports commentator will question whether a particular athlete's newfound faith has taken away his "drive" to excel in the sport.[4] An athlete considering the Christian faith knows that he or she will have to deal with a persistent prejudice from a segment of the sports world. It's true in other circles, too. Those in the academic and artistic fields also know that if they commit to a biblical worldview it may cause some colleagues to question their objectivity, depth and motives.

Our fear of losing life, love, or respect may be real or exaggerated. Either way, Jesus told his followers that they would have to face down these fears if they intended to take him seriously. He said, "Don't imagine that I came to bring peace to the earth! No, I came to bring a sword" (Matthew 10:34 NLT). He was not advocating violence; he was using the image of a sword as a metaphor. A sword cuts and separates and Jesus was warning those who wanted to follow him to be prepared for heart-breaking conflict, even with those dearest to them. To those who would let their fears keep them from taking him seriously, Christ's words sound like a drill sergeant toughening his troops or a football coach at halftime bracing his team to overcome a first-half deficit. Jesus warned, "If you cling to your life, you will lose it; but if you give it up for me, you will find it" (Matthew 10:39 NLT).

You May Have Had Bad Experiences With a Church or with Christians

For some, the strongest case against a relationship with Christ is their relationship with Christians. Their only memory of attending a church is of a boring and irrelevant service. Their only experience with Christianity has been with a family member or a colleague at work who deeply disappointed them. Their only knowledge of the faith comes from news segments of church squabbles and scandals. These experiences, piled one on top of another, create a formidable barrier that blocks any consideration of belief.

In another chapter, we'll look closer at this subject of the Christians and their churches that fail to paint a good picture of the Christian life. For now, though, let me make this analogy. As I write this, my youngest son is in another part of the house practicing on his drum kit. One of his favorite musicians is Carter Beauford, the famed drummer of *The Dave Matthews Band*. My son is a good percussionist, but working out Beauford's complicated syncopated rhythms is proving to be a real challenge for him. He'll eventually get it, but it would be completely unfair for anyone to judge the quality of Beauford's drum work based on my son's ability to play it right now. In the same way, it's unfair for people to draw conclusions about Christ's teaching simply based on how well the Christians they know have practiced them. To draw any fair conclusions about Christ, one has to examine the words and life of Christ himself.

Acknowledge the Barriers to Belief

I have found few people who have thoroughly examined Christianity and rejected it. But many have rejected the faith before really examining it. They have let questions remain unanswered, they have maintained unrealistic expectations, they have held misconceptions of the faith, they have hesitated in fear of what will happen if they became interested in Christianity, or they have let disappointing relationships with Christians keep them from considering Christ himself.

As you continue to read the explanation of the Christian faith in this book, be ready to identify any barriers that are blocking you from serious consideration of Christianity.

Chapter 3
Trust the Bible

For over eighteen hundred years we Christians have recited the Apostles Creed as a brief summary of our basic beliefs. It is not, however, the *foundation* of those beliefs. It is not the Apostles' Creed but the Apostles' teaching as found in the Bible that dictates our convictions. The Apostles were eyewitnesses of Christ's deeds and words, and Jesus chose them to teach in his name.[1] The Bible, then, is a reliable resource for understanding Jesus and his precepts.

Some seekers, however, question the Bible's reliability. Maybe they have been told that the Bible as we have it was not written until long after Jesus lived, and thus many of the biblical stories are the result of legends and myths that developed in the centuries after his life.[2] Maybe they have read the claims of the Jesus Seminar, a group of fifty media-savvy panelists under the late Robert Funk who garnered widespread publicity for their doubts about the Bible as an accurate guide to understanding Jesus.[3] Maybe they have read Dan Brown's *The Da Vinci Code*, the runaway bestseller that claims to be based on alternate views of Jesus that have recently come to light in the discovery of ancient writings "suppressed" by the early church.[4] After being exposed to all these claims, some seekers aren't sure they can rely on the Bible for accurate information about who Jesus really is or what he really taught.

> *It is not the Apostles' Creed but the Apostles' teaching as found in the Bible that dictates our convictions.*

A little investigation will reveal that many of those who cast doubts on the Bible's reliability have their own axe to grind. It is not, as some claim, that they simply let the "facts" take them to their controversial conclusions. Instead, by discounting the Bible's description of Christ's life and teaching, they can re-write the accounts and thus present a version that suits them. At the end of this process, then, it's no surprise that a radical feminist scholar ends up with a radical feminist Jesus, for example, or a teacher attracted to Eastern mysticism ends up with a pantheistic Jesus.[5]

In reality, the Bible is far more reliable than these writers and teachers claim. There are five things you can trust about the Bible.

You Can Trust That Contemporaries of Jesus Wrote the New Testament

Some claim that a long time passed before views developed regarding Jesus' divinity, his virgin birth, his miracles, and his resurrection. But in fact, contemporaries of Jesus wrote the New Testament documents where these views are found. For example, the Apostle Paul began writing within twenty years after the earthly life of Jesus, and most of the New Testament is comprised of his letters.[6] Many of his letters are filled with lines from creeds and hymns used by the early church, which of course would have existed even earlier than Paul's letters. This places the fundamental statements of Christian faith at the earliest days of the church, just a few years after the earthly life of Jesus. In the fifteenth chapter of First Corinthians, Paul said (verses 3-4):

> For what I received I passed on to you as of first importance: that Christ died for our sins according to the Scriptures, that he was buried, that he was raised on the third day according to the Scriptures.

To "receive" and to "pass on" are technical terms that refer to a subject that is formally and officially passed from one teacher to another, like the baton runners pass along in a relay race. Since Paul's first letter to the Corinthian congregation was written within twenty years of Christ's earthly life, we can conclude that the formal teaching that Paul "received" and "passed on" was even earlier than that.[7] In fact, considering that Paul became a believer just two or three years after the death and resurrection of Jesus and was formally instructed in the faith at that time, what Paul says he "received" and "passed on" to the Corinthians would have been shared with him within five years after the dramatic events took place.

Again, in the second chapter of his Philippians letter, Paul was clearly quoting from a hymn or some other formal statement that would have been familiar to his readers.[8] He wanted to make the point that believers become like Christ when they humbly serve each other. So, he reminded them of what was the common teaching about Christ in the churches by quoting from a favorite worship song (verses 6-11):

> Being in very nature God,
> he did not consider equality with God
> something to be grasped,
> but made himself nothing,
> taking the very nature of a servant,
> being made in human likeness.
> And being found in appearance as a man,
> he humbled himself
> and became obedient to death—
> even death on a cross!
> Therefore God exalted him to the highest place
> and gave him the name that is above every name,
> that at the name of Jesus every knee should bow,
> in heaven and on earth and under the earth,
> and every tongue confess that Jesus Christ is Lord,
> to the glory of God the Father.

In a later chapter, we'll look at what the Bible means when describing Jesus as "in very nature God." For now, it's important to note that this wasn't a view that developed centuries after the Bible was written. Instead, it was the view of the earliest Christians.

Furthermore, the four Gospels that we find at the beginning of the New Testament were written by, or under the guidance of, the apostles themselves, who were eyewitnesses of the events the Gospels describe. After reviewing the arguments both for and against apostolic authorship, award-winning journalist Jeffery Sheler concluded, "The evidence and arguments that persist suggest that the traditional claim of the gospels to apostolic origins is a most plausible one."[9] What's more, these memoirs from the apostles circulated among the churches very early. Recent evidence dates the Gospel of Matthew, for example, as early as AD 50, less than 20 years after the life of Christ.[10]

The fact that we can read documents about Jesus' life written by his contemporaries is all the more remarkable when you consider the information we have on other ancient figures. For example, the earliest biographies on Alexander the Great were written more than four hundred years after Alexander's death, and yet historians consider them generally trustworthy.

These things were not only passed around among contemporaries of Jesus, but they were passed around *publicly*. The stories weren't passed secretly from one member to another like the lore of a reclusive society. Just days after Jesus' execution, Simon Peter publicly announced Jesus' resurrection before thousands, encouraging his listeners to recall the things they had seen and heard during the recent days of Jesus' arrest and crucifixion (Acts 2). In addition, Paul said that more than five hundred people saw the risen Christ, and then he added—"most of whom are still living" (1 Corinthians 15:6).

Why is it important to point out that the astonishing stories of Jesus' life circulated publicly among those who lived in the days of Jesus? It is because enough people were still alive who could say, "It's just the way I saw it happen" or "It didn't happen that way at all." It was as if the early Christians were inviting people to examine the stories.

The Bible preserves an accurate record of what the eyewitnesses of Jesus said about his words and actions. Their conclusions about him serve as important evidence for any seeker to consider. In fact, as we will see in a later chapter, their conclusions about Jesus are founded in what Jesus said about himself.

You Can Trust that the Bible Was Faithfully Copied

The original texts of the Bible, of course, have long succumbed to the effects of nature, and what we have today are copies. How can we be sure these versions are accurate? The vast number of early copies is one way. The more often we find copies that say the same thing, especially if they come from a wide range of geographical locations, the more confident we can be that what we read in the New Testament is what the original authors wrote. Scholars have catalogued more than five thousand Greek-language manuscripts of the New Testament.[11] One of these is a small portion of the Gospel of John dated as early as A.D. 100, putting it just a few years after the original would have been written.[12] In addition, translations of the Gospels into other languages occurred very early.

No other ancient document has so many copies dated that close to the original. Other documents that scholars routinely accept as reliable are supported by far fewer copies separated from the original by many more years than those of the Bible. Our knowledge of Homer's *Illiad*, for example, depends on less than 650 copies, and the closest to the original is separated by about a thousand years.[13]

Still, some doubt that copies could be transferred accurately in an age before photocopiers, an age where copies had to be handwritten in painstaking detail. Didn't clerical errors slip in? A few should be expected, for it was an age before eyeglasses, with scribes working in poor lighting and perhaps depending on documents with faded ink. As a result, there are what scholars call "variants" between one copy and another. But when scholars talk about variants, they are referring to misspellings of some words, or a word that turns up out of order in a sentence. In a few cases, a story that appears in some copies does not appear in other copies. However, there are no variants in the copies regarding how a biblical teaching ought to be understood. In other words, you will not find one copy claiming one thing to be the truth and another copy claiming a contradictory thing to be the truth.[14]

You Can Trust that Archaeology Verifies the Stories of the Bible

The stories don't begin with the line, "Long, long ago in a land far, far away. . . ." Instead, they are anchored to history with references to things like rulers and towns and social customs that existed at a specific point in time. Now, in the nineteenth century, liberal scholars were skeptical of the accuracy of the Bible because some of these historical references were not easily and quickly verified by archaeological research. This skepticism still shows up in religious studies at some universities. But archaeological discoveries through the twentieth century and to date have confirmed the stories of the Bible where skepticism once reigned.

For example, in John 5:2 we're given an account of Jesus healing at the Pool of Bethesda. (The Bethesda Naval Hospital in Maryland was named after this biblical story.) For a long time, some scholars doubted the reliability of John's Gospel because such a place had not been found in Jerusalem. Now that the Pool has been excavated (about forty feet below ground), that challenge to the historical reliability of John's Gospel isn't raised.[15]

Other archaeological work has also increased confidence in the Bible's references to towns and rulers and customs. Furthermore, no archaeological discovery has refuted a biblical claim.[16]

Since you can trust the Bible in terms of what an archaeological dig can validate, doesn't it stand to reason that some of the book's more remarkable claims deserve a more serious look?

You Can Trust the Consistency of the Bible

Some claim that the stories of Jesus in the four Gospels contain contradictions, and in one sense this is true. An event that appears early in one Gospel appears late in another Gospel, for example; a statement that one Gospel reports was said in one setting is reported in another setting by another Gospel; in one Gospel a man asks Jesus to come heal his servant while in another Gospel the man sends someone to make this request of Jesus.

However, these contradictions are relatively minor when compared to the biblical accounts as a whole. They even strengthen the Bible's claim to be eyewitness testimony. In a courtroom trial, for instance, it is not unusual for eyewitnesses to differ somewhat on things like sequence of events or the type of clothing someone wore. What's more, if two witnesses shared every detail in exact order, a jury could reasonably suspect that they had conspired ahead of time to make sure to get their story straight. Simon Greenleaf of Harvard Law School studied the consistency among the four Gospels and concluded:

> There is enough of a discrepancy to show that there could have been no previous concert among them; and at the same time such substantial agreement as to show that they all were independent narrators of the same great transaction.[17]

Altogether we have an accurate accounting of the earliest Christians' remembrance of Jesus' life and teaching. In fact, considering that the entire Bible was written across a span of thousands of years, by various authors in diverse settings across the Near East, it's remarkable how *consistent* we find the Bible's concept of God, the Bible's concept of what God expects from us, and the Bible's concept of the world's Savior. As we explore these concepts throughout the book, you will see this amazing consistency. This strengthens my trust in the Bible as a reliable source for truth.

You Can Trust the Selection of the Bible's Writings

It is fashionable in some circles to suggest that there were competing accounts of Jesus' life and teaching that circulated in the early church along with the stories that we find in our Bibles. The so-called "Gospel of Thomas" is a popular example. These accounts, we are told, were "suppressed" in the fourth century when the emperor Constantine convened a council of the church leadership to create the views of Jesus Christians now hold.

While it is true that some of these documents existed, they cannot be dated any earlier than 150 years after Jesus, and most have been dated more than 200 years after his life.[18] As we have already seen, this is much later than the biblical accounts. For that reason, when lists of the writings that were considered reliable started appearing in early second-century Christian documents, accounts like the Gospel of Thomas were not in these lists. These accounts were not "suppressed" by the church; they simply did not *exist* in the earliest churches. Later councils of Christian leaders did not create the Bible books but rather documented the Bible books that Christians had long relied on for their understanding of Jesus. So, later councils of church leaders did not *fabricate* the Christian view of Jesus. Rather, they *defended* it against heretical views of Jesus' nature and teaching that had cropped up long after the apostles had died.

At the end of this book, I've provided a list of books for those who want to dig deeper into the fascinating topics of the archaeological and textual integrity of the Bible as an historical document. The point is that you can trust that the books of the New Testament are reliable books of eyewitness testimony to Jesus. Jesus called the Apostle Paul to be "a witness for Him to all men of what you have seen and heard" (Acts 22:15 NASB). The Apostle Peter said, ". . . we were eyewitnesses of his majesty" (2 Peter 1:16). The Apostle John said, "What we have heard, what we have seen with our eyes, what we have looked at and touched with our hands, concerning the Word of Life . . . we proclaim to you also, so that you too may have fellowship with us" (1 John 1:1-3 NASB).

Read that last line again: *"so that you too may have fellowship with us"*—that's the reason the Bible was written. The earliest followers of Jesus wanted you and me to share in their remarkable experience with Jesus. By reading their words, we can enter into a fellowship with these people who actually walked and talked with this historical figure that has intrigued and inspired millions—Jesus of Nazareth.

Chapter 4
Use the Bible

In one of her reports for MTV, political correspondent Tabitha Soren said, "No matter how secular our culture becomes, it will remain drenched in the Bible. Since we will be haunted by the Bible even if we don't know it, doesn't it make sense to read it?"[1]

She's right. Why has the Bible made such a profound impact on our world? Believers would say it is because of the Bible's divine origin and daily usefulness. The Apostle Paul wrote (2 Timothy 3:16-17 Msg):

> Every part of Scripture is God-breathed and useful one way or another—showing us truth, exposing our rebellion, correcting our mistakes, training us to live God's way. Through the Word we are put together and shaped up for the tasks God has for us.

Did you catch how he described the Bible? He said it is both "God-breathed and useful." Christians pay attention to the Bible because it is both remarkable and practical. It is remarkable in that God inspired it; it is practical in that it is useful for daily life.

Believers Take the Bible Seriously Because We Believe it is God-breathed

Some translations refer to the Bible as "inspired," which means the same thing as the phrase "God-breathed." Today, if we call a poem or a novel "inspired," we usually mean that it has made a profound connection to our heart and mind. While this is certainly true of the Bible, the earliest Christians meant much more when they called the Bible "inspired." If I were speaking to you right now, you would be hearing Tom-breathed words: My words would be carried to you upon my exhaled breath. To refer to the Bible as "God-breathed" means that we believe it has been carried to us upon the very breath of God himself. As a result, we see it as a reliable resource for information about God.

Christians pay attention to the Bible because it is both remarkable and practical

This poetic image of God "speaking" the words of the Bible does not ignore the fact that real human beings formed the Bible. The Bible consists of sixty-six separate books written by many different writers who brought their own unique experiences, personalities and artistic styles to their writing. Clearly, the Bible writers were not like secretaries passively taking dictation from God: Luke said he wrote his Gospel after painstaking research (1:1-4); the author of the book of Ecclesiastes was described as someone who "searched to find just the right words" (12:9-10); the psalmist said he put his artistic skills to work in creating the psalms (45:1). In addition, the Bible is made up of common forms of human literature: history, poetry, legal code, proverbs, personal correspondence—even the strange visions in the book of Revelation are in common with an ancient form of writing called apocalyptic literature.

So, the *form* of biblical literature is like any other human literature. When Christians refer to God "speaking" the Bible into existence, however, it's the *nature* of the Bible that's being addressed. Although God used the background, personality, scholarship and artistic style of human writers, we believe that the end result is a Bible that accurately reveals what he wanted us to know. The Bible is the word of human authors and fully the word of God at the same time. "You received the word of God," Paul reminded the new Christians at Thessalonica, and then he added, "which you heard from us" (1 Thessalonians 2:13).

Believers today have this understanding of Scripture because Jesus—and the people Jesus chose to carry on his message—had this understanding.

Jesus regarded the Bible as authoritative. He said that the Old Testament writers spoke "under the inspiration of the Holy Spirit" (Mark 12:36 NLT). To those who questioned his instruction, he said, "Your problem is that you don't know the Scriptures" and "the Scripture cannot be broken" (Matthew 22:29 NLT; John 10:35). He made his decisions in accordance with the Bible, saying, "The Scriptures must be fulfilled" (Mark 14:49). Since Jesus had such a high view of Scripture, he did not want people to think his teaching and actions contradicted it. He said (Matthew 5:17-18 NLT):

> Don't misunderstand why I have come. I did not come to abolish the law of Moses or the writings of the prophets. No, I came to fulfill them. I assure you, until heaven and earth disappear, even the smallest detail of God's law will remain until its purpose is achieved.

In addition, as his earthly ministry came to a close, he made sure that the Bible would be completed through his apostles. Jesus told the apostles that they would be equipped to communicate his teaching with accuracy and when people accepted their message it would be the same as accepting the very words of Christ (John 14:26; Luke 10:16).

The first Christians sustained the view of Scripture they learned from Christ. The early disciples, like Jesus, regarded the Old Testament as God's Word. Its *transmission* was human but its *origin* was divine:

> They considered the first five books as both "the Law of Moses" and "the Law of the Lord" (Luke 2:22-23).
>
> They regarded the Psalms that David wrote as in fact "spoken" by God (Hebrews 3:7; 4:7).
>
> They maintained that the prophecies were from men who "spoke from God as they were carried along by the Holy Spirit" (2 Peter 1:20-21).

Also, the first Christians considered the New Testament writings as part of "the other Scriptures" (2 Peter 3:16). They "devoted themselves to the apostles' teaching" and accepted it "not as the word of men, but as it actually is, the word of God" (Acts 2:42; 1 Thessalonians 2:13).

We can learn a few things about our Creator through carefully observing the natural world, just like we can draw some conclusions about an architect by looking at the buildings he or she has designed. It's only through Scripture, however, that God has "spoken" and revealed his character, his will, and his ways to us. The first reason to pay attention to Scripture, then, is because it is God-breathed.

Believers Take the Bible Seriously Because it is Useful

When Paul described the Bible, he regarded it as not only God-breathed but also useful for "showing us truth, exposing our rebellion, correcting our mistakes, training us to live God's way." The Bible contains much practical guidance on money management, marriage, parenting, employer-employee relationships, getting along with others, victory over addictions, and many other matters of daily living.

In the film *Castaway*, Tom Hanks played the lone survivor of a FedEx jet crash marooned on a deserted island in the south Pacific. A few packages from the jet washed up on the shore with the castaway, and he opened them in hopes of finding something that would help him survive. When he came to the last package, though, he chose to keep it intact. His determination to eventually deliver that package to its owner was his thin connection to the hope of rescue. In fact, the film ended with the delivered castaway delivering that package to its recipient five years later.

During Superbowl XXXVII, FedEx ran a commercial that spoofed the movie. In the send-up, after the FedEx employee delivered the package he had protected for so long, curiosity got the best of him. "Excuse me," he asked the recipient, "what was in that package after all?"

She opened it and showed him the contents, saying, "Oh, nothing really. Just a satellite telephone, a global positioning device, a compass, a water purifier, and some seeds."

No doubt, those items would have been useful to a man stranded on a deserted island! In the same way, God has provided many practical things in the Bible, but many of us discover the value of its contents only after years of trying to make life work on our own terms. If you want to join other believers in benefiting from the Bible's practical content, there are three things you should do.

First, read it. For years, Christians south of Korea's demilitarized zone have released balloons with Bibles attached in hopes that the gifts would find their way into the hands of their northern neighbors. Likewise, members of a Christian group called the Gideons have placed Bibles in hotel rooms for guests to find. These actions reflect a confidence that by simply reading the Bible, the average reader can understand enough of it to draw some life-changing conclusions. Why not test this conviction yourself? You can purchase a modern translation from any Christian bookstore, and many churches will offer copies for free. I love the story that presidential speechwriter, Peggy Noonan, told of a friend who bought a beautiful old Bible from a quaint New England bookstore. When Noonan's friend thanked the shop owner for selling it to him at such a good price, she replied softly, "I don't sell Bibles. I find good homes for them."[2] Bring one home this week.

Once you have your own copy, how do you begin reading the Bible? Actually, the Bible is a *collection* of books, so don't think you have to treat the Bible like you would a novel and start at page one. Feel free to do that, of course, but I suggest you start with the story of Jesus by choosing one of the four "biographies" of him at the beginning of the New Testament—Matthew, Mark, Luke or John. After that, you may want to read through one of Paul's letters, such as Ephesians. You can also ask Bible-reading friends what book they like best and read it for yourself.

Most biblical books can be read in less time than it takes to watch a television program—between twenty and forty-five minutes. Even a commitment to read through the entire Bible is easier if you tackle a little bit each day. By reading an hour a day, you can complete the Bible in less than three months. Several publishers have arranged the Bible into daily readings so that a commitment of fifteen minutes a day will enable you to read the entire Bible in a year.

Another way to get familiar with the Bible is to look up the biblical references that I provide in *The Anchor Course*. The references are listed by the title of the biblical book, then the chapter, and then the verse. For example, a reference to "1 Timothy 3:16," means that you can find the text I'm referring to in the book of First Timothy, the third chapter, and the sixteenth verse. The Bible was not originally written with book titles and divisions into chapters and verses, but these were added later to make it easier to study the Bible.

Second, think about it. In order to understand the meaning of the biblical text and its potential impact on our lives, we'll have to do more than read it. "Reflect on what I am saying," Paul wrote, "for the Lord will give you insight into all of this" (2 Timothy 2:7). In other words, the God who inspired the Bible will help us understand it, but only as we engage in meditation, reflection, and study.

Those who neglect this step of careful study end up using the Bible in some strange ways. The author of one book claimed he had found a detailed diet and exercise plan in the Bible. A drilling company persuaded people to invest in their company because they said a passage in the Bible discloses an oil reserve in the Middle East. A few years ago, a popular book announced the discovery of the Bible's "code" that unlocked all kinds of startling things, including assassinations of twentieth-century world leaders by name. A little responsible study of the Bible will keep you from falling for such irresponsible claims.

The forms of biblical literature are like what we find in any other human literature, and so we can interpret them like we do any other literary forms:

- When you run across metaphors and symbols, you should interpret them as you would in any other writing. So, when we read about the "eyes" and the "arm" of the Lord, we should not insist that the Bible is telling us God is a big man—unless we're also ready to conclude that the promise that he will cover you with his "feathers" (Psalms 91:4) is the Bible's way of telling us that God is a big chicken!

- On the other hand, what the Bible presents as eyewitness history should be judged as the testimony of eyewitnesses and not interpreted as allegory.

- When you read a biblical proverb, you should understand that it is stating what is "generally" true, just as modern proverbs are "generally" true. I mean, does anyone think that our so-called "Murphy's Law" proverbs apply in absolutely every case? Does the toast *always* fall butter-side down?

- Context is important when trying to understand any writing, including Scripture. People misuse the Bible when they yank individual verses out of their textual and cultural setting.

In addition to reflecting on the Bible on your own, many of us have found it helpful to study Scripture by joining Bible studies in our community or a local church. We can also benefit from listening to sermons and reading commentaries. "As iron sharpens iron," according to a biblical proverb, "so people can improve each other" (Proverbs 27:17 NCV). Find a group of people who can hone your understanding of Scripture.

Third, live it. As important as it is to read the Bible and think about it, we profit from the Bible's practical content only by putting it into practice.

It's interesting to read about people who have put their favorite books into practice. After reading *The Vikings*, Elizabeth Janeway's biography of Leif Ericson, W. Hodding Carter decided to follow the same sailing route from Greenland to Newfoundland in the same kind of Viking ship Ericson used. He raised $300,000 in corporate sponsorships, built an open longboat, enlisted a crew of eight, and set sail wearing a helmet with pointy horns and everything. Then there's Rick Werner, who decided to try climbing Everest after reading *Into Thin Air*, Jon Krakauer's account of the disastrous 1996 Everest expedition. Again, after reading Sebastian Junger's *The Perfect Storm*, some readers have tried to convince Sam Novello, a Gloucester fishing captain, to take them out in tempests like the one in the book (the captain has declined every request so far).[3]

Likewise, the life of a believer can be described as putting into practice the adventurous life we read about in Scripture. Daniel's steadfast faith under fire, for example, can inspire us to resist compromising our convictions. When we read about the sacrificial love of Hosea, the prophet who patiently waited for his faithless wife to return to him, we can commit to remain loyal to a spouse who has disappointed us. When we read about the bold leadership of Nehemiah, the man who mobilized a demoralized nation, we can follow his example in our own leadership roles. The romantic passion that the two lovers so openly expressed in the Song of Solomon can lead us to renew our commitment to our own marriage partners. Queen Esther's courage on behalf of her people can cause us to take a worthwhile risk for others. Even if you don't share the same view of the Bible as your believing friends at this point, I suggest you at least put into practice those portions of your reading that make sense. It's the best way to "test" the validity of the Bible.

Priming the Pump

Hopefully this chapter and the one before it have given you a new appreciation for the Bible and have whetted your appetite to examine it for yourself. Why would anyone think he knew enough about Christian truth to accept it or reject it before studying the primary document of the faith? Reading the Bible for yourself is an essential step in getting to the point of saying, "I believe."

Part Two: "I Believe in God"

~~I believe~~
in God the Father Almighty,
Maker of heaven and earth;
And in Jesus Christ his only Son our Lord;
who was conceived by the Holy Spirit,
born of the Virgin Mary,
suffered under Pontius Pilate,
was crucified, dead, and buried.
The third day he rose again from the dead.
He ascended into heaven,
and sits at the right hand of God the Father Almighty.
From there he shall come
to judge the living and the dead.
I believe in the Holy Spirit;
the one holy church;
the communion of saints;
the forgiveness of sins;
the resurrection of the body;
and the life everlasting.
Amen.

Chapter 5
Don't Ignore the Evidence for God

When believers say, "I believe in God," they mean more than simply, "I believe God exists." To "believe in" God means to rely on his leadership and to trust him to provide all that we need. Still, acknowledging the existence of a personal Supreme Being of willpower and creativity is a big step for some, so let's begin there.

It's interesting that the Bible never lists "proofs" for God's existence. Jesus gave evidence for his unique relationship to God and the apostles and prophets gave proof that they spoke for God. But apparently the Bible's writers considered that God's "existence" simply was not a proposition needing proof. We read in Scripture that the world around us reveals not only God's existence but also a measure of his character and expectations. The Old Testament poet put it this way (Psalms 19:1-4):

> The heavens declare the glory of God;
> the skies proclaim the work of his hands.
> Day after day they pour forth speech;
> night after night they display knowledge.
> There is no speech or language
> where their voice is not heard.
> Their voice goes out into all the earth,
> their words to the ends of the world.

Though the natural world can't give people a *complete* picture of God, it gives people a *sufficient* picture of God to draw some conclusions. In Scripture, we are told that evidence for God from the natural world is so obvious that people have to suppress it in order to ignore it.

The Apostle Paul wrote (Romans 1:18-20):

> What may be known about God is plain to them, because God has made it plain to them. For since the creation of the world God's invisible qualities—his eternal power and divine nature—have been clearly seen, being understood from what has been made, so that men are without excuse.

If the evidence from the world around us is so obvious, what signs of God's existence are non-believers overlooking? To come to the point where you can say, "I believe in the existence of God," there are at least five realities to stop ignoring.

Stop Ignoring the Reality of Cause and Effect

At every birthday party, you celebrate a beginning. Small children are often amazed to find out that their parents were once babies. As we grow and mature, we see that the world around us also is essentially a cycle of beginnings and endings, a process of cause and effect. If we look at this process logically, we can see that everything in the universe came from some prior cause. We can conclude that ultimately, there must have been a first "cause" that got everything started. And since, according to our most recent knowledge, matter could not have brought itself into existence, something or someone independent of this physical world must have launched the entire process. What caused the birth of the universe?

This idea that the universe had a beginning was nothing more than speculation and religious conviction until scientists in the twentieth century began to make some discoveries. Telescopes aimed at the sky revealed what scientists concluded were galaxies moving away from us at high speeds, as if everything had come from a point of origin and was now expanding like an inflating balloon or an explosion. One early critic derisively labeled this interpretation "the big bang," and the term stuck. Scientists did not easily give up the concept that the universe was infinite and unlimited, but the evidence kept mounting. From Edwin Hubble's research in the early 1900s to the results from the Cosmic Background Explorer (COBE) satellite of the late 1900s, it seemed inevitable that the universe had a beginning.[1] If it had a beginning, then it makes sense to ask if there is a Beginner behind the beginning. Science is making it easier to say, "Of course."

Stop Ignoring the Evidence of Design

Scientists have marveled at how the universe "burst" from its point of origin in such a way that made human life inevitable. Freeman Dyson wrote, "The more I examine the universe and the details of its architecture, the more evidence I find that the universe in some sense must have known we were coming."[2]

To what "details" is he referring? It seems that the fundamental physical laws that eventually made life possible were in place within a small fraction of the first second of its big-bang beginning. Scientists have identified more than a hundred parameters required for life to develop, and more are being discovered. John Leslie compiled a large number of these parameters in his book, *Universes*.[3] If any of these constants, values and relationships in nature had been even slightly different, you and I would not be around to comment on them.

It seems that someone went to a lot of trouble to get the universe ready for us. The name for this perspective is the "anthropic principle," a term derived from the Greek word, *anthropos*, which means "man." This principle states that the universe was apparently fine-tuned from the very start to make human life possible. As Patrick Glynn wrote in the New York *Times* bestselling autobiography of his spiritual search:

What twentieth century cosmology had come up with was something of a scientific embarrassment: a universe with a definite beginning, expressly designed for life. Ironically, the picture of the universe bequeathed to us by the most advanced twentieth-century science is closer in spirit to the vision presented in the Book of Genesis than anything offered by science since Copernicus.[4]

Evidence for design exists not only in the field of physics but also biology. For nearly two hundred years, this field of science has maintained that all life came about through natural selection, a process of numerous, successive, slight modifications over many years. Its main flaw, however, is that it does not take into account the presence of key elements required to make such select systems work.

These elements are at the root of an intriguing new theory that challenges natural selection as a comprehensive explanation for life. Some scientists are now concluding that at every level of existence, there are systems of *irreducible complexity*. This is a phrase that biochemist Michael Behe first used to describe systems that require several components to function.[5]

Behe's favorite analogy of irreducible complexity is a mousetrap. A common mousetrap requires several components to function properly: a wooden base, a hammer, a spring to provide force for the hammer, a catch to activate trap, and a bar between the catch and the hammer to set the trap. All of these components have to exist and be set in the right relationship to each other (by a person who is designing it) before they are of any use at catching mice. In nature, numerous systems are like this. Even at the cellular level, many components combine to enable the cell to perform. According to the theory of natural selection, impersonal processes are biased toward systems that are already working and would have had no use for these components prior to their interaction with each other. So, the existence of these irreducibly complex systems challenges evolution as a comprehensive explanation of life.

Thankfully, there is a growing body of credentialed scientists speaking in the language of their various fields to point out evidence for intelligent design. Most of us, however, come to the same conclusion in more intuitive ways. For example, a medical doctor once told his story of how his agnosticism broke down while he held his newborn daughter. Such moments are reverent, as any parent will admit. The baby lay sleeping in her physician-father's arms, and he was admiring the little wonder. Her tiny ear caught his attention, and he marveled at its intricacy—the way it was curved to catch sounds and direct them to the protected eardrum. He knew that inside there were microscopic hairs that would interpret the sounds to the brain. The moment overwhelmed him and the realization broke in: "There *must* be an intelligent power behind the universe." At that point, he had not drawn any conclusions about Christ (that came later); but he quit suppressing the truth about the existence of God.

Stop Ignoring Your Awareness of Right and Wrong

No matter the cultural background, selfishness is not lifted up as an admirable quality. Nor are actions such as incest, theft, murder, or abandoning responsibilities. In short, there is a universal acknowledgement that we should be ashamed of certain behaviors. This sense of what we "ought" or "ought not" to do is a bright sign pointing to our origin in God. Where do we get the idea, for example, that prison guards at Iraq's Abu Ghraib compound "shouldn't" use the humiliation of human beings for the guards' personal enjoyment? Or that an uncle "shouldn't" sexually exploit his little niece or nephew? Or that someone "shouldn't" slip into our parking spot after we politely waited and provided room for a departing car to back out? Admitting that we have a sense of what is right and wrong can lead us to acknowledge a Lawgiver.

All too often, however, this idea of the way things "should" be is one of the most persistent objections against the existence of God. How many times have you heard someone say, "Well, if there is a god, why do so many bad things happen to the innocent? Why would a good god allow pain and suffering?"

While these protests seem valid and understandable on the surface, they are actually strong arguments for the reality of the divine. You see, these questions are questions of justice—we observe something that is not right and seek to correct it or cast blame. But what makes us see some act as unjust in the first place? Where did our definition of unjust and just originate? To call a stick crooked, you have to have in mind what a straight stick looks like. To complain that life is *unfair*, you have to have some idea of the way things *ought* to be in the universe. If human life is just an accidental byproduct of blind natural selection, then our moral outrage at its mishaps is nothing less than irrational. The fact that we feel a sense of outrage at injustice actually points to the existence of God.

Stop Ignoring Your Sense of Self

Biologist and philosopher Leon Kass remembers standing at the bedside of a brilliant man he deeply respected just moments after the man's death. He said:

> One day I went to visit him in the hospital, as I'd done a number of times before. On the way into the room, I asked the nurse, who was coming out, how he was doing. She said, "Didn't you know? He died about an hour ago." I walked into the room, and there he was, lying in bed, very peaceful. Had I not been told by the nurse, I would have assumed he was asleep. I don't really know what happened in the next few moments, but I found myself on my knees at the end of the bed. I was thunderstruck. Here he was, but he wasn't there at all. There was almost a smile on his face. All I could think of was—where is he? Where is this mind? What's happened to him?[6]

Kass had a sense that there was more to his friend than simply the now-lifeless muscles, bones and tissue in the bed. Many of us have had that same sensation as we stand next to the lifeless body of a loved one.

While some would say that such feelings are merely sentimentalism, the research into what makes you "you" is raising some of the strongest challenges against the naturalistic explanations for life. Where do you get your sense of self—your introspection, feelings, hopes, and subjective viewpoint? Advocates of naturalistic explanations would say that self-consciousness is merely the product of highly-evolved brains, which one MIT professor famously called "computers made of meat."[7]

Is the brain alone sufficient to account for our sense of self? Scientists have researched the stubborn human conviction that there's a nonmaterial reality called the "soul," or "self," or "mind." One neurosurgeon found when working with epilepsy patients that by stimulating certain parts of the brain he could make the patients swallow or blink or turn their heads. In every case, however, the patients would say, "I didn't do that; you did." The patients knew they had a separate existence from whatever was happening to their bodies. The neurosurgeon added that there was no place in the brain where electrical stimulation could make a patient believe or decide, and thus these mental actions had to originate in something other than simply the physical brain.[8]

Recent studies in a field called *neurotheology* seem to contradict that last statement. Proponents claim that that there's a physical basis for religious thoughts—our minds are "wired" for God, as one book puts it. But instead of assuming that electrical impulses in a portion of the brain generate what we call consciousness of God, couldn't it be the other way around? It's just as likely that our consciousness of God impacts the activity of our brain.[9]

Certainly, no one argues against a *correlation* between the brain and the sense of self. But the research calls into question *causation*—it's not conclusive that the brain *causes* consciousness. One person likened the relationship between the brain and the mind to the way a television set manifests pictures and sounds from waves in the air.[10] There is a connection between the television set and the waves it turns into pictures and sounds, but the waves exist independently of the TV. Research continues to run into signs that the immaterial mind or soul exists independently of the material brain. These indicators lead us toward a creator who is personal, purposeful, and creative himself. We are, the Bible says, made in his image (Genesis 1:26).

Stop Ignoring Your Innate Impression of Permanence

The Bible says God has "planted eternity in the human heart" (Ecclesiastes 3:11). Even if we had very little religious training, we intuitively know that life cannot end here. After some sixty to eighty years of laughing, hoping, dreaming, crying, relating, exploring the "what" of existence through engineering and the sciences, examining the "why" of existence through philosophy and the arts—after all this, are we to become nothing more than decaying fertilizer in the ground? We have eternity in our hearts, and our hearts tell us there's more to life than this life.

Go Fish

People have to ignore a lot in order to deny that a personal God exists: the reality of cause and effect, the evidence for design, our awareness of right and wrong, our sense of self, and our stubborn impression of permanence. The evidence for God is so clear that the Old Testament poet observed, "Only fools say in their hearts, 'There is no God'" (Psalms 14:1 NLT). If a man casts a line on a lake all day and fails to catch fish, does that prove there are no fish to catch, or does it prove that he is an inept fisherman?[11]

Chapter 6
Clear Up Your Misunderstandings of God

When our first child turned four, it was time for him to start sitting with his mother in church services instead of attending the preschool care. After a few weeks of observing the hour-long services of songs, prayers, and my teaching, he told me at lunch, "I know what your job is, Daddy."

"Oh?"

"Your job is to tell people about God."

"Well, that's right, son. I'm a pastor, and my job is to tell people about God."

"Daddy?" he continued.

"Yes, son."

"It takes a lo-o-o-ong time to tell people about God, doesn't it, Daddy?"

Well, I guess it does; there's a lot to say about God. The Apostles' Creed, though, summarizes the Bible's teaching about the nature of God in just three statements: he is "God the Father," "Almighty," and "Maker of heaven and earth." In the last chapter we looked at some reasons to believe in the existence of God, but

Christian belief involves more than merely believing in the reality of a Supreme Being. It involves certain convictions about the nature of God: He is our Father, our Ruler, and our Creator.

These three statements challenge some popular misunderstandings of God. Some people look upon God as a tyrant whom we must constantly calm with unpleasant acts of sacrifice. By contrast, others see God as an indulgent grandfather figure that grants our every request and overlooks our bad behavior. Some people see him as a spoiler, sort of like a cop forever in our rearview mirror. Still others understand "God" as the impersonal life force that animates the universe. In contrast to the various ways people perceive God today, the believer says, "I believe in God the Father Almighty, Maker of heaven and earth." Let's look at those three statements, starting with the last one first.

"God is my Maker"

The first line of the Bible tells us, "In the beginning, God created the heavens and the earth" (Genesis 1:1). This conviction has a personal impact and a cosmic impact. Personally, the fact that God made *me* tells me how valuable I am. I am not an accidental by-product of an impersonal evolutionary process; the Bible says I am "fearfully and wonderfully made" (Psalms 139:14) and therefore God *intended* me to be part of this epic adventure of his.

God made *me*, and that tells me how valuable I am; on a much larger scale, God made *everything*, and that tells me that I am just one part of a vast epic adventure that God is directing. In the 1976 film, *Star Wars: A New Hope*, Luke Skywalker was introduced to the concept of "the Force." His mentor, the Jedi knight Obiwan Kenobi, explained that the Force was that which animated all things and bound them all together. Remarkable feats could be accomplished, he told young Skywalker, by letting the Force flow through him. But, he warned, "beware the dark side of the Force."

Although Obiwan's view of "God" was new to many American moviegoers in 1976, it's an ancient and persistent view called *pantheism*. "Pan" is a Greek word that means "all," and pantheism is the belief that everything is God. It contends that rocks, trees, spiders, planets, and people are all simply extensions of the divine. Events in life and even human behavior are manifestations of this force as well. Some events and behavior display the life-affirming side of this animating mind, but there is also a dark side to the force that menaces life and order. Everything we experience is simply the manifestation of the competition of these opposing sides to reality.

By contrast, Christians believe that God is "Maker of heaven and earth." He made the world but exists apart from it, like an architect who designs a building but exists independently of the building. This view of God is announced from the first book of the Bible to the last. As we have seen, the first line of the Bible speaks of God's creative act, and in the last book of the Bible we find people praising God because of his creative work (Revelation 4:11):

> "You created all things,
> and by your will they were created
> and have their being."

When believers say that God created "all things," this includes "things in heaven and on earth, visible and invisible, whether thrones or powers or rulers or authorities" (Colossians 1:16[1]). In other words, God created even the invisible "powers" that shape world events and influence human behavior. Many of these powerful beings are loyal to God, but some have rebelled.

According to pantheism, bad things will *always* be a part of reality because the eternal animating "force" is made up a menacing side as well as a life-affirming side: Yin and Yang, Good and Evil, Light and Darkness . . . forever. While pantheism tries to give us an *explanation* as to why we experience bad things, however, Christianity promises us a *solution*. We look forward to a future without pain and evil because evil only exists as a result of rebellion within the ranks of the visible and invisible beings God has created. In other words, the devil that is described in Scripture is not God's co-equal evil counterpart. Rather, he is a rebellious created being—a fallen angel. Therefore he and his forces cannot stop their future final defeat as it is described in the last book of the Bible. That which has been made cannot eternally resist the intentions of the Maker—especially one that is Almighty, which is the second way that God is described in the Apostles' Creed.

"God is my Ruler"

"Almighty" is one of the favorite titles for God in the Bible. In the Old Testament alone, the Hebrew word for "God Almighty," *El-Shaddai*, shows up 330 times. God rules the world he made.

Now, this conviction impacts life in a lot of ways but let me call attention to two: *how we talk to God*, and *how we live for God*.

How we talk to God. When we want to talk to God in prayer, the fact that he is ruler over all can be intimidating. But it can also be liberating. God is "Almighty," and so when we pray to him we can be confident that, as the angel said in the Christmas story, "Nothing is impossible with God" (Luke 1:37).

Of course, if you've ever prayed for something that wasn't granted, or if your heart has ever been broken in a personal tragedy, this conviction that God is "Almighty" is unsettling. Why do tragedies happen if God is all-powerful? In fact, some have tried to resolve the tension between God's rule and life's disappointments by saying that God is not all-powerful. There are things he wants to do for us, some say, but he simply cannot do them.

As for me, I would rather wrestle with the mystery of a God who could have answered my request and did not, than to conclude that God really wants to answer my request and could not. No matter why I face disappointments now, at the end of time I want to stand before a God that is not only good enough to *want* to set everything right but is powerful enough to *be able* to set everything right. He is *El-Shaddai*, God Almighty, and that conviction impacts our prayer life.

How we live for God. If "God is my Ruler," the second way that reality affects Christians is in the matter of obedience. God says,

"I am the Almighty God. Obey me and always do what is right" (Genesis 17:1 TEV). Believers' obligation to do what God wants comes from the fact that he is *El-Shaddai*, and it counters the "greeting-card" concept of him that many people hold. In this mindset, God is non-threatening, safe and responsive to our every desire. He has no strong views on our behavior. He opens a parking space when we are late for an appointment, and responds to our failures with an indulgent pat on the head as a reprimand. But if I believe he is my Ruler, I am reminded that my goal should be to honor his intentions for my life. The fact that he rules the world he made means that he has the right to rule my life as well. So, his wish is my command—in my relationships, my business practices, my finances, my forms of entertainment, and my decision-making.

"God is my Father"

The fact that God is my Maker and my Ruler does not complete the biblical picture of God. The remarkable truth of scripture is that my Maker and Ruler is also my Father. I don't relate to him as a slave relates to a master but rather as an obedient and loyal child relates to a loving father. Some see God as the perpetual spoiler, the constant cop in our rearview mirror. Others envision God as some sort of impossible-to-please tyrant. But the Apostle Paul wrote, "We should not be like cringing, fearful slaves, but we should behave like God's very own children, adopted into the bosom of his family, and calling to him, 'Father, Father'" (Romans 8:15 LB). Paul used the tender, intimate Aramaic word "Abba" in that verse, which is closer to our word "Daddy." In fact, Paul was simply echoing the teaching of Jesus, who made the idea of fatherhood central to his teachings about God.

> *Some have suggested that this picture of God as Father isn't helpful today*

Some have suggested that this picture of God as Father isn't helpful today because many people have known abusive or neglectful fathers. A bad experience with an earthly father, they say, could cause some to think of a heavenly Father with revulsion instead of reverence.

It's true that our earliest impression of God is shaped on the anvil of our relationship with an earthly father. That's why fathers are so important in our lives. But, while I don't want to belittle the concern, I think it falls short. To think of God as "Father" does not mean we should see God as fathers *are* but rather as fathers *ought to be*. God relates to us as earthly fathers should.

There is a universal expectation of behavior which earthly fathers try to meet. Earthly fathers ought to be protectors, nurturers, and responsive to the basic needs of their children. God perfectly fulfills that image of the responsive, protective, nurturing father. Many have discovered this, as Barbara Curtis so beautifully described in a magazine article:

> I remember the day my dad left. He knelt and hugged me and cried. The skimpy dress of a five-year-old girl could not protect me from the chill that gathered around my arms and legs. The scratchy whiskers—would I feel them no more? The arms that felt so safe—would they be gone forever?
>
> What would it be like not to have a father?
>
> The years to come provided harsh answers to those questions. . . . I guess you might say with no one to believe in, I learned to believe in myself.
>
> Only when this unsustainable strategy dropped me down and out—and more alone than ever—did I finally face my fatherlessness. . . .
>
> So it was in my 30s, sensing a spiritual vacuum, that I finally launched a search for God. . . . How ready I was the moment I first understood that God was my father. At last, I was someone's little girl! To this day, 10 years later, I cannot approach God intellectually, but only as a child and with no reservations. I feel such love. . . .

> I remember once, before he left, my father carrying me home in his arms as blood gushed from a jagged cut on my foot. I was four and I was frightened, hoping that my father could take care of me. But though that day he stopped the bleeding, no earthly father could have healed the wounded heart he later left behind.
>
> That hurt cried out for the love of a Heavenly Father. And so I will always be God's grateful little girl—trusting, dependent, and filled with faith in the arms that will never let me go.[2]

What a world of love, security, and self-worth opens up to us when we discover that God is our Father!

Bragging Rights

God is our Maker, our Ruler, and our Father. How firmly you hold these truths will determine whether you seek the company of God through prayer, Bible study and daily living. Embracing these truths will change the way you handle stress, anxiety and unanswered prayer. It will also impact your sense of personal value, as well as the value you give to "life ethics"—issues like euthanasia, war, abortion, and capital punishment. What you believe about the nature of God will determine if you will live under the awareness that you are accountable to God. These truths about God put limits on the authority human government can claim over us, which explains why totalitarian governments try to stamp out Christianity. In short, you tell me a world about yourself when you say, "I believe in God the Father Almighty, Maker of heaven and earth."

According to the prophet Jeremiah, God said (9:23-24):

> "Let not the wise man boast of his *wisdom*
> or the strong man boast of his *strength*
> or the rich man boast of his *riches*,
> but let him who boasts boast about this:
> *that he understands and knows me* . . . ."

It's not our intelligence, power, or wealth that should fill us with security and wholeness. Many have chased after the first three options only to discover that they cannot completely satisfy. In the passage above, God said, "Let a man boast that he *understands* and *knows* me."

Many people say, "I believe in God"—and what they are saying is "I believe that God exists." But our goal should be to *know* God—to have a relationship with him, to "improve our conscious contact with God" as those in recovery groups put it. A.W. Tozer once said, "I want deliberately to encourage this mighty longing after God. . . . He waits to be wanted. Too bad that with many of us He waits so long, so very long, in vain."[3]

Part Three: "I Believe in Jesus"

*I believe
in God the Father Almighty,
Maker of ~~heaven and~~ earth;
And in Jesus Christ his only Son our Lord;
who was conceived by the Holy Spirit,
born of the Virgin Mary,
suffered under Pontius Pilate,
was crucified, dead, and buried.
The third day he rose again from the dead.
He ascended into heaven,
and sits at the right hand of God the Father Almighty.
From there he shall come
to judge the living and the dead.
I believe ~~in the Holy~~ Spirit;
the one holy church;
the communion of saints;
the forgiveness of sins;
the resurrection of the body;
and the life everlasting.
Amen.*

Chapter 7
Jesus is Everything It Means to Be God

"Who do you say that I am?"

Jesus once asked this question of his followers, and it's still the most important question we have to answer. Jesus asked this at a rare lull in his busy ministry. The crowds weren't pushing in, asking to be fed or healed. Jesus had some private teaching time with his closest followers, and he probed their understanding of his identity. The question wasn't asked in ignorance, because he knew the hearts of his men. Neither was it asked in insecurity. Sometimes we feel we need to ask our marriage partners, "Do you still love me?" Or if we're a leader we're sometimes tempted to ask, "What are people saying about me?" Jesus had none of this insecurity. Instead, he asked them that question because the answer makes all the difference in the world. It was Simon Peter who spoke for the group: "You are the Christ, the Son of the Living God" (Matthew 16:15).

Believers recite this same statement of faith in the Creed. Just as Christians say, "I believe in God the Father Almighty, Maker of heaven and earth," they also say, "I believe in Jesus Christ, his only Son." What does it mean to say, "I believe in Jesus?" As a lifelong student of theology, I've read a lot of complicated ways to explain what Christians believe about Jesus, but if someone asked me to describe him I would use a simple image: Jesus is the ultimate freediver.

A freediver's only equipment is a mask and perhaps a wetsuit. She draws one breath of air and sees how far down that one breath will take her. As of this writing, the world record in freediving is held by Tanya Streeter, who plunged 525 feet deep on August 17, 2002. Sports Illustrated named her "The World's Most Perfect Athlete" in 2002. Born in the Cayman Islands, Streeter now lives in Austin, Texas, promoting conservation causes and training for her next freediving challenge.[1]

Today freediving is an extreme sport designed to test the body's limits, but it came from more practical uses. For thousands of years, pearl divers would draw in one breath of air and plunge to the sea bed and from there they would bring back treasures to the surface. In Tahiti they were known to dive as deep as 100-130 feet.

Like a pearl diver, Jesus plunged down from heaven to the depths of human experience, and then he returned to the heavens. The Apostles' Creed captures this freediving motion. We begin at the heights:

> *I believe... in Jesus Christ [God's] only Son our Lord;*

Then we see the descent to the depths of human experience. Down and further down the words take us:

> *who was conceived by the Holy Spirit,*
> *born of the Virgin Mary,*
> *suffered under Pontius Pilate,*
> *was crucified, dead, and buried..*

And then we celebrate the ascent back to heaven again:

> *The third day he rose again from the dead.*
> *He ascended into heaven,*
> *and sits at the right hand of God the Father Almighty.*

These phrases speak of the divinity of Jesus, the virgin birth of Jesus, the conscious existence of Jesus in death, the resurrection of Jesus, and the living presence of Jesus in heaven. These concepts may cause our head to spin, but the words capture the Christian convictions about Jesus: Jesus left the heights of heaven, plunged down into the experiences of humanity even into human death, and then rose back up to the heights of heaven.

What if Jesus asked you what he asked his disciples—"Who do you say I am?" For the next three chapters, I'll compare the life of Jesus to that of a pearl diver. In this chapter we'll begin with this conviction: *"Jesus is everything it means to be God."*

Imagine one of those Tahitian pearl divers at the surface, preparing for her deep plunge. Her experience is very different on the surface than the experience she's about to have down below. Above, she breathes air, feels the wind and hears the words of encouragement from her friends, she squints at the bright sunlight in a blue sky. All of that will be left behind when she descends for her prize below. That's the image I get when I think about the paradise from which Jesus came to live our kind of life on this earth. In the Creed, believers state that Jesus is Christ, God's only Son, and our Lord. All of those phrases speak of the unique nature of Jesus. He was and is much more than another prophet or a great moral teacher: he is everything it means to be God.

Jesus is the ultimate freediver

Some scholars claim that, like the barnacles that attach to the hull of a ship, the concept of the divinity of Jesus evolved over time and if we would simply scrape away these barnacles we would get down to the ship's hull. In other words, if we removed the elaborate nonsense about a divine Jesus, the historical Jesus would become obvious—a remarkable but simply human Jesus. The problem is, if we scraped away the fourth-century church debates over the divine nature of Jesus, we would find second-century references to Christians who worshipped him as God. And if we scraped away the second-century references, we would find the biblical comments about his divinity from his first-century followers. And even if we stripped away those barnacles right down to the hull of the ship, we would find Jesus himself making these astonishing claims.

Have you read what Jesus said about himself? Jesus applied to himself many of the things that were said of God in the Old Testament:

- Jesus depicted himself as a shepherd—specifically *the* shepherd—which was a familiar image of God (compare John 10:11-15 to Ezekiel 34).

- Numerous times the Old Testament referred to God as a bridegroom to Israel, which was one of Jesus' favorite ways to describe his relationship to believers (compare Isaiah 54:4-8 to Matthew 9:15).

- Just as the prophet Zechariah looked forward to God coming with his angels on the day of judgment, Jesus pictured himself coming with his holy angels on the final day (compare Zechariah 14:5 to Matthew 25:31).

- Old Testament verses tell us that God alone gives life, and Jesus expanded this to include himself, saying, "In the same way that the Father raises the dead and creates life, so does the Son. The Son gives life to anyone he chooses" (compare 1 Samuel 2:6 to John 5:21 Msg).

- He said that his mission was to "seek and to save that which was lost," which his listeners knew to be God's mission from hearing Old Testament readings (compare Luke 19:10 to Ezekiel 34:11-22).

- In addition to the permanence of *God's* word, Jesus insisted on the permanence of *his own* word. He said, "Heaven and earth will pass away, but my words will never pass away," which is the way God's own words were described in earlier Scripture (compare Mark 13:31 to Isaiah 40:8).

- When his enemies criticized children for praising *him*, Jesus defended the praise by quoting a psalm about how children learn to praise *God* (Matthew 21:16, quoting Psalms 8:2).

Some of the things Jesus said about himself may seem obscure to us. But to many of his listeners, his comments came through loud and clear, judging from their reaction. When he claimed to be able to forgive sins, the leaders of his community became enraged: he had claimed to do what only God had the right to do, and therefore he had made himself equal with God (Matthew 9:1-8). At one point his enemies even tried to stone him because of his claims: when they asked him to explain who he was, Jesus said, "I am!" The leaders immediately took up stones to kill him. You see, Jesus had used the holiest name for God to describe himself. In the Old Testament story of Moses and the burning bush, when Moses asked him for his name, God had said, "I AM WHO I AM." From that point on, the title "I AM" became the holiest name for God. Reverent Jews did not even speak the name aloud, and yet here Jesus not only spoke it but also used it as a title for himself (John 8:58-59; Exodus 3:14-15). The immediate reaction was to take up stones to kill him. To them, he had committed blasphemy, which was a capital crime.

Jesus made claims that would have been absolutely inappropriate—that is, unless he was God. I still remember the powerful impact an observation by C.S. Lewis had on me when I read it in my university years:

> I am trying here to prevent anyone saying the really foolish thing that people often say about Him: "I'm ready to accept Jesus as a great moral teacher, but I don't accept His claim to be God." That is the one thing we must not say. A man who was merely a man and said the sort of things Jesus said would not be a great moral teacher.... You must make your choice. Either this man was, and is, the Son of God: or else a madman or something worse.... [L]et us not come with any patronising nonsense about His being a great human teacher. He has not left that open to us. He did not intend to.[2]

No wonder the New Testament writers considered Jesus divine. Just look at the way they talked of him and in the way they related to him.

The way they talked of him. The apostles used the title "Lord" interchangeably to refer to God and to Jesus. They even took sacred texts that referred to God as "Lord" and applied them to Jesus (for example, Acts 2:20-21; Romans 10:13). They called Christ "God over all" (Romans 9:5) and "our God and Savior" (Titus 2:13). Paul wrote, "By him all things were created," which is what the first sentence in the Bible says about God (Colossians 1:16; Genesis 1:1). Paul also said he was "in very nature God" (Philippians 2:6), that "God was pleased to have all his fullness dwell in him" (Colossians 1:19), and that "in Christ all the fullness of the Deity lives in bodily form" (Colossians 2:9). John respectfully called Jesus "the Word," and said of him, "In the beginning was the Word, and the Word was with God and the Word was God" (John 1:1 NKJV). In recounting his astonishing visions in the book of Revelation, John heard Jesus declare, "I am the Alpha and the Omega, the First and the Last, the Beginning and the End" (Revelation 22:13), the very title God twice claimed for himself earlier in the same book (1:8 and 21:6-7).

The way they related to him. The early Christians prayed to Jesus (Acts 7:59-60) and claimed that to be "in him" made you "a new creation" (2 Corinthians 5:17). This worship of Jesus was mocked among nonbelievers of the time. The Kircherian Museum in Rome has in its collection a crude drawing preserved from the second century. It depicts a cross upon which hangs the body of a man with the head of a donkey. At the foot of the cross is another man with his hand raised up to the crucified man in worship. Under the drawing are the Greek words, *Alexemenos cebete theon*—"Alexemenos worships his god."[3] The drawing, despite being a mocking reference to Christians, shows that even those outside the faith recognized the special status Jesus held in the hearts of believers.

Jesus is everything it means to be God. Why should that matter? Note two implications.

Knowing Jesus is the
Best Way to Know God

The Bible says, "In the past God spoke to our ancestors many times and in many ways through the prophets, but in these last days he has spoken to us through his Son" (Hebrews 1:1-2 TEV). Jesus said, "Anyone who has seen me has seen the Father" (John 14:9). Jesus wasn't simply a man filled with the presence of God—Jesus was the presence of God. So, if you want to know what makes God smile, look at what made Jesus smile. If you want to know what captures the attention of God, look at what captured the attention of Jesus. If you want to know what enrages God, look at what made Jesus angry.

It wasn't that the prophets before Jesus were inaccurate. What they had to say was completely true, but not truly complete. Jesus came to complete the picture. The prophets gave us *principles* about God; Jesus gave us the *person* of God! And so any claim about who God is and what God likes must be measured by the words and life of the man who was God-in-the-flesh: Jesus Christ. This truth is especially relevant for those exploring the Christian faith. I like the encouragement from John Stott, an English pastor and popular author:

> If you find it hard to believe in God, I strongly advise you to begin your search not with philosophical questions about the existence and being of God, but with Jesus of Nazareth. . . . If you read again the story of Jesus, and read it as an honest and humble seeker, Jesus Christ is able to reveal himself to you, and thus make God . . . real to you.[4]

At the Cross God Bore the
Penalty for Sin Himself

Since Christ's crucifixion is the most important event in the Christian worldview, we will wait until a later chapter to examine it in detail. In brief, though, the Bible writers explained that the crucifixion was God's way of removing the sin that separates us from him. All of us have broken God's laws and we deserve the consequences for doing so, but the amazing truth of the gospel is that God came to bear the punishment himself: "God was in Christ reconciling the world to Himself" (2 Corinthians 5:19 NASB). The astonishing claim of the gospel is that the man hanging upon the cross was the Creator himself giving himself up to save his prized creation.

Imagine standing before a judge's bench to hear him bang the gavel and say, "Guilty!" And then, to your amazement, the judge steps down from the bench, removes his robe, and he stands beside you saying, "But I will bear your sentence myself; you are free to go." Believers have always looked upon the crucified Christ in that manner: as God himself paying the penalty for the sins we've committed. As a 19th-century Southern folk hymn put it:

> What wondrous love is this
> that caused the Lord of bliss
> To bear the dreadful curse for my soul!

The Bible teaches that it was, in the words of the song, "the Lord of bliss" who bore the dreadful curse to save us.

If Jesus were standing before you asking, "Who do you say that I am?" what would you say? Simon Peter issued the life-changing challenge: "You must worship Christ as Lord of your life" (1 Peter 3:15 NLT).

After his death and resurrection, Jesus appeared to his disciples. The Apostle Thomas, who had doubted the earlier reports of those who had seen Jesus alive, was astonished to see him. With all doubt vaporized, Thomas stammered, "My Lord and my God!" (John 20:28)

Jesus did not rebuke or correct him for this outburst of praise. Neither will Jesus rebuke us for ours.

Chapter 8
What If God Was One of Us?

"Jesus wept."

The New Testament wasn't written with chapter-and-verse divisions. A French printer named Robert Stephens placed chapters and verses in his 1551 edition of the New Testament, and we've had them ever since. For reasons known only to him, the printer assigned just two words to John 11:35—"Jesus wept." When I was a kid, my friends and I chose this verse whenever a teacher at church challenged us to recite a scripture from memory. Obviously, we had other and less noble reasons for picking that verse, but without knowing it we had actually selected one of the most revealing texts about Jesus. John tells us about Jesus' tears in a setting that's natural for tears. Jesus' good friend Lazarus had died, and Jesus did what you and I do at funerals for good friends: he cried.

In her hit song, "One of Us," Joan Osborne sang, "What if God was one of us . . . just a slob like one of us?"[1]

Some consider the song irreverent, but Osborne was asking an important question: does God know what we're dealing with down here? The answer is found in the life of Jesus. In the last chapter, we covered the idea that Jesus is everything it means to be God. In this chapter we'll look at another conviction: *Jesus is everything it means to be human.* God was one of us.

Imagine again one of those pearl divers I described in the last chapter. On the surface she breathes air, feels the wind, squints at the bright sunlight in a blue sky, and hears the words of encouragement from her friends. But then she plunges below the surface into a very different world. Deeper and deeper she goes until colors fade . . . then light fades . . . warmer surface water gives way to the black and cold . . . and still further down she goes until she's at the oyster bed, digging her hands into the muck and ooze to pull out the gnarled shells of oysters.

That's the image that comes to mind when I read about what we call the "incarnation"—the act of God becoming man. The Apostle John reverently described Jesus as the "Word" and said of him, "In the beginning was the Word and the Word was with God and the Word was God." That's not the end of John's comments about Jesus, though. John goes on to say, ". . . and the Word became flesh and dwelt among us" (John 1:1, 14 NKJV).

With the Apostles' Creed believers say that the one who was "Christ, God's only Son and our Lord," was conceived, born, suffered, and died. In other words, our creator visited his creation in person and experienced everything it means to be human.

Since the Apostles' Creed is supposed to be a *short* summary of Christian belief, it's remarkable that the longest part of the Creed emphasizes the humanity of Jesus. Maybe that's because we have a harder time *appreciating* his humanity than we do *understanding* his divinity. The earliest Christians were captivated by the truth that God was one of us: the ancient words recount that he was conceived, he was born, he suffered, and specifically he suffered under a named man—Pontius Pilate. The God of the universe suffered injustice and torture in a specific place and time.

Reciting the Creed, Christians state rhythmically that Jesus was "crucified, dead, and buried." As if that weren't enough to emphasize his experience with human suffering and death, many versions of the Creed point out that he "descended into Hades" or "descended to the dead." Over the years, some have developed elaborate speculations about what Jesus did in "Hades," but to say he descended into Hades simply means that he really did die. The word "Hades" was a Greek word that means "unseen," and it was the ancient way of speaking of death. In the very first Christian sermon, Simon Peter said that Jesus was not "abandoned to Hades." Other modern translations of this verse say he was not "left among the dead" or "abandoned to the grave" (Acts 2:31 NASB, NLT, NIV). In other words,

> *The earliest Christians were captivated by the truth that God was one of us*

he was among the dead, but he was not left there because God resurrected him.

In short, all the words of this section of the Creed vividly describe the Lord of heaven experiencing everything it means to be human, not only *up to* the point of death but *into* the experience of death itself. His conception was remarkable, of course—conceived by the Holy Spirit in the womb of a virgin. But beyond that, his birth involved all the blood and pain and exhaustion of any other birth, and he grew up facing all the experiences of any other man—*physically, emotionally,* and *spiritually.*

He Was Human Physically

A few years ago *Popular Science* magazine ran a cover story in the Christmas season called "The Real Face of Jesus." The story assumed that, since Jesus had to be pointed out to the Roman soldiers who arrested him, he looked no different than other Semites of his time. Examining the skull of a man who lived in the time and region of Jesus, they used special software to build computer-generated features that would have fit on the skull. In the end they had a face with dark features, short brown curly hair, and a beard.

I have no argument with the assumptions of the research, because Jesus was a man. Jesus said to his enemies, "Now you seek to kill me, a *man* who has told you the truth" (John 8:40). Simon Peter referred to him as "Jesus of Nazareth, a *man* attested to you by God with mighty works and wonders and signs" (Acts 2:22).

Paul used the phrase, "the *man* Christ Jesus" (1 Timothy 2:5). He grew up like any boy of his day, learning his lessons and developing through puberty and adolescence into manhood (Luke 2:52). Until he began his teaching ministry at the age of 30, he worked in the carpenter's trade of his adoptive father, Joseph. No doubt, when he hit his thumb with a hammer, it would throb and a black bruise would rise. His feet blistered when he walked, he sneezed at pollen, and his stomach grumbled at dinnertime. When he was beaten and tortured, he suffered and died like any other human would under the same circumstances.

He Was Human Emotionally

The Bible says Jesus lived "enjoying life," his enemies accused him of going to too many parties, and he enjoyed the pleasant surprise of being "amazed" at times (Matthew 11:19 Ph; Luke 7:9 NLT). In addition to the more pleasant aspects of human experience, though, he also knew the gloomier side of earthly life. In the Bible we read about moments when he was bitterly disappointed with people (Mark 3:5), "irate" at his own followers (Mark 10:14 Msg), and "filled with anguish and deep distress" at the thought of suffering an agonizing death (Matthew 26:37 NLT). He knew loneliness: The night before he was crucified, he urged his closest followers to remain awake and stay with him (Mark 14:32-42). The next day he moaned from utter loneliness on the cross, asking, "My God, My God, why have you forsaken me?" (Mark 15:34) As Isaiah predicted, hundreds of years earlier, Jesus would be "a man of sorrows and acquainted with grief" (Isaiah 53:3 NASB).

He Was Human Spiritually

More remarkable than his connection with our physical and emotional experiences, he identified with our spiritual experiences. He sought strength and wisdom from his Father in his times of prayer, moments that sometimes lasted long into the night. Scripture also lets us know that he experienced temptation to rebel against his Father, just as we do. The Bible repeats over and over that Christ "committed no sin" (for example, 1 Peter 2:22), but it equally emphasizes the man's struggle to stay aligned with God's will (for example, Matthew 4:1-11). Amazingly, the Bible says he was "at all points tempted, yet he did not sin" (Hebrews 4:15). Imagine someone experiencing "all points" of human temptation. We have a hard time imagining someone who successfully resists all temptation as being really human, but doesn't that tell us more about *our* spiritual failure than about *Christ's* spiritual success?

Physically, emotionally, and spiritually, Jesus was everything it means to be human. Now, why should that matter? I want to note two important implications.

He is Our Example

Simon Peter said, "Christ suffered for you, *leaving you an example*, that you should follow in his steps" (1 Peter 2:21). We will later discuss how Christ was doing much more on the cross than simply setting an example for us. Still, several times the New Testament states that Christ's faithfulness through his suffering is a standard and benchmark that we should imitate. In other words, the way Jesus handled mistreatment is the way we ought to act when we're mistreated. The patience and refusal to retaliate, the forgiveness, the trust in Father God—all that Jesus did when he suffered is how we ought to act.

We should not only copy the way he approached dying, but also the way he approached living. He was compassionate and attentive to others, especially to those whom others overlooked. His relationships with others were not complicated with jealousy, insecurity, and sexual tensions. Through prayer, he expressed his need of the Father's help and wisdom. He loved people but did not let their opinions of him determine his course of action, and this was his attitude toward his own earthly family as well. Life's experiences left him troubled at times but never hopeless, and he maintained clarity in his life's mission. These are just a few of the ways that Jesus lived a life worth imitating. Although the fad of wearing "WWJD" bracelets has come and gone, the question the letters represented will never go out of style: We should determine our every course of action by asking, "What would Jesus do?"

When we fail, our typical excuse is, "Hey, I'm only human." We seem to equate weakness, inconsistency, and lack of self-control with what it means to be human. Since Jesus is everything it means to be human, it should force us to reconsider that line of thought. In response to moral failure we should not say, "I'm only human," but rather, "I'm less than human, I'm not everything a human should be, because I'm not everything Jesus was." Though he was divine, his perfection wasn't so much a sign of his *divinity* as it was a sign of his completely obedient *humanity*. The way he lived does not make him *superhuman*, but rather *fully human*. He is the picture of everything God intended women and men to be. We're the ones who fall short of what it means to be human. Our humanity has been corrupted by our rebellion, and our aim should be to follow the example of Jesus in order to get back to being the men and women God intended us to be. That is what it means to be a "disciple" of Jesus: it means to be an imitator of him. In fact, the word "Christian" was not a label the early believers gave themselves. Instead, it was what the community said of them after observing them. The word "Christ-ian" means "Christ follower." He was no Greek deity floating in effortless ease around the serenity of Mount Olympus. Jesus was the Word-made-flesh that lived our kind of life to show us how to do it right.

He is our Encourager

The fact that Jesus is our example could be intimidating if he was not also our encourager.

The Bible says, "For we do not have a high priest who is unable to sympathize with our weaknesses, but we have one who has been tempted in every way, just as we are—yet was without sin. Let us then approach the throne of grace with confidence, so that we may receive mercy and find grace to help us in our time of need" (Hebrews 4:15-16). Sometimes we want to pray, "Lord, I'm tempted" or "Jesus, I'm struggling down here," or "Lord, life just hasn't been fair to me recently." It's good to know that we can bring those things to a Lord who can say, "I *know* what you mean. Follow my example and hang in there."

I read about fifteen-year-old Douglas Maurer of Missouri, whose mother took him to the emergency room after he had suffered high temperature and flu-like symptoms for several days. Blood work revealed that Douglas had leukemia. For days, Douglas endured blood transfusions, spinal and bone marrow tests and chemotherapy. The doctors were blunt about the seriousness of his condition. They said he would have to undergo chemotherapy for three years. They told Douglas that he would go bald and his body would swell up. The news sent him into deep depression.

One of his aunts ordered an arrangement of flowers to be sent to Douglas. "I want the planter to be especially attractive," she told the florist. "It's for my teenage nephew who has leukemia." The boy appreciated the floral arrangement and the card from his aunt, but it was the second card attached to the vase that really caught his attention. The second card read: "Douglas—I took your order at the florist shop. I had leukemia when I was seven years old. I'm 22 years old now. Good luck. My heart goes out to you. Sincerely, Laura Bradley."

Douglas' face lit up. His mother said, "For the first time since he had been in the hospital, he had gotten some inspiration. He had talked to so many doctors and nurses. But this one card, from the woman at the florist who had survived leukemia, was the thing that made him believe he might beat the disease."[2]

Laura Bradley's words of encouragement had authority because she had experienced what Douglas was going through. In the same way, Jesus has experienced everything that we as humans face: the temptations, the injustice, the misunderstanding, the loneliness, and the pain. He's even experienced what it's like to hear his Father say "no" to a prayer request: the night before he went to the cross, he asked the Father to remove the "cup" of suffering so that he would not have to drink it, but then he yielded to his Father's will. What's more, he's already gone through a part of the human experience that you and I haven't come to yet: He's already experienced what it's like to die. Those who talk to him in prayer, worship him in song, and study his words from Scripture find encouragement from someone who knows.

Immanuel

In the Christmas story, the angel told Mary that people would see her child and exclaim, "Immanuel!" which means, "God with us" (Matthew 1:23).

Joan Osborne asked an important question, and Jesus has firmly answered it. God was one of us.

Chapter 9
What Does the Resurrection Prove?

Several years ago *Time* magazine ran a cover story with this title: "Who Was Jesus?" For the next several weeks the magazine received hundreds of letters from people writing in to say that the magazine raised the wrong question. The question, they said, should not be "Who *was* Jesus." Instead, it should be, "Who *is* Jesus."[1] Jesus is not some dead historical figure but the living Lord. Jesus was raised to life again—life that continues to this day. In the words of the Apostles' Creed:

> *The third day he rose again from the dead.*
> *He ascended into heaven,*
> *and sits at the right hand of God the Father Almighty.*

I want to take us again to the image of the pearl diver. Do you recall where she's been so far? At the surface, she was breathing fresh air, feeling the wind, squinting at the bright sunlight in a blue sky and hearing the words of encouragement from her friends. Then she plunged below the surface. Deeper and deeper she went until colors faded, light faded, and warmer surface water gave way to dark, cold water. She's been down along the oozy muck of the ocean bed digging up gnarled oyster shells, the dark water heavy on her limbs. She's been under water for several minutes now, and her lungs are beginning to burn as she turns to head for the surface. With her oysters in her hands, she slowly and methodically pumps her legs to keep pace with the rising bubbles. Finally she breaks the top of the water with a smile of triumph to her companions, and she holds up her prizes—oysters filled with pearls.

That's what Jesus did for us. He came down to our depths so that he might bring us up to his heights. We are the treasures he descended to get!

As we've seen in the past two chapters, the Creed explains who Jesus is by taking us from the apex of heaven down into the darkest reaches of human experience. The ancient words describe Jesus as "Christ," "God's only Son," and "our Lord," who was "conceived," "born," "crucified" and "buried." The One who was everything it means to be God became everything it means to be man. But the words "crucified, dead, and buried," don't complete the story of Jesus. The Bible says Jesus rose up from the dead, ascended into heaven, and today intercedes for us at God's right hand.

Many people prefer to think of Jesus as Thomas Jefferson thought of him. Our nation's third president regarded Jesus as nothing more than a remarkable man of the past whose teachings provided guidance for earthly life. He even formed his own personal edition of the Bible by cutting out the verses that referred to anything supernatural. The only things left were Christ's teachings and the record of his death. Jefferson's "Bible" is still available today, and in it the gospel story ends with people placing Jesus' body in the tomb and walking away. To Jefferson, belief in the resurrection was more than just irrational; it was irrelevant. To him, Jesus' example and teaching was the heart of the story, not Jesus' crucifixion and resurrection.

Though very few keep a copy of Jefferson's Bible on their nightstand, many share his understanding of the life of Christ. A few years ago on her radio program, Dr. Laura Schlessinger asked a caller about the value of believing in the resurrection. At the height of her popularity, Dr. Laura was heard on 430 radio stations by an estimated listening audience of 18 million people. One caller asked for advice regarding her fiancé, who attended a different church than the caller attended. The sharp differences in what the two churches taught were causing a problem in the relationship. When Dr. Laura pressed for an example, the caller answered that her fiancés church did not affirm the resurrection. "Tell me something," Dr. Laura replied, "I don't understand all these ins and outs. What difference does the resurrection make?"[2]

The caller didn't have an answer. Do you?

Numerous good books offer proof for the resurrection, but what does the resurrection prove? It's not just the *rationality* of the story, but its *relevance* that needs to be addressed. The *value* of the resurrection centers on three words: *validation, victory,* and *vigilance.*

Validation of His Words

Like Jefferson, many people will respectfully refer to Jesus as a great moral teacher. One thing this great moral teacher taught, however, was that he would be killed and would rise again. Before it all happened, he warned his followers (Matthew 20:18-19 NLT):

> "When we get to Jerusalem, the Son of Man will be betrayed to the leading priests and the teachers of religious law. They will sentence him to die. Then they will hand him over to the Romans to be mocked, whipped, and crucified. But on the third day he will be raised from the dead."

Jesus didn't just say this just once; he said it over and over. His predictions about his execution and resurrection saturated his teachings. If what he predicted is true, it strengthens our trust in the other things he said. If what he taught about his death and resurrection is false, he's not really a trustworthy teacher after all.

That's why the resurrection is the linchpin in the whole Christian worldview. As the Apostle Paul wrote (1 Corinthians 15:14-20 Msg):

> Face it—if there's no resurrection for Christ, everything we've told you is smoke and mirrors, and everything you've staked your life on is smoke and mirrors.... If all we get out of Christ is a little inspiration for a few short years, we're a pretty sorry lot. But the truth is that Christ has been raised up, the first in a long legacy of those who are going to leave the cemeteries.

Critics down through the years have attacked the reality of the Easter story, but fabricated stories just don't have the characteristics of the Easter story. Let me put it this way: If I were making up something like the Easter story, I would do several things differently.[3] Here's what I'd do:

First, I'd use a different time and location. I would have waited a while before I spread the story, and then told the tale far from where it was supposed to have happened. That way, fewer people could disprove me. But within fifty days of the Resurrection, and in the same city where Jesus died, the disciples were preaching that he had been raised from the dead (Acts 2). Paul wrote that more than five hundred people had seen Jesus alive after the crucifixion and he added that most of them were still around as of his writing (1 Corinthians 15:6). In other words, "talk with them yourself if you need to."

Second, I'd use different eyewitnesses. Several biblical accounts of Jesus' first post-resurrection appearances were to women, but in the first-century world women were not regarded as reliable witnesses in a court of law. If I were making up a story, I'd probably make sure to use the kind of witnesses the culture of that time considered credible. Furthermore, I wouldn't have used any specific names for my eyewitnesses, especially famous names of influential people. The Bible writers, however, mention at least 16 individuals by name as witnesses to the Easter story, and one of those is Joseph of Arimathea (John 19:38). He was a wealthy, influential member of the Sanhedrin, the Jewish high court. If I were making up a story, I certainly wouldn't include a famous man who was still living.

Third, I'd remove the variation of details between eyewitness accounts. If I made up a story like the resurrection, I'd like to think I'm smart enough to make sure that all the parts of my story correlate, sort of like a good crook would when forming an alibi with his partner. Accomplices in a lie make sure they can all give the same details so no one will question their account. But when you read the various Gospel accounts of Jesus' death, resurrection and post-resurrection appearances, they differ in some of the details. For example, while Mark wrote that three women walked together to the tomb and found it empty, John only mentioned one of the women. Also, while Mark mentioned that an angel announces Christ's resurrection to the bewildered women, Luke reported the presence of a second angel. Likewise, while John reported that Simon Peter and another of the Apostles ran to the tomb to confirm the report of the women, Luke only mentions the actions of Simon Peter. However, instead of making the Gospel accounts unreliable, differences such as these lend credibility because they are more in line with how actual eyewitness accounts unfold.[4]

Fourth, I'd stop short of dying for my lie. Countless people willingly die for their religious beliefs if they sincerely believe them to be true, but people won't die for their religious beliefs if they know their beliefs are false. The disciples claimed to have seen Jesus alive. It is one thing to spread these kinds of claims as long as it generates interest, but totally another to keep expressing these beliefs under persecution and martyrdom—which is exactly what the disciples did. In his remarkable book, *Loving God*, Charles Colson said that one of the things that strengthened his confidence in the Apostles' claims that they had seen the resurrected Christ was how they maintained that story down through decades of hardship and martyrdom. By comparison, Colson pointed out that he and his fellow Watergate conspirators couldn't maintain their stories under just a few months of investigation.[5]

In fact, the actions of the Apostles following the crucifixion were very different than their behavior in the days leading up to it. When Jesus was arrested and crucified, his disillusioned followers fled for their lives. Then, little more than a month after the crucifixion, they were out in the public eye again in boldness. They faced opposition, they endured persecution, and they even accepted martyrdom. These actions cannot be discounted. There was something that happened that transformed them from disillusioned men to confident men, from frightened men to bold men. They claimed it was the fact that they had seen Jesus alive, just as he had promised.

The point is, fabricated stories have different characteristics than what we find in the Easter story. Throughout history, brilliant men and women have concluded that the resurrection accounts in the Bible ring true. As recently as 2002, Oxford philosophy professor Richard Swinburne presented his case to a Yale audience that a reasonable mind can be ninety-seven percent sure that the resurrection of Jesus happened. The fact that such a distinguished professor in such a distinguished setting would defend the resurrection was intriguing enough to make the *New York Times*.[6]

The first thing that the resurrection proves, then, is validation. Easter proves that Jesus is trustworthy. Woven throughout his great moral teachings was the prediction that he would be killed and would rise again. The fact that he was killed and he rose again adds validity to everything else he taught.

Victory for His People

The Apostle Paul wrote, "Just as Christ was raised from the dead . . . we too may live a new life" (Romans 6:4). Notice two important phrases in that verse: "Just as," and "we too." The hope of a fresh start is tied to the reality of the resurrection.

The Easter story proves it's not too late for anyone. The Bible states that when a man or woman believes in Christ, a union takes place between that life and the Lord's life. When we become believers, our old life with its frustration, regret and guilt dies with Christ. And, since we unite with a Christ that was raised from the dead, we can have a new life with hope and expectation and confidence.

In the film "City Slickers" Mitch consoles his friend Phil, a character who has lost his marriage and his job, and he wants to throw in the towel. Mitch tells him, "Take a do-over. Like when we were kids playing ball and the game went bad. Just start over. You can have a clean slate." The reason that line connected with so many moviegoers is that we've all experienced the desire to "just start over." If this is true and God can enable us to make a fresh start, what would you like to do over? If you wrote your answer in the margin of this page, some of you would write: "I'd like to be a better influence with my kids." Or, "I'd like to be a better example to my sister or brother." Or, "I'd like to be more attentive to the needs of people around me." Or, "I'd like to make better choices." Or, "I'd like to show stronger self-control." We can't go back and reverse all the mistakes and sins of the past, but we can say, "That was the old me, and in Christ people will see a new me. I get a do-over."

Not only is the *hope* of a fresh start tied to the reality of the resurrection; the *power* for a fresh start is tied to that event, too. Paul wrote, "God's power is very great for us who believe. That power is the *same* as the great strength God used to raise Christ from the dead. . ." (Ephesians 1:19-20 NCV). The Easter story is remarkable, of course: a dead man walked out of a tomb to live again forever. But according to this verse, what God did in that tomb is no different than what God is doing in every believer's life. Easter power is still at work today in those who want to fix a troubled marriage, break a destructive habit, change a crippling attitude, develop a needed skill, or pursue a worthy dream.

Of course, no matter how many things we can straighten out in this life, it's probably the *end* of life itself that troubles us most. The Bible promises victory for believers in this battle, too. Paul wrote, "If all we get out of Christ is a little inspiration for a few short years, we're a pretty sorry lot. But the truth is that Christ has been raised up, the first in a long legacy of those who are going to leave the cemeteries" (1 Corinthians 15:19-20 Msg). In a later part of the book, we'll examine more closely the meaning of this great promise. For now, note again how the Bible connects the truth of the Easter story with victory—in this case, victory over our future death.

Vigilance Beside His Father

Reciting the creed, Christians state that Jesus is now at "the right hand of God the Father Almighty."[7] What is he doing there? The Bible says he's bringing our needs to the Father's attention:

> "He is able to save completely those who come to God through him, because he always lives to intercede for them" (Hebrews 7:25).

> "Christ Jesus, who died—more than that, who was raised to life—is at the right hand of God and is also interceding for us" (Romans 8:34).

> "My dear children, I write this to you so that you will not sin. But if anybody does sin, we have one who speaks to the Father in our defense—Jesus Christ, the Righteous One" (1 John 2:1).

I love to meditate on that thought. One day this Pearl Diver is going to bring me personally before his Father, but even now he's bringing my name before his Father. I've prayed for people and afterward they say, "Thank you, pastor. I feel a bit better, I feel stronger already." If we draw comfort from the prayer of a common pastor, imagine the Lord Jesus himself praying for you! He is praying for your marriage right now. He is praying for your success in school right now. He sees your discouragement and prays for fresh hope; he sees your fear and prays for courage; he sees you weakening to a temptation and he prays for strength. And when we fail, Jesus says, "Father, remember I died for them, and forgive."

Treasure Hunt

We are God's treasure. Jesus, as I've illustrated in the last three chapters, dove down from the heights of heaven, descended into even the deepest, darkest experiences of human life, and rose back up to heaven with our lives in his hands.

Because Jesus lives again we can trust him, we can ask him to help us prevail over what troubles us about life and death, and we can have someone to watch out for us. Thomas Jefferson was wrong: Cutting the resurrection out of Christ's story ruins the whole story. That's why the Bible says, "If you confess with your mouth, 'Jesus is Lord,' and believe in your heart that God raised him from the dead, you will be saved" (Romans 10:9).

What a person concludes about the *reality* and *relevance* of Christ's resurrection makes all the difference. It always has.

When Paul shared the story of Jesus with the intellectuals of Athens, Scripture says they listened politely until he began to describe how Jesus was raised from the dead (Acts 17:32-34 Msg):

> At the phrase "raising him from the dead," the listeners split: Some laughed at him and walked off making jokes; others said, "Let's do this again. We want to hear more." There were still others, it turned out, who were convinced then and there.

Some cut off any further consideration of the Christian claims. Some expressed interest in continuing the conversation. Some crossed the line of faith. What about you?

Chapter 10
The Return of the King

After Jesus spent another forty days with his disciples following his resurrection, he ascended before their eyes. Their astonished silence was broken by the words of two angels. "Why do you stand here looking into the sky?" the angels asked. "This same Jesus, who has been taken from you into heaven, will come back in the same way you have seen him go into heaven." (Acts 1:11). It was something Jesus himself had often promised them.

The disciples' approach to life changed because of this promise. The thought of Christ's return motivated the first Christians to make the right moral choices, to be patient, and to keep their faith during persecution. Because it so deeply impacted their view of life, they often referred to their Lord's return in scripture. There are more than 500 references to the return of Christ and they occur in 23 of the 27 books in the New Testament; in fact, his return is mentioned on nearly every page of the New Testament. The Apostle Paul even summarized the expectations of the Christian life as simply "to serve the living and true God, and to wait for his Son from heaven" (1 Thessalonians 1:9-10).

As believers around the world have recited the Creed down through the centuries, they have continued to express the same conviction:

"I believe ... he shall come to judge the living and the dead."

It's remarkable how someone's promise to return can change our perspective. It happened to the Filipino people during the Second World War. I learned about this when I was in middle school, and my family lived in the Philippine Islands where my father worked in the U.S. Embassy in Manila. One of my most memorable experiences was making a fifty-mile march with Boy Scouts from both the Philippines and the United States to commemorate the tragic Bataan Death March. We marched in the early 1970s along the same trail that Japanese invaders used in the early 1940s to bring Filipino and American POWs to concentration camps. Many of those soldiers died along the way.

Japan had invaded the Philippines in December 1941, shortly after the bombing of Pearl Harbor. The American general in the Philippines, Douglas MacArthur, chose Bataan peninsula and Corregidor Island at the mouth of Manila Bay as defensive strongholds. But the Japanese could not be stopped: Bataan fell April 9, 1942; Corregidor fell twenty-seven days later.

General MacArthur was ordered to leave the Philippines and he barely escaped to Australia, where he set up the Allied offensive against Japan. He told reporters that a primary goal of the war in the Pacific was to liberate the Philippines. He vowed to personally return. Speaking of his narrow escape from Japanese pursuers, he said, "I came through and I shall return."

That casual comment, "I shall return," galvanized the Filipino opposition. In his book *Reminiscences*, MacArthur remarked:

> The phrase 'I shall return,' seemed a promise of magic to the Filipinos. It lit a flame that became a symbol which focused the nation's indomitable will. . . . It was scraped in the sands of the beaches, it was daubed on the walls of the barrios, it was stamped on the mail, it was whispered in the cloisters of the church.

Three words—"I shall return"—became the rallying cry for millions. They clung to those words, found hope in those words, and drew strength from those words. In 1944, MacArthur did return with Allied forces to successfully liberate the islands, just as he promised.

Jesus said he would return, and when we believe that promise, it changes our perspective on this life. There are at least four ways that life is different for those who anticipate the return of Christ.

We Know We're Wanted and Valued

Before he returned to heaven, Jesus told us what he would be doing there. "I am going to prepare a place for you," he said. "When everything is ready, I will come and get you, so that you will always be with me where I am" (John 14:3 NLT).

The Son of God himself is personally overseeing the preparations for our eternal home. When everything is ready, he will return to escort us there. As we saw in the last chapter, Jesus is the ultimate pearl diver who descended to our depths to raise us to his heights. He descended for us—we are his treasure! And his pearl-diving work won't be complete until he shows us the magnificent place he has prepared for us in heaven.

It's remarkable how someone's promise to return can change our perspective

Have you ever looked forward to seeing someone who was obviously looking forward to seeing you? It makes a college semester or business trip more bearable if you know that someone's getting ready for your return home. Maybe you've returned from a long college semester to find that your mom remembered to cook your favorite meal. Or maybe you've walked in the door after a business trip to the delighted squeals of your small children or the wagging tail of your dog. There's nothing like the feeling of being *wanted*. That's the way a believer looks at life. No matter what we experience in this life, things are more bearable knowing that the sovereign Lord of the universe is preparing a marvelous place for us and will come back to escort us there himself.

We Know That Things Will Be Set Right

Christians believe that Christ will return to fix all that has gone wrong with this world. I've talked with people who can't believe that a loving and just God rules a universe where so many painful and unjust things happen. They cannot believe in a faith like Pippa's in the Robert Browning poem, "Pippa Passes"—a faith that simply looks at the beauties of a fresh spring morning and contentedly sighs,

> God's in his Heaven—
> All's right with the world!

Some people assume that this is the Christian view of the world, and since they can't reconcile that view with the pain and injustice they see around them, they reject Christianity. But that's not the best summary of the Christian faith. Instead, a believer takes a clear-eyed look at the heartbreaks of this life and says, "Things *aren't* right in our world—but they eventually *will be*."

According to the Christian worldview, long ago rebellion against God altered the way we now experience the created order. As Scripture says about Christ: "at present we do not see everything subject to him" (Hebrews 2:8). But the day is coming when "Christ will overcome all spiritual rulers, authorities, and powers, and will hand over the Kingdom to God the Father. For Christ must rule until God defeats all enemies and puts them under his feet. The last enemy to be defeated will be death" (1 Corinthians 15:24-26 TEV). Scripture promises that on that day, our God "will wipe every tear from their eyes. There will be no more death or mourning or crying or pain, for the old order of things has passed away" (Revelation 21:4). Paul wrote, "The Lord himself will descend from heaven with a shout," thus beginning the whole process of setting things right (1 Thess. 4:16 HCSB).

Looking at that last verse, what do you think Jesus will shout? That question surfaced in one minister's classroom as he taught at the West African Bible College. "Reverend," one of Gregory

Fisher's students asked, "Scripture says that Christ will descend from heaven with a commanding shout. I would like to know what that command will be."

Fisher wanted to leave the question unanswered, or to say something about the symbolic nature of literature that describes the end of time, or to remind the student that we must not go past what Scripture has explicitly revealed. But suddenly there came into the minister's mind an encounter with a refugee from the Liberian civil war. The refugee was a high school principal who had faced inhuman cruelty at the hands of death squads. Then the beggars came into the mind of the professor: numerous homeless people that he passed on his way to school every day. The vacant eyes of the hopeless, helpless beggars haunted him throughout his days in Africa.

"Reverend," came the student's voice again, "You haven't given me an answer. What will Jesus shout as he returns?"

"Enough," said the professor.

"Enough?" echoed the student.

"Yes, he will shout 'Enough! Enough suffering! Enough starvation! Enough third-world terror. Enough death. Enough injustice! Enough lives trapped in hopelessness! Enough sickness and disease! Enough time!' He will shout *Enough!*"[1]

It's a beautiful thought. Regardless of what his battle cry will be, though, we look forward to the day we hear it. It will signal the start of setting right all that's wrong with the life we know. A question mark may still hang over why we suffer pain and injustice in the present, or why it's taking so long for God to come and set things straight. But it's good to know that human history has a happy ending.

As Billy Graham once made his way to a meeting in the U.S. Senate dining room, he was stopped by a group of senators at a table. "Say, Billy," said one, "We're having an argument over whether it's right to look on life as an optimist or a pessimist. Which one are you?"

"I'm an optimist," the famous evangelist said, "because I've read the last chapter of the book."

We Know That Life Has a Purpose

Just as MacArthur's promise to return galvanized the Filipinos to action, Christ's promise to return does not lead to *idleness* but to *faithfulness*. When Jesus gave his most detailed teaching about the events leading up to his return, he concluded with a call to action. Jesus said, "Who is the wise and loyal servant that the master trusts to give the other servants their food at the right time? *When the master comes and finds the servant doing his work*, the servant will be blessed. I tell you the truth, the master will choose that servant to take care of everything he owns" (Matthew 24:45-47 NCV).

Believers want to be found in the middle of faithful work upon our Commander's unexpected return. The author and Oxford professor, C.S. Lewis, once wrote:

> Happy are those whom [Christ] finds laboring in their vocations, whether they were merely going out to feed the pigs or laying good plans to deliver humanity a hundred years hence from some great evil. The curtain has indeed now fallen. Those pigs will never in fact be fed, the great campaign against . . . slavery or governmental tyranny will never in fact proceed to victory. No matter; you were at your post when the inspection came.[2]

It makes a difference to live under that expectation. As Lewis said, our work could be as noble as bringing an end to some social injustice or as common as feeding hungry pigs on the farm. If Christ should come in the midst of that work, the social cause would remain unfinished and the pigs would remain unfed, but what is important is to be found at work.

When Jesus tells us to *wait* for his return, then, that doesn't mean we passively sit around. Instead, those who anticipate Christ's return jump into life with an active faithfulness. We want to *carpe* every *diem* as if it's our last chance to make a difference!

This reality hit home with me early in my calling as a pastor. When I was in my early twenties and attending seminary, a fellow student succumbed to a brain tumor and died suddenly. That sent a number of us on some soul searching. I remember one of my friends who began to wonder what we were all doing wasting our time in seminary. My friend decided that if death could snatch us away before he even began to serve a church, then it would be better for him to drop out of school and start fulfilling his calling immediately.

I drew another conclusion, however. Though it was tragic that a seminary colleague died, he had not wasted his time. When death took him, he was in the middle of doing exactly what God wanted him doing at that particular moment. Ever since, that's how I've tried to approach life: I always want to be in mid-project when I'm called away. I want to be at my post when the inspection comes.

We Know That Our Lives Will Be Reviewed

Set this book down for a moment and think: what would you go back and change about yesterday—just *yesterday*—if you knew that yesterday's attitudes and actions will eventually be evaluated by the God who made you? Would you have been more compassionate? Would you have caught yourself before you said those hateful things behind a co-worker's back? Would you have backed away from behavior that has been bringing you closer and closer to infidelity? Would you have been more generous? More disciplined?

It makes a difference when we live under the awareness that God will hold up yesterday and every day for inspection. In the words of our Creed, Christians believe that Christ will return "to judge the living and the dead." You may have recited older versions of the Creed that speak of him judging "the quick and the dead." The word "quick" is an old English way of speaking of what is "living." Mercury is called *quicksilver* because it's a metal that moves. Explorers fear falling into *quicksand*, which is moving ground. Mothers used to speak of the first movement of the unborn child as the *quickening*. So, it's the *living* as well as the dead whom Christ will judge. This means that Christ will return to an entire generation that will be alive to see him. At that time, the dead will be raised, too, so that whether we're alive or dead at Christ's return, we'll all face the evaluation of our days.

This line in the Creed about the living and the dead simply summarizes the Apostles' teaching in Scripture—teaching that began with Jesus himself. Speaking of himself in the third person, Jesus said (Matthew 25:31-32 Msg),

> "When he finally arrives, blazing in beauty and all his angels with him, the Son of Man will take his place on his glorious throne. Then all the nations will be arranged before him and he will sort the people out, much as a shepherd sorts out sheep and goats."

Elsewhere he said (John 5:26-29 CEV),

> "The Father has the power to give life, and he has given that same power to the Son. And he has given his Son the right to judge everyone, because he is the Son of Man. Don't be surprised! The time will come when all of the dead will hear the voice of the Son of Man, and they will come out of their graves. Everyone who has done good things will rise to life, but everyone who has done evil things will rise and be condemned."

In a future chapter, we'll look more closely at Christ's teaching about the resurrection and eternity. For now, our focus is on Christ's promise to "judge the living and the dead" upon his return. Life is different for those who operate within this worldview. As they make their decisions, hold their opinions, and correct their mistakes, they ask themselves, "What will God eventually say about this?"

Two Extremes

It changes the way you view life when you look forward to the return of the King. You know you're wanted and valued, you know that things will be set right, and you live with a commitment to faithfulness, knowing that a thorough review is coming. Because of these advantages, the Apostle Paul told us to "eagerly wait for the return of our Lord Jesus Christ" (1 Corinthians 1:7 NLT). Jesus taught us to pray for his arrival. In fact, that's what you're praying when you say, "Thy kingdom come," as you recite the Lord's Prayer. However, in any study of Christ's promised return, make sure you keep to a path between two extremes: *speculation* and *skepticism*.

On the one extreme, we must avoid *speculation*. The same Jesus who told us to hope and pray for his return also told us not to try to predict it. Faithfulness in following him is the proper response of believers, not idle conjecture. Sadly, though, there's no shortage of those who speculate about the timing of Christ's return. When such wild predictions make headlines, people turn away from the rest of the Christian message.

Don't let fanatical speculations about Christ's return make you cynical. Jesus himself warned against predicting a date for his return. "No one knows about that day or hour," he said, "not even the angels in heaven, nor the Son, but only the Father" (Mark 13:32). During his time on earth, under the limitations of being human, he admitted that even *he* did not know this information. So, it's the height of arrogance for some to claim to know what Jesus himself said he could not know.

On the other extreme, we must avoid *skepticism*. We need to make sure that the embarrassing incidences of failed speculations don't make us turn away from a serious look at Christ's frequent promises to return.

A few decades after Christ's earthly life, Simon Peter wrote, "It is most important for you to understand what will happen in the last days. People will laugh at you. . . . . They will say, 'Jesus promised to come again. Where is he?'" The Apostle went on to point out that, "With the Lord a day is like a thousand years, and a thousand years are like a day" (2 Peter 3:3-4, 8 NCV). In other words, though it's been nearly two millennia since Jesus left with his promise to return, from the perspective of eternity, beyond the confines of time, it's been little more than a couple of days.

Some would say that Christ's promised return has lost its relevance after so many years, but that reminds me of what a research scientist said after the eruption of the Philippine volcano Pinatubo. Hundreds of people lost their lives, in part because they had built their homes and businesses on the side of this active volcano. When asked why so many had built up a domestic life on the slopes of a volcano, the scientist said the matter had an easy explanation. For six hundred years, Pinatubo had shown no signs of activity. "They forgot it was a volcano," he said, "and they began treating it like it was a mountain."[3]

Likewise, we can build our lives within a universe that has remained the same for many centuries, forgetting that our homes, our businesses, and our nations are all in the realm of a King who has promised to return.

So, we must chart a course between the extremes of *speculation* and *skepticism* as we try to understand what this great moral teacher named Jesus said about his return.

Believers are convinced that, in the words of the Creed, "he shall come to judge the living and the dead." We have concluded that since we cannot run *from* God we should run *to* him, asking him to be our Forgiver and Leader. "I am coming!" Jesus said. In the last words of the Bible, we are given the right reply to this news: "Amen! Come, Lord Jesus!" (Revelation 22:20 HCSB).

Part Four: "I Believe in the Holy Spirit"

*I believe
in God the Father Almighty,
Maker of heaven and earth;
And in Jesus Christ his only Son our Lord;
who was conceived by the Holy Spirit,
born of the Virgin Mary,
suffered under Pontius Pilate,
was crucified, dead, and buried.
The third day he rose again from the dead.
He ascended into heaven,
and sits at the right hand of God the Father Almighty.
From there he shall come
to judge the living and the dead.
I believe in the Holy Spirit;
the one holy church;
the communion of saints;
the forgiveness of sins;
the resurrection of the body;
and the life everlasting.
Amen.*

Chapter 11
The Hound of Heaven

Three-year-old Joseph Leffler told his mother he was going fishing. She thought the idea was cute, and smiled as she watched him walk out into the backyard with his three-foot-long plastic pipe—his favorite pretend fishing rod. That was Friday at 1:00 p.m. When she couldn't find him an hour later, she became worried.

When she had not found him by sundown, she became frantic.

Joseph Leffler was lost in the woods outside Estacada, Oregon. A massive search began, and the progress of the search dominated the news throughout the weekend. As Friday night gave way to Saturday, and Saturday passed into Sunday morning, worries only intensified. How long could a three-year-old survive in the wild forest?

Then, just before noon on Sunday, little Joseph came out of the woods and walked straight up to one of the searchers. "I had to look twice," said Judy Magill, who was coordinating the search dogs. "I couldn't believe this little boy was walking toward me. He stretched out his arms and I picked him up," she said.

A front-page picture showed little Joseph in his mother's arms. He looked bewildered but well. Above the picture in bold black letters the newspaper headline read: "Lost Boy Finds Searcher."[1]

I love that headline. It's a perfect way to describe the beginning of a relationship with God. We think of ourselves as "seekers" when we explore faith issues like the ones described in this book. In reality, when we finally start reaching out to God, we discover that he's been reaching out to us all along.

Francis Thompson called God "The Hound of Heaven." In his famous 1893 poem, Thompson described the way God chased him through his struggle with addiction. He wrote:

> *I fled Him, down the nights and down the days;*
> *I fled Him, down the arches of the years;*
> *I fled Him, down the labyrinthine ways*
> *Of my own mind; and in the mist of tears*
> *I hid from Him…*

Thompson goes on to write about how he sought fulfillment in various things, only to be disappointed in them one by one. Nothing seemed to satisfy. Then the reality of things became clear to him, and he heard the call:

> *Is my gloom, after all,*
> *Shade of His hand, outstretched caressingly?*
> *"Ah, fondest, blindest, weakest,*
> *I am He Whom thou seekest!"*[2]

Thompson could have entitled his poem, "Lost Boy Finds Searcher." He pictured God as pursuing him until Thompson finally yielded to him.

According to the Bible, this is the work of the Holy Spirit in the world. In the Apostles' Creed, after believers recite that we believe in "God the Father Almighty, Maker of heaven and earth," and that we believe in "Jesus Christ, His only Son our Lord," we then express our belief in "the Holy Spirit."

What—or *who*, more exactly—is the Holy Spirit? The Bible says, "The Lord is the Spirit" (2 Corinthians 3:17-18). The Spirit is not some "influence" or "force," but the presence of God himself.

We've already seen that Jesus considered himself to be God and to be *sent* by God. We can say the same thing about the Spirit: he is God and sent by God. This is a difficult concept and in Chapter 13 we'll cover this more thoroughly. Before we get to the *nature* of the Spirit, though, we need to understand the *impact* of the Spirit upon our lives. In fact, the men Jesus chose to lead and teach his church first *experienced* the Holy Spirit and then *drew conclusions* from their reflections on those experiences. We want to follow that same order in this book. So, in this chapter we'll look at how God works upon those who do not yet believe in Jesus. In the next chapter we'll look at how God works within those who do. Then, in Chapter 13, we'll draw some conclusions about what it means to say, "I believe in the Holy Spirit."

What—or who, more exactly— is the Holy Spirit?

According to the Bible, the Spirit does two things among nonbelievers: he *convicts* and he *converts*. As Francis Thompson put it, he is the Hound of Heaven.

The Spirit Convicts

Before his arrest and execution, Jesus told his followers that when he went away he would "send" them the Spirit. Before he told them how the Spirit would impact their own lives, though, he told them the Spirit "will prove to the people of the world [nonbelievers] the truth about sin, about being right with God, and about judgment" (John 16:8 NCV).

Jesus said the Spirit will "prove the truth," which means to persuade or convict. In a sense, the Spirit's work is like a prosecuting attorney, but with an important distinction. Prosecutors in a court of law try to convince a judge or jury of an accused person's guilt; the Holy Spirit works to convince the *accused person* of his wrongdoing.

According to Jesus the Spirit is at work to prove the truth about three things: sin, being right with God, and judgment. Let's look at this work carefully.

People need to be convinced of sin. People need to squarely face the attitudes and choices they've made and they need to draw some conclusions about their true selves in light of it all. Specifically, though, Jesus said they need to be persuaded of the sin of unbelief. There's a difference between honest seeking and a reluctance to do something with the information that seeking has provided. Every seeker who has become a believer will tell you that, in the end, they found an important distinction: They realized that their failure to accept Christ's claims was more a moral issue than an intellectual one. Their reluctance had less to do with unanswered questions and more to do with unwillingness to admit their need of a forgiver and leader. The Spirit is actively at work upon every nonbeliever to press home that nonbelief is moral failure—sin.

People need to be convinced of what it takes to be right with God. It's one thing to admit that we sin and another thing to understand the seriousness of it and what to do about it. How do we set things right with God? The Apostle Paul said of his unbelieving countrymen: "They did not know the righteousness that comes from God and *sought to establish their own*" (Romans 10:3). He knew something about this effort personally, because he said he had to get to a point where he considered all his efforts at being right with God as "rubbish" (Philippians 3:8-9). He found that being right with God did not come from all his religious activity and rule-keeping but through accepting the forgiveness and leadership of Jesus. "He saved us," Paul said, "not because of the good things we did, but because of his mercy" (Titus 3:5 NLT).

People need to be convinced of the reality of judgment. According to Jesus, the Spirit is actively reminding people that history is moving toward a time when life will be audited. The Spirit uses the circumstances of life to remind people that life is limited and the clock is counting down on their spiritual search. They need to draw some conclusions about God before God draws some conclusions about them.

I have dentists and doctors as friends, but I have to admit that I'd rather visit with them socially instead of professionally. Visits to their offices usually result in a lot of uncomfortable poking and humiliating prodding and unpleasant recommendations. Naturally, the only reason anyone would submit to such treatment is because it's the only way to make an unhealthy body whole again. Jesus said that the Holy Spirit pokes and prods, too. He convicts of sin, righteousness, and judgment, with the aim of bringing us to spiritual health and wholeness.

The Spirit Converts

According to the Bible, the Spirit is behind conversion as well as conviction. Jesus said when we cross into faith, it's like starting life all over again, and he said that "born again" experience was the Spirit's work (John 3:5-8). Paul also described conversion as "renewing by the Holy Spirit" (Titus 3:5 NASB). God is not up in the bleachers dispassionately observing us compete in the game of life. God is part of our process of returning to him. That is the heart of what believers teach about the Holy Spirit: God is passionately, intimately involved with our lives.

Conviction isn't the same as conversion, of course. When Paul was a prisoner under Felix, the Bible says the Roman governor would occasionally send for Paul and ask him about "a life of believing in Jesus Christ." The Bible says (Acts 24:24-25 Msg),

> As Paul continued to insist on right relations with God and his people, about a life of moral discipline and the coming Judgment, Felix felt things getting a little too close for comfort and dismissed him.

Felix was convicted as the Spirit pressed the truth of Paul's words home, but he responded to the uncomfortable experience by simply sending Paul away. Thousands of people do the same thing today by turning off a radio program, closing a book, or cutting off conversation with a friend if any of those things strike too close to home. "You are always against what the Holy Spirit is trying to tell you!" one of the Bible's martyrs said (Acts 7:51 NCV). It was his last appeal before the mob killed him.

For many, though, this resistance finally gives way to the Spirit's persuasions. When this happens, conviction leads to conversion.

What if He Responds?

God the Father said, "I will seek the lost" (Ezekiel 34:16 NASB). God the Son said his mission was "to find and restore the lost" (Luke 19:10 Msg). That work now continues by God the Spirit (Acts 8:26-40; 10:9-48). This activity of the Spirit should prompt some people to seriously consider if they're ready to meet the God they say they want to know.

I remember an experience on a fishing trip from many years ago. I must have been only 9 or 10 when it happened, but I still remember how weak my knees got and how hard my heart pounded.

My uncle had baited my line and dropped it over the railing of a walkway that ran along a Gulf coast causeway in Pensacola, Florida. The bridge had been decommissioned for anything but foot traffic, and it was a rickety old thing. The wooden planks were weather-beaten and rough under my bare feet, and the whole contraption shuddered with every footfall.

My uncle had walked ahead of me, trolling his line over the handrail as he went. Soon he was a hundred yards away, and it was quiet enough to hear the rhythmic slapping of the seawater upon the pylons twenty feet below.

Little boys love to "go fishing" but they can quickly get bored without any action on the line. I had fallen into that bored state, dully letting my bait sway upon the surface of the rolling swells. Suddenly, a huge fish emerged from the murky waters and shot toward my line. Fearing that such a magnificent fish would pull me off that old wooden walkway and into the wild, deep sea far below, I panicked and yanked my line out of the water. The fish disappeared into the deep as quickly as it had appeared, and I was left alone again with unsteady legs and a thumping heart.

While many of the people I've talked to are on a sincere search, others merely "troll" for God. They have no anticipation of finding what they say they're searching for. If God's presence actually welled up from out of the mysterious deep, they would abandon their search for fear of being pulled away and overwhelmed. This is what Felix did in his conversations with the Apostle Paul.

At this stage in your spiritual search, it's important to settle the question of what kind of "fisherman" you are. What will you do if what you've been searching for responds?

Chapter 12
You Can Live Strong

"The Spirit... will be in you."

Jesus gave this remarkable promise to those who follow him (John 14:17). As we saw in the last chapter, the Spirit pursues and persuades those who have not committed themselves to Christ. While the Holy Spirit works *upon* nonbelievers, though, he works *within* believers. At conversion, the work of the Spirit continues, but he moves *indoors*, so to speak, to engage our thoughts, our attitudes and our motivations. In this chapter, we'll focus on the impact of the Spirit within believers.

I'm inspired by the work of Lance Armstrong. Following his cancer scare, the seven-time Tour de France winner wanted to raise attention and funds for cancer research, as well as raise the spirits of those fighting the disease. So, in the spring of 2004, the Lance Armstrong Foundation launched a fundraiser that has become a phenomenon. He began selling yellow rubber wristbands bearing the phrase "LiveStrong." At a dollar a bracelet, he expected to raise six million dollars for his foundation's work. Within five months, twenty million bracelets had been sold and the fad showed no sign of abating.[1]

No doubt, the effort became a national craze in part because people began spotting the bracelets on the wrists of high-profile celebrities. Still, a large part of the popularity is due to the slogan that is both upbeat and pointed: "LiveStrong." For those wearing the bracelets, the phrase became more than just a way to identify with those fighting cancer. It became a rallying cry for facing any setback: *defy the odds... rise above your circumstances... live strong.*

The campaign slogan resonated with so many people because we all face times when we need our courage renewed, our poor attitudes challenged, our resolve freshened, our options clarified. According to the Bible, this is precisely what the Holy Spirit does within believers. When Christians say with the Apostles' Creed, "I believe in the Holy Spirit," it's not merely compliance with some dull theological line. Instead, it's a way of saying, "I can live strong."

The Apostle John wrote that at one point in his teaching ministry, Jesus stood in the Jerusalem Temple and called out loudly to the crowd:

> If anyone is thirsty, let him come to me and drink. Whoever believes in me, as the Scripture has said, streams of living water will flow from within him.

John went on to explain what Jesus was referring to: "By this he meant the Spirit, whom those who believed in him were later to receive" (John 7:37-39). In the days of Jesus, people called water "living" if it flowed. In contrast to stagnant standing water, "living" water was typically fresher and certainly more powerful. Jesus promised that the Holy Spirit would work "within" believers in the same way, providing refreshment and power.

Other Bible texts also point to the presence of the Holy Spirit. We read that the Spirit "dwells" in those of us who believe and lives "in our hearts" so the believer's very body can be called a sacred thing—"a temple of the Holy Spirit" (see Romans 8:9-11, 2 Corinthians 1:22, and 1 Corinthians 6:19 NASB).

This is a remarkable truth, because the Bible says, "The Lord is the Spirit" (2 Corinthians 3:17-18). The Spirit is not a "force" or an "influence" or even God's invisible errand-runner. Instead, he is the presence of God himself. The same God who created us can show us how to live in hope and joy and peace. The same

God who died for our sins can empower us to overcome them. The same God who inspired the Bible can help us apply his instructions to daily life. You may think you can't deal with the troubles of life or can't be victorious over the things that frustrate you. But if God lives in you, you can live strong.

Scripture reveals four things that the Holy Spirit does within believers: he *empowers*, he *enlightens*, he *equips*, and he *encourages*.

He Empowers Us When We're Weak

Believers and nonbelievers have something in common: we get frustrated with ourselves. Some of us let words fly before thinking of the consequences. Others return again and again to routines that don't really satisfy us. Still others seem to be helpless against depressed moods and sour attitudes. Even when we know that all these things hurt us relationally, emotionally, and physically, we can't seem to live in consistent victory over them.

If we're honest, this defines us all, whether we believe in Jesus or not. But Jesus said that whoever believed in him would have help to overcome these weaknesses: when we "walk by the Spirit" and are "led by the Spirit" we "will not do what our sinful selves want" (Galatians 5:16-17 NCV). The work of the Holy Spirit is called "sanctifying work" (2 Thessalonians 2:13). To "sanctify" something means to purify it. As we depend upon the Spirit, the acts of our sinful nature are "put to death" (Romans 8:13). Knowing that God actively wants to help his people overcome our natural inclinations, the Apostle Paul confidently told one group of believers, "I pray that out of [the Father's] glorious riches he may strengthen you with power *through his Spirit in your inner being*" (Ephesians 3:16).

This "sanctifying work" is not completed overnight, and once a battle is won against one area of weakness, we find another area that needs addressing. That's why the Bible describes the spiritual life with words like "fight," "race," and "wrestle" (see 1 Corinthians 9:26, 2 Timothy 4:7, and Colossians 4:12). The good news, though, is that God is not some detached observer in the stands as we engage in this Olympic-level contest for victory. The Lord is the Spirit who empowers us from within to win over our weaknesses. Christians who have experienced this power talk about how, with the help of the Spirit, they have broken harmful habits, they have changed patterns of relating to others, and they have re-aligned attitudes.

He Enlightens Us When We're Confused

Just as every one of us needs strength, we also need better insight. We lie awake at night wondering about what college major to pursue, or whom to marry, or how to fix a troubled marriage, or whether to accept that job offer, or what to say to our rebellious daughter, or how to make sense of heartbreak.

We can become immobilized by confusion, but Jesus promised that the Holy Spirit would be "the Counselor" who "will teach you all things and will remind you of everything I have said to you" (John 14:26). He also called him "the Spirit of truth" who "will guide you into all truth" (John 16:13). Paul knew the source of the truth he taught, and he said, "God has revealed it to us by his Spirit" (1 Corinthians 2:10). In *The Acts of the Apostles*, the biblical history of the early church, we see God's Spirit leading people into strategic opportunities, directing the selection of men for a mission trip, and preventing leaders from going to one place so they would be free to go to another (see Acts 8:29, 13:2, and 16:6-7). Clearly, God *wants* to enlighten those who need wisdom.

The Bible is an important resource in this work. God will never lead us to do something that he has already prohibited. Someone who says that the Spirit has "led" him or her to do something the Bible forbids is unstable. Likewise, be careful of any religious organization that has a history of claiming certain "revelations" from God that actually contradict earlier claims. The Spirit who inspired the Bible enables us to understand it and apply it to life's situations. What Paul wrote to his young protégé, Timothy, is applicable to any of us who want to understand God's will: "Consider what I say, for the Lord will give you understanding in everything" (2 Timothy 2:7 HCSB). We must "consider" what has been said in Scripture, which means to give careful thought to it. But as this study and examination proceeds, we can be sure that God will give us "understanding in everything." Assured that God *wants* to enlighten us, Paul did not hesitate to pray for God to do this work in believers. He wrote, "I keep asking that the God of our Lord Jesus Christ, the glorious Father, may *give you the Spirit of wisdom and revelation*, so that you may know him better" (Ephesians 1:17).

He Equips Us When We're Inadequate

Just as the Spirit can *empower* us when we're frustrated by weaknesses and the Spirit can *enlighten* us when we're immobilized by confusion, the Spirit can *equip* us with what we need to handle our responsibilities.

The Bible tells stories of the Spirit of God endowing a craftsman with "skill, ability and knowledge in all kinds of crafts" (Exodus 31:1-5), equipping people with leadership skills (e.g., Genesis 41:38[2]), and supplying the courage to speak (e.g., 2 Samuel 23:2[3]). Jesus even said that when we defend Christian convictions in difficult settings we are not to worry about "what to say or how to say it" because "you will be given what to say, for it will not be you speaking, but the Spirit of your Father speaking through you" (Matthew 10:18-20). When God's people show competence in things like administration, teaching, hospitality, and generosity, the Bible calls this a "manifestation" or "gift" of the Spirit (1 Corinthians 12:7-11; Romans 12:6-8; 1 Peter 4:10).

God is active within believers, enabling them to handle what life throws at them.

He Encourages Us When We're Anxious

Christians tell stories of uncanny peace that has settled over them in the midst of fearful news. Believers report that they sensed an inner prompting to pick up and keep going after circumstances left their world in ruins around them. This also is the work of God's Spirit. Paul wrote, "If the Holy Spirit controls your mind, there is life and peace" (Romans 8:6 NLT). Returning to the image of living water, Paul also prayed that God would enable believers to "overflow with hope by the power of the Holy Spirit" (Romans 15:13).

Grief, anxiety, and numb shock are common to everyone from time to time, but God works within believers to carry them through. The Bible promises that, "the peace of God, which transcends all understanding, will guard your hearts and your minds in Christ Jesus" (Philippians 4:7).

This is the Life!

While the Spirit works *upon* nonbelievers, he works *within* believers by empowering, enlightening, equipping, and encouraging. Christians attest that dependence upon God gets them through life. Of course, the key word is "dependence." The Bible says believers can "grieve the Holy Spirit of God" and "put out the Spirit's fire" when they fail to trust and obey God (see Ephesians 4:30 and 1 Thessalonians 5:19). Instead, believers need to "keep in step with the Spirit" and "be filled with the Holy Spirit" (see Galatians 5:25 and Ephesians 5:18).

I occasionally reflect on the "fruit," or by-products that the Bible says my life will bear if I depend on God's Spirit: "love, joy, peace, patience, kindness, goodness, faithfulness, gentleness and self-control" (Galatians 5:22-23). Who would not want this kind of life? This is a description of life under the influence of the Spirit, and Jesus told us how to begin experiencing the present of the Spirit's presence. "God will give the Holy Spirit," Jesus said, "to those who ask him" (Luke 11:13).

Ask.

Chapter 13
Great is the Mystery of Our Faith

In one of her hit songs, Bette Midler sang, "God is watching us from a distance."[1] It's a pretty song, but it doesn't tell the whole story of how God relates to us. The song correctly pictures God evaluating whether we show compassion and kindness to others, but he does much more than simply watch us from a distance. Believers run life's race knowing that their heavenly Father is watching from the grandstands, but believers also experience God running *with* us as our model, and we experience God *within* us to empower us in our race. The Father above us, the Son beside us, and the Spirit within us—this is how Christians describe their experience with God.

As we've seen in the past six chapters, believers are convinced that God is intensely, intimately involved in life. Experiences with Jesus showed the earliest Christians that Jesus was God incarnate: he was everything it means to be God and yet he entered into everything it means to be human. As the angel promised Mary in the Christmas story, "They will call him Immanuel—which means, "God *with* us" (Matthew 1:23). But after Jesus left the first believers, they found him somehow *within* them. In his teaching, he had promised that they would not be left alone when he departed. He said, "I will not leave you as orphans; I will come to you" (John 14:18). He shared this promise in the context of what he taught them about the Holy Spirit.

So, with the Creed Christians recite belief in "God the Father," in "Jesus Christ his only Son our Lord," and in "the Holy Spirit." This conviction is captured in the words of a famous hymn, almost two hundred years old now:

> *Holy, Holy, Holy*
> *Merciful and mighty*
> *God in three persons*
> *Blessed Trinity!*

When you read the biblical explanations of the earliest Christians' experiences with God, it clearly isn't a "unitarian" explanation of God. Unitarians see Jesus as merely a man God created and the Spirit is merely the "influence" or "force" of God upon our lives. Neither did the first Christians believe they were interacting with three gods. Instead, the word "trinity" is the best way to summarize the nature of God as the first Christians experienced him. He is the Father who hears the prayers of his Son and he is the Son who prays; he is the Son who sent the Spirit to live within believers and he is the Spirit who lives within us.

The Apostle Paul wrote that our faith is a "great mystery" (1 Timothy 3:16), and it's certainly true in relation to the nature of God. As we have seen in the past chapters about the Father, the Son, and the Spirit, though, this mysterious understanding of God is vitally practical. There are at least three important implications about the "blessed Trinity."

God Wants to be Known, Not Just Known About

As we've already seen, it's not adequate to describe God as simply sitting up in the bleachers observing us compete in the race of life and neutral to its outcome. Through Jesus we experience God *with* us as our example, and through the Spirit we experience God *within* us as our encourager. God is passionately, intimately involved with our lives. He has not remained aloof from the pain and problems of this world but has experienced them on our level as one of us. He has not left us alone but he works among nonbelievers to convict and convert, and he works within believers to equip and encourage. He has experienced our human nature in Jesus and wants us to experience his divine nature in the Holy Spirit. Other religions teach that God has given us *rules* to follow, but Christianity goes deeper, teaching that God wants a *relationship* with us.

God does not want to be solved like a Rubik's Cube or answered like a math problem or contemplated like an academic curiosity. Instead, he wants us to trust him as we would a loving parent ("I believe in God the Father"), he wants us to enjoy him as we would a good friend ("and in Jesus Christ his only Son our Lord"), and he wants us to follow him as we would a wise leader ("I believe in the Holy Spirit").

Paul beautifully expresses this full experience with God as he closed one of his letters: "May the grace of the Lord Jesus Christ, and the love of God, and the fellowship of the Holy Spirit be with you all" (2 Corinthians 13:14). Many Christians around the world close their worship services with this phrase, often simply called, "The Grace." We can speak truly of our experience of God only by speaking at the same time of Jesus Christ and the Holy Spirit.

God *is* Love

Most of us have been told the reassuring news that God loves us. In reality, the Scriptures teach us something much more profound: In the Bible we don't just find a God who loves, but a God who *is* love (1 John 4:8 and 16). Love is a description of his *being*, not just his *activity;* love is not simply what God *does*, but what God *is*.

Love is what we find in the eternal relationship between Father, Son and Spirit. I like the way C.S. Lewis put it: "In Christianity God is . . . a dynamic, pulsating activity, a life, almost a kind of drama. Almost if you will not think me irreverent, a kind of dance."[2] The dance Lewis pictured was the relationship of giving and receiving, of surrender and affirmation, among the Father, the Son, and the Holy Spirit. You can see this interaction in the following verses:

"Christ . . . through the eternal Spirit offered himself unblemished to God" (Hebrews 9:14).

"Now is the Son of Man glorified and God is glorified in him. If God is glorified in him, God will glorify the Son in himself" (John 13:31-32).

"I [Jesus] will ask the Father, and he will give you another Counselor to be with you forever—the Spirit of truth" (John 14:16-17).

In these verses we see one asking and another responding, one sending and another surrendering, one affirming and the other returning the glory.

Now, if God *is* love, eternally love, then we can say two things about the universe and our part in it. First, it's all about relationship. It is not enough to describe God as, in the words of various philosophers, the "Prime Mover," "First Cause," or "Ground of All Being." Instead, God is love. The interaction between Father, Son, and Spirit means that at the very heart of the universe, at the core of the way things are, you find relationship.

Since this is so, relating to God and to others is not simply *nice* but *necessary* if we want to know the purpose of life. When Jesus was asked to name the most important of all commands, he told us to love God with everything we've got and to love others as ourselves (Matthew 22:36-40). Keeping this commandment aligns us with the heart of reality itself.

Here's the second thing we can say about the universe and our part in it: It's all about grace. The description of God as love was true long before you or I arrived on the scene. Although I like a lot of James Weldon Johnson's folksy poetry, he missed the heart of God in his famous poem, "The Creation"—

> And God stepped out on space,
> And he looked around and said:
> I'm lonely—
> I'll make me a world.[3]

If God *is* love, eternally relating as Father, Son, and Spirit, loneliness has never been a mood he has known. In one of his prayers to the Father, Jesus said, "You loved me before the creation of the world" (John 17:24). *We* may marry or give birth or buy a pet because of loneliness, but *God* did not create us because he felt something was missing. Instead, because God is Father, Son, and Spirit, love was a characteristic of God long before he had angels, animals, or people to love. You and I were created by God—and we can enter into a relationship with him—because of God's grace: God does not *need* us, but he *wants* us. This holy dance—this sacred relationship of Father, Son, and Spirit—did not start with us. God graciously pulls us into a dance that has been going on forever, and we're *given* the experience of what Paul called "the grace of the Lord Jesus Christ, and the love of God, and the fellowship of the Holy Spirit" (2 Corinthians 13:14).

The Full Picture of God Must Include Father, Son, and Holy Spirit

On college campuses, Muslims hand out tracts claiming that Christians believe in three gods,[4] but Christians are monotheists, which means we believe that there is only one God to know and worship. Jesus affirmed this conviction, quoting the solemn Jewish *Shema* in his teachings: "Hear, O Israel, the Lord our God, the Lord is one" (Mark 12:29-30).[5]

As we saw in this book's chapters on Jesus, however, Jesus revealed his divinity to his followers. And as we saw in the chapters on the Holy Spirit, "The Lord is the Spirit" (2 Corinthians 3:17-18). So, to describe God as Father, Son and Holy Spirit does not question the oneness of God, but it says something about the *nature* of the one God.

It seems impolite in our world to insist that one way of understanding God is better than another. No doubt, those in other religions correctly describe certain aspects of God's nature: his eternity, for example, and his power, authority, and loving attention. But, as Timothy George puts it, "The God of the Bible is the God who has forever known himself, and who in Jesus Christ has revealed himself to us, as *the Father, the Son*, and *the Holy Spirit*."⁶ We can appreciate the stirring and inspiring words about God from the writings of other religions, but no explanation of God really gets the full picture if it's missing this mysterious trinity.

The full picture includes the *Fatherhood* of God, the *Lordship* of Christ, the *personhood* of the Holy Spirit, and the *eternal relationship* of all three. Let's summarize everything we've seen of God from Chapters 5-13:

The Fatherhood of God. The Apostle Paul wrote, "We should not be like cringing, fearful slaves, but we should behave like God's very own children, adopted into the bosom of his family, and calling to him, 'Father, Father'" (Romans 8:15 LB). God relates to us as an earthly father should: as a nurturer, provider and protector.

The Lordship of Jesus. The earliest "creed" was the simple declaration, "Jesus is Lord" (see Romans 10:9 and 1 Corinthians 12:3). Expressing this conviction was more a reference to his *divinity* than to his *authority*. The biblical writers called Christ "God over all" (Romans 9:5) and "our God and Savior" (Titus 2:13). John respectfully called Jesus "the Word," and said of him, "In the beginning was the Word, and the Word was with God and the Word was God" (John 1:1 NKJV).

The Personal Nature of the Spirit. The Spirit is not some "influence" or "force," but the personal presence of God. Jesus used the personal pronoun "he" in his references to the Holy Spirit (for example, see John 16:13-14). This is particularly striking since normally pronouns in the Greek language of the New Testament have to match the gender of their nouns. A neuter Greek word like "Spirit" (*pneuma*—pronounced "nooma") would call for a neuter pronoun, but Jesus deliberately used a masculine pronoun—"he." Following his Lord, Paul used the personal pronoun when referring to the Spirit: "And when you believed in Christ, he identified you as his own by giving you the Holy Spirit, *whom* he promised long ago" (Ephesians 1:13-14 NLT). The Bible speaks of actions of the Spirit that cannot be carried out by an impersonal force: teaching, determining, and even grieving (See Acts 15:28, John 14:26, 1 Corinthians 12:11, Ephesians 4:30, and Isaiah 63:10). It takes a *person* to perform these actions, and the Bible tells us who that person is: "The Lord is the Spirit" (2 Corinthians 3:17-18). Simon Peter taught that to lie to the *Holy Spirit* was to lie to *God* (Acts 5:3-4). Paul used the phrases "the *Spirit's* power" and "*God's* power" interchangeably (1 Corinthians 2:4-5). And he said that believers have become "a dwelling in which *God* lives by his *Spirit*" (Ephesians 2:22).

The Eternal Relationship of God Between Father, Son, and Spirit. The earliest Christians celebrated the mysterious nature of God by using numerous Trinitarian statements. Note the interaction of Father, Son, and Spirit in the following verses:

> "There are different kinds of gifts, but *the same Spirit*. There are different kinds of service, but *the same Lord* [i.e., the Son]. There are different kinds of working, but *the same God* [i.e., the Father] works all of them in all men" (1 Corinthians 12:4-6).

> "Pray in *the Holy Spirit*; keep yourselves in the love of *God*, waiting for the mercy of *our Lord Jesus Christ* that leads to eternal life" (Jude 1:20-21 ESV).

> We "have been chosen according to the foreknowledge of *God the Father*, through the sanctifying work of *the Spirit*, for obedience to *Jesus Christ* and sprinkling by his blood" (1 Peter 1:2).

> "*God* sent the *Spirit* of his *Son* into our hearts" (Galatians 4:6).

> "For this reason I kneel before the *Father*, from whom his whole family in heaven and on earth derives its name. I pray that out of his glorious riches he may strengthen you with power through his *Spirit* in your inner being, so that *Christ* may dwell in your hearts through faith" (Ephesians 3:14-17).

"May the grace of *the Lord Jesus Christ*, and the love of *God*, and the fellowship of *the Holy Spirit* be with you all" (2 Corinthians 13:14).

Some try to say that the whole idea of the Trinity didn't develop until centuries after Christ in some esoteric theological debates rife with politics. Instead, these verses clearly show that the very first followers of Jesus and those Jesus authorized to teach in his name taught that God's very nature was a dynamic relationship between Father, Son and Spirit. Indeed, it all started with Jesus himself, who taught that believers were to be baptized "in the name of the Father and of the Son and of the Holy Spirit" (Matthew 28:19).

The Father above us, the Son beside us, and the Spirit within us—this is how Christians describe our experience with God. With the Creed, we say that we "believe in God the Father," in "Jesus Christ his only Son our Lord, and in "the Holy Spirit."
The fourth-century Latin poet Prudentius captured the believer's wonder at being invited into life with this kind of God:

> Christ, to Thee with God the Father
> And, O Holy Ghost, to Thee,
> Hymn and chant and high thanksgiving
> And unwearied praises be.
> Honor, glory and dominion,
> And eternal victory,
> Evermore and evermore! Amen.[7]

Part Five: "I Believe in the Church"

*I believe
in God the Father Almighty,
Maker of heaven and earth;
And in Jesus Christ his only Son our Lord;
who was conceived by the Holy Spirit,
born of the Virgin Mary,
suffered under Pontius Pilate,
was crucified, dead, and buried.
The third day he rose again from the dead.
He ascended into heaven,
and sits at the right hand of God the Father Almighty.
From there he shall come
to judge the living and the dead.
I believe in the Holy Spirit;
the one holy church;
the communion of saints;
the forgiveness of sins;
the resurrection of the body;
and the life everlasting.
Amen.*

Chapter 14
Don't Go It Alone

The church is "one"

Geese in the autumn fly in V-formation as they make their southern migration. Starlings take to the air—hundreds of them, swirling, swooping, and turning this way and that, as if they were all communicating with each other at once. Blackbirds fly in long tornado-like swirls, thousands at a time, like a tentacle up from one field and down into another.

We've all seen this flocking phenomenon among birds, but only recently have scientists begun to discover the reasons for it. Two researchers at the California Institute of Technology did the math and estimated that a bird could fly as much as seventy percent farther in a V-formation that allows birds to use the rising air currents streaming off the wings of its neighbors. Scientists have also surmised that flocking helps with navigation, since several birds—not just one bird—would be looking for the landmarks to guide them on a long journey. Birds in flocks can also better protect themselves from predators. Starlings, for example, "group up" in the air when a hawk makes a dive toward them. A predator can snatch a single starling out of the air, but by uniting, and darting right and left in unison, the starlings can successfully confuse the hawk and make their escape.

We Christians have learned that we gain the same advantages by flocking together as believers. We enjoy greater endurance, we navigate through life better, and we find protection from destructive choices when we flock together. So, even as we recite together, "I believe in God the Father, I believe in Jesus Christ his only Son our Lord, I believe in the Holy Spirit"—so also we profess together: "I believe in the one holy church" and "the communion of saints."

Even though the Creed covers such miraculous things as the virgin birth and the resurrection, the hardest thing for some people to say is, "I believe in the church." They respect Jesus, they may even put their faith in him, but they're just not too thrilled with church. The Lord has not given us that option, though. Loving someone means sharing in that person's passions—and Jesus is passionate about his church. The Bible says, "Christ loved the church and gave himself up for her" (Ephesians 5:25). We need to understand why Jesus loved the church so deeply if we're going to take him seriously.

Many seekers have been attracted to the lifestyle of their Christian friends and they have been impressed by the work of a local church. Other seekers, however, have stories of hypocritical Christian neighbors, judgmental Christian relatives, and churches in their past that left them either bored or emotionally beaten up. This disillusionment shows up in polls and census information which reveal growing numbers of people who identify themselves as "spiritual" are not attached to any particular religious body.

When seekers look at Christ's *intent* for his church, though, it is not the church but what some have made of it that bothers them. Once you become a believer, Jesus expects you to join other disciples in pursuit of an inspiring vision of what "church" is supposed to be. In this chapter and the next two, we'll look at this hope-filled blueprint designed by Christ himself. Our ancient Creed summarizes the vision in three words: the church is to be *one, holy,* and a *communion.*

Note that these three words work best to describe an assembly of people rather than a building or a corporation. This corrects a major misconception right away. Many understand "the church" as a building they go to or an organization that can do things for them. As I get into conversations about faith during the week, often someone will ask, "Where's your church located?" I know that all the person wants is directions to our building, so I provide that. Still, what I really want to say is, "Well, it's 1 p.m. on Monday afternoon so that means the church I lead is located in several hundred homes and businesses all around town." In other words, I'll give them directions to the building where our church meets on the weekend, but if they want to know where my church is they need to look for *believers* and not *bricks*. The church is not a building you go to but a body you belong to. A building or an institution cannot really be described with words like "one" and "holy" and "communion"—but *people* can, and Jesus intended his people to be worthy of those titles.

The first word to capture his intent is the word "one"—"I believe in the *one* holy church." If you've spent time in a church that regularly quotes the Apostles' Creed, you've probably heard the word "catholic"—"I believe in the holy catholic church." The word is an English transliteration of the Latin *catholicam*, which itself derived from the Greek word *katholikos*. The word means "universal" and it speaks of the oneness of all believers around the world, across cultural lines, and down through the ages. Today, though, most people understand the word "catholic" to refer to a specific branch of Christianity: the Roman Catholic Church. Since a word that once referred to the oneness of *all* Christians is now identified with only a segment of the Christian body, I prefer simply to speak of the church as *one* instead of as *catholic*.

Jesus intended his church to be one. On the night before he went to the cross, he prayed that his Father would bring believers to "complete unity" (John 17:23). It's meaningful that the night before he was killed, he prayed that those whom he united to God through the cross would be united to each other. After praying for the tiny band of disciples who had ministered with him, his thoughts turned to the future (John 17:20-23):

> "My prayer is not for them alone. I pray also for those who will believe in me through their message, that all of them may be one, Father, just as you are in me and I am in you. May they also be in us so that the world may believe that you have sent me. I have given them the glory

that you gave me, that they may be one as we are one: I in them and you in me. May they be brought to complete unity to let the world know that you sent me and have loved them even as you have loved me."

As we saw in the last chapter, God is love, in an eternal relationship of Father, Son, and Holy Spirit. In the prayer quoted above, Jesus speaks of that union between himself and the Father as something that is to be extended to the community of believers. His desire was that his disciples would experience a deep connection with God and with each other. To enter into fellowship with God is to enter into fellowship with everyone who shares in the fellowship of God (see 1 John 1:3).

In one sense, Christ's intent is already fulfilled. Down through the ages and around the world, God's church transcends cultures, generations, languages, and governments. In one of his letters, Paul uses the word "one" seven times in just three verses to speak of what we experience in church: "There is *one* body and *one* Spirit—just as you were called to *one* hope when you were called—*one* Lord, *one* faith, *one* baptism; *one* God and Father of all, who is over all and through all and in all" (Ephesians 4:4-6).

Seekers sometimes wonder why there are so many denominations and varieties of worship styles, but when you peel back the thin surface of our differences, you will see that what unites believers is far more profound than what divides us. There is oneness among God's people because our message does not change from generation to generation or from passport to passport.

So, in one sense, we can speak of the oneness of the church as a present reality. Still, Jesus prayed, "May they be brought to complete unity," and that implies an unfinished process. Disciples of Jesus have the responsibility to move toward the vision of oneness Jesus intended. It's remarkable to see how much can be accomplished when believers pursue that intention. As small as they are, when snowflakes get together they can stop traffic. I've reminded my church how that image applies to us: It's amazing what a bunch of flakes can do when we stick together!

Christ-followers do three things to fulfill our Lord's vision: we *connect* with a specific congregation, we *protect* the unity of that congregation, and we *intersect* our congregation with other congregations for meaningful causes.

Believers Connect With a Specific Congregation

Since Jesus intended believers to experience life together, we won't get very far in our spiritual development without interaction with others who love Jesus. John Wesley discovered this. Wesley's teaching sparked a spiritual awakening in eighteenth-century England, but as a young man he needed an awakening himself. He was under the sway of mystics who taught that the spiritual search was that of a solitary soul in lonely pursuit of God. He was hit between the eyes, however, with the practical advice in a friend's letter. His friend wrote, "Remember, you cannot serve God alone. You must try to find companions or make them. The Bible knows nothing of solitary religion."[1]

It's true. In the New Testament, you will not find a disembodied collection of isolated people who had met Christ. Instead, Christian activity and belief are always spoken of in collective figures. In the Bible, Christians are addressed and described as "fellow citizens," "members of the household of God," a "priesthood," a "nation," a "flock," a "fellowship," and the "members of the Body." Most of the letters which make up the New Testament are addressed to "'the church which is at"—and cities or regions would be named.

Other religions may say, "To know the purpose of life, obey these rules," or "take this path," or "meditate in this manner," or "practice this routine." Jesus says, "To know the purpose of life, gather with others who love me. *Where two or three come together in my name, there I am with them*" (see Matthew 18:20).

In her book, *The Unauthorized Guide to Choosing a Church*, Carmen Renee Berry recalled the crisis that drew her into fellowship with other believers: "When a friend committed suicide, I realized I could become too cynical, too lost, and too alone. I needed a church, a community of believers.... Something happens there that simply doesn't when you are alone in prayer or on the Internet. As much as I hate to admit it, my faith is enhanced and enlarged when in relationship to other less-than-perfect human beings."[2]

It's impossible to work at the oneness that Jesus intended you to have with other believers if you don't plug into a specific congregation. No church is perfect, but since you aren't either, you're a good match! It's unlikely you'll find a group where everybody aligns with your politics, your interests, and your preferences. Then again, if such a group existed, what opportunities for growth would it provide? Our rough edges are smoothed out only in the "sandpaper experiences" of interacting with those who are different from us. Even if you're still deciding about the faith, you'll learn more about the faith through interaction with Christ-followers than by simply reading a book, listening to a lecture, or browsing the Internet.

Believers Protect
The Unity of the Congregation

The Bible tells believers, "Make every effort to keep the unity of the Spirit through the bond of peace" (Ephesians 4:3). It takes work to achieve and to guard the oneness Jesus intended us to have.

Nuclear reactors have "scram switches"—emergency power-off switches that can be activated in the event of a runaway chain reaction. According to one story, "scram" is an acronym for "Safety Control Rod Ax Man." In the early days of nuclear power plants, control rods were raised and lowered on ropes. If the core overheated, these ropes could be cut, dropping the control rods and stopping the chain reaction. In this case, "scram" didn't mean that the personnel abandoned the plant to a meltdown. Instead, "scram" referred to a specific and proactive solution to the emergency. Any gathering of human beings will "overheat" on occasion, and when that happens we're tempted to think "Scram!" when instead we need to think "S.C.R.A.M." We need to be the "System Control Rod Ax Man." We have to take the steps to mend broken relationships.

The Apostle Paul heard of a conflict in one of his favorite churches, the church at Philippi. Writing to them, he addressed the battling believers by name: "I plead with Euodia and I plead with Syntyche to agree with each other in the Lord." Obviously, clashes between believers arose even in the earliest churches two thousand years ago. Then he addressed someone else whom he simply called "loyal yokefellow." It may have been a specific reference to a church leader or a broad reference to the entire congregation. He wrote, "Yes, and I ask you, loyal yokefellow, help these women who have contended at my side in the cause of the gospel" (Philippians 4:2-3).

Sometimes believers are like Euodia and Syntyche: we have to lay aside our animosity and distrust so we can work out our differences. But other times believers are called to be like this "loyal yokefellow" and bring battling believers to the negotiating table.

When reciting the things Christians say we believe in, we say, "I believe in the *one* holy church." Being a believer includes pursuing Christ's vision of oneness among his followers. So, we need to *connect* to a specific congregation and *protect* the harmony of that congregation. Third—

Believers Intersect
Their Congregation with Other Congregations
For Meaningful Causes

On the one hand, believers are wrong if they acknowledge their membership with the universal body of all believers without any real connection with a particular congregation. Such people are like little Linus in the *Peanuts* comic strip who said, "I love humanity; it's people I can't stand." They love the idea of the church, but don't do anything to make it a reality among living, breathing people with differing opinions and irritating faults. The universal church of all God's people around the world and across the ages is made real to you in one congregation that you make your church home.

On the other hand, believers are wrong if they simply affiliate with a particular band of fellow Christians without acknowledging their union to the other congregations. Paul's perspective was the right perspective. He addressed his first letter to the Corinthians with these words: "To *the church of God in Corinth*," but then he added, "*together with all those everywhere who call on the name of our Lord Jesus Christ—their Lord and ours*" (1 Corinthians 1:2).

That ought to be our attitude. Our commitment ought to be to a specific congregation even as we have consideration for "all those everywhere who call on the name of our Lord Jesus Christ."

The congregation I lead bands together with other congregations for many activities. Together our united congregations support schools where ministers can be trained. We fund missionaries and aid workers. We pool our resources to launch evangelistic campaigns. We gather for worship opportunities. We unite for community development such as food banks and home construction. By banding together, we can accomplish more than we could as solitary congregations, and we enjoy learning from the insights and practices of other Christian groups. It's one way we fulfill Christ's vision of unity among all believers.

"Here's the Church, Here's the Steeple . . ."

If you spent some of your childhood days in church, or if you're taking your children to a church now, you've probably come across the little hand motions that teachers use to teach kids the habits of church attendance. You weave your fingers together, palms up, and then fold your hands together so that the thumbs are before your face. With your index fingers pointing upward as a kind of steeple, you say to the kids you're teaching, "Here's the church, here's the steeple," and then you open your hands and wiggle your linked-up fingers as you say, "Open the doors and see all the people." I love Randy Frazee's reminiscence about that little rhyme. He writes:

> I have a son who was born without a left hand. One day in Sunday school the teacher was talking with the children about the church. To illustrate her point she folded her hands together and said, 'Here's the church, here's the steeple; open the doors and see all the people.' She asked the class to do it along with her—obviously not thinking about my son's inability to pull this exercise off. Yet in the next moment it dawned on her that my son could not join in. Before she could do anything about it, the little boy next to my son, a friend of his from the time they were babies, reached out his left hand and said, "Let's do it together." The two boys proceeded to join their hands together to make the church and the steeple.[3]

I can't think of a better way to illustrate the truth of that little children's rhyme. Paul prayed, "May the God of steadfastness and encouragement grant you to live in such harmony with one another, in accord with Christ Jesus, that together you may with one voice glorify the God and Father of our Lord Jesus Christ" (Romans 15:5-6). Deciding to become a Christ-follower means joining other believers in fulfilling the vision of *oneness* that Christ set out for life together.

Chapter 15
Lost in Translation

The church is "holy"

The *Wall Street Journal* reported on some signs at overseas businesses. The signs were translated into English for American tourists, but the signs lost their meanings in the translations. Here's one from a Swiss restaurant: "Our wines leave you nothing to hope for." Then there's the posted notice in front of a Budapest zoo: "Please do not feed the animals. If you have any suitable food, give it to the guard on duty." One dental office boasted: "Teeth are extracted by the latest Methodists." In Copenhagen at least one airline was up front in how it handled luggage. Its sign read: "We will take your bags and send them in all directions." Or here's another from a Japanese hotel, which led to some misunderstandings, I imagine: "You are invited to take advantage of the chambermaid." That's like the laundry in Rome that advertised: "Ladies, leave your clothes here and spend the afternoon having a good time." Finally, there was the sign at a Paris hotel that advised: "Please leave your values at the front desk."[1]

It could be that even the lines of the Apostles' Creed we're now studying strike you like one of those mistranslated signs. While many seekers have been impressed with the lifestyle of Christian friends and have been inspired by the work of a particular church, we believers don't always live up to the high expectations Jesus set for us. When that happens, to call the church "one" and "holy" and "a communion," strikes people as odd. Between reading the Creed's definition of the church and seeing the church in action, something seems to be lost in the translation.

Though these lines in the Creed don't always describe what believers *are*, they do describe what believers *should be*. The words summarize Christ's *intent* for his followers. Once you become a believer, Jesus expects you to join other disciples in pursuit of an inspiring vision of what "church" is supposed to be.

I talked with a man once who was active in a church until he saw behavior in the leadership that disillusioned him. When I asked him what he did about it he shrugged his shoulders and said, "I left." It never occurred to him that he was expected to work with others to find a remedy for the situation. For him, the church was merely an institution under someone else's responsibility, not his. He drew benefit from it until the institution no longer pleased him. The man did not understand that Christ expects his followers to actually pursue Christ's vision for a church that is "one," "holy," and "a communion."

In the last chapter, we looked at what believers can do to foster unity with each other. In this chapter, we'll look at Christ's desire that his church be *holy*.

"Isn't That Special?"

What do you think of when you hear the word "holy?" For some, it's just another word for "sanctimonious," and conjures up images like Dana Carvey's "Church Lady" character from re-runs of *Saturday Night Live*. In Carvey's skits, the Church Lady would draw her lips into a disapproving pucker and sarcastically say, "Well, isn't that *special*?" as she began her rant against behavior she disliked. For others, the word "holy" brings to mind not so much sanctimonious people as it does impractical people, like gurus on lonely mountaintops or hermits in isolated desert lodges who withdraw from the realities of daily life the rest of us face. Both of these ideas are exaggerations. A person who truly pursues holiness is interested in *righteousness*, but not in smug *self-righteousness*. A person who really wants to be holy is *different*, but not *indifferent* to the world.

In the Bible, the word we translate as "holy" means to *cut* or to *set apart*. In a way, the word we translate "church" carries this meaning, too. The Greek word is *ecclesia*, and it combines the word *ek* meaning "out," and *kaleo* meaning "to call." Greek politicians called their assembly an *ecclesia* because the participants were "called out" of their normal routines so they might come together temporarily for deliberations. The believing community is to be a "called out" people in the fullest sense of that term. In the Bible, believers are reminded that God "*called you out* of darkness into his wonderful light" (1 Peter 2:9).

Though these lines in the Creed don't always describe what believers are, they do describe what believers should be

We believers, then, have been "called out" and "set apart" by the Lord we follow, and our lives are to be different from the way we used to live. Most of us admit that no matter how many admirable things we did before committing to Christ, other forces drove our former life. We gave in to peer pressure, natural inclinations, or ego satisfaction. We had dysfunctional ways of relating that were picked up from our family background. We had unexamined biases absorbed from our friends and culture. We nod in recognition when we read that the Bible calls this kind of life a form of slavery (see Romans 6:16-23). In Scripture, followers of Christ are reminded that our Lord "bought" us out of this kind of slavery and we belong to him now: "You are not your own; you were bought at a price. Therefore honor God with your body" (1 Corinthians 6:19-20).

In a future chapter we will look closely at the high price Jesus paid on the cross to "buy" us out of our former slavery. Because of the price he paid, we have been "set apart" from the things that used to drive us. Other impulses drive us now. Paul spoke of the church as a cherished bride, and he said Jesus "gave up his life for her *to make her holy and clean*" (Ephesians 5:25-27).

When I was a boy, my father disciplined me for something that I felt was entirely unfair considering that the parents of my friends took no action on the matter.

"The Perry boys got to do it," I said of my friends, "Their parents don't mind."

My dad replied, "Yes, but you're a Goodman."

He was saying, "There may be other standards in other houses, but you bear my name and your behavior should reflect what's important in our household." In the same way, we believers have been brought into God's family, and we are expected to live by his standards now. Our natural impulses don't have the last word. Our ego's satisfaction is no longer our goal. The opinions of our peers and the prejudices of our culture don't govern us. We can rise above any dysfunctional patterns that we learned in our childhood home. Our lives are to be different . . . set apart . . . *holy*.

This definition of holiness corrects the misunderstandings of holiness I mentioned earlier. In the pursuit of biblical holiness there is no call to be smug like the Church Lady or aloof like a hermit. Unlike the Church Lady's brand of holiness, the pursuit of biblical holiness brings about a deep humility. We recognize our former way of life as a kind of slavery, a bondage we would still be under if it weren't for the intervention of God. In addition, we also realize that our priorities and motivations and behavior still don't consistently align with God's intention—which is why we call the Christian life a *journey* toward maturity. So, the combination of an enslaved past and an imperfect present should be enough to make us humble in our responses to the imperfections of others.

Also, while some may only think of the guru on a lonely mountain or the hermit in the secluded desert when they think of "holy men," they should consider that to live a "set apart" life refers to behavior, not to relationships and practical obligations. The biblical definition of holiness assumes a new way of living in the context of ordinary life. After people cross the line into faith, it's their priorities, motivations, and behavior that should change and not necessarily their jobs, friendships, families and pastimes. A holy life is not an aloof life, which is obvious when we look at the life of Jesus. He told jokes, he liked to go to parties, and he built close friendships. In short, as Jesus said of himself, "The Son of man came, enjoying life" (Matthew 11:19 Ph). This is the example of holy living he set for us: a pure life that is still fully engaged in the joys and relationships and responsibilities of ordinary life.

Unlike the aloof hermit or the smug Church Lady, we believers also understand that we have to work *together* in order for the community of believers to pursue holiness. We give each other encouraging challenges to keep going. We intervene with loving confrontation when necessary. In the event a believer stumbles and falls morally, we should work to restore him or her.

The Bible says that when God set us *apart*, he set us apart *together*. He did so for a specific purpose: "His intent was that now, *through the church*, the manifold wisdom of God should be made known to the rulers and authorities in the heavenly realms" (Ephesians 3:10). I love that verse, because it tells me that God's wisdom is on display through my mutual interaction with other believers—in short, "through the church." Cosmic unseen authorities gain insight into the ways of God by looking at the body of common, ordinary people who follow Jesus. Astonishing.

Earlier, I mentioned an acquaintance of mine who abandoned all church involvement because of a disillusioning experience with a church leader. By walking away, he forfeited his part in displaying the manifold wisdom of God through the church. He should have prayed for guidance in how to handle the situation, he should have used his access to the leader to do the hard work of confronting and restoring the leader, and he should have encouraged others who were impacted by the situation. Through these proactive steps, he would have fulfilled the intent God had for setting us apart together.

"The Church Is Full of Hypocrites"

No doubt, the church often falls short of these high expectations, and that can lead to one of the most common objections against Christianity: "The church is filled with hypocrites." It should be obvious from what has been said so far, though, that this objection comes up empty on three counts.

First, it fails to take seriously Christ's vision for the church. When seekers look at the intentions Jesus had for his church, they find that it's not Christ's vision that bothers them, but what some people have done with it. Jesus' design for the community of believers we call "the church" is worth pursuing.

Second, it fails to acknowledge all the ways believers have boldly pursued that vision. Sadly, we could compile a long list of ways that churches have fallen short—and since I am a longtime "insider" to church work, I imagine I could compile a longer list than many. At times in history, for example, Christians have been part of bloody crusades, intolerant inquisitions, pro-slavery positions, and racist policies. But Christians have also led the way in the abolition of slavery, the civil rights movement, the end of apartheid, the formation of the hospice movement, prison reform, and many other efforts that have made the world a better place. In hundreds of thousands of churches, members give generously of their time and money to help people in need. To turn away from any consideration of Christ with a dismissive claim that all Christians are hypocrites does not do justice to the facts.

Third, this criticism fails to properly define a hypocrite. It's important to identify hypocritical living, because Jesus had particularly strong words against it (see Matthew 6:1-18 and 23:13-32). A hypocrite is someone who claims to be something he's not. A perfect example of this comes from an "awareness picnic" hosted by a drunken-driving prevention organization. Attendees saw police administering a field sobriety test to the coordinator of the organization. Assuming it was all part of the program, they gathered around to watch the "demonstration." It wasn't a demonstration. When the coordinator had arrived, the police officers grew suspicious at the way she drove up to the picnic site. When they smelled alcohol on her breath, they insisted she take a breath test, which recorded her blood-alcohol level over the legal limit. She also failed four of five coordination tests. She was arrested in front of the onlookers and charged with driving while intoxicated.[2] When the director of a program designed to tell others not to drive drunk drives drunk, you have a perfect illustration of hypocrisy!

Jesus said a hypocrite is someone who claims to have a close relationship with God and yet ignores areas of his life that are not aligned with God's rules. A hypocrite focuses on the public activities that will impress his peers. A hypocrite decides which of God's rules are more important (usually the ones he has no trouble following), and then he considers himself better than those who do not follow the selected rules—never mind that he fails at the rules he considers less important.

You will occasionally run into people like this and when you do, you have every right to turn away from their kind of Christianity. According to the Bible, Jesus already has! This kind of religiosity, however, is vastly different from the Christian life as Jesus intended it. Jesus intended to *lead* us, not just *forgive* us. The most common title for Jesus in the Bible is "Lord." While this is a declaration of his divinity, believers never forget that the word means "boss," "ruler," or "master." When I became a believer, I began a lifelong process of aligning my life with the will of God. Spend a day in my head and you will see me fall short in that process. That does not make me a hypocrite; that just makes me imperfect. God isn't finished with me yet. As I continue to set his expectations before me and as I depend on the transforming power of his Spirit within me, my life becomes a better and better example to others. That's what Paul said about his life (1 Timothy 1:15-16 NLT):

> Christ Jesus came into the world to save sinners—and I was the worst of them all. But that is why God had mercy on me, so that Christ Jesus could use me as a prime example of his great patience with even the worst sinners. Then others will realize that they, too, can believe in him and receive eternal life.

In the book, *Of Whom The World Was Not Worthy*, Marie Chapian wrote about the sufferings of believers in Yugoslavia under Nazism and Communism. Despite the unyielding stance of many believers, the actions of corrupt church officials disillusioned many from giving any consideration to the faith. One of Chapian's main characters, a believer named Jakov, commiserated with an elderly man named Cimmerman on the tragedies he had experienced. When Jakov tried to talk to him about the love of Christ, though, Cimmerman cut Jakov off and told him that he wanted to hear nothing more about Christianity. He reminded Jakov of the dreadful history of the church in his town, a history that included plundering, exploiting, and even killing innocent people.

"My own nephew was killed by them," he said angrily. "They wear those elaborate coats and caps and crosses signifying a heavenly commission," he said of the church officials' clothing, "but their evil designs and lives I cannot ignore."

Jakov replied, "Cimmerman, can I ask you a question? Suppose I were to steal your coat, put it on, and break into a bank. Suppose further that the police sighted me running in the distance but could not catch up with me. One clue, however, put them onto your track; they recognized your coat. What would you say to them if they came to your house and accused you of breaking into the bank?"

"I would deny it," said Cimmerman.

" 'Ah, but we saw your coat,' they would say." This analogy annoyed Cimmerman, and he ordered Jakov to leave his home

Jakov continued to befriend Cimmerman and share the love of Christ with him. Finally one day Cimmerman asked, "How does one become a Christian?" Jakov taught him the simple steps of repentance for sin and of trust in what Jesus did on the cross. Cimmerman bent his knee on the soil with his head bowed and surrendered his life to Christ. As he rose to his feet, wiping his tears, he embraced Jakov and said, "Thank you for being in my life."

Then he pointed to the heavens and with a voice choked with emotion he said to Jakov, "You wear his coat very well."[3]

As you examine the Christian faith, I hope you have a few believing friends who wear Christ's coat very well. It's a powerful thing to see the difference in a life that has accepted the forgiveness and leadership of Jesus. Still, between our expectations of believers and the actual lives of believers, sometimes something gets lost in translation. If you've been disappointed with Christians you know, don't let it derail you in your examination of the faith. Study the vision Christ set for his people and see if it's worth pursuing in your own life.

Chapter 16
Life Together

The church is a "communion"

In the 1985 film, *Witness*, Harrison Ford played John Book, a Philadelphia detective investigating a murder. His only witness was an Amish boy on his first visit to the city. As the plot thickened, Book was wounded during an attempt on his life. Knowing that his little witness faced the same threat, he returned the boy and his mother to the safety and anonymity of their Amish farming community. Upon reaching their home, however, Book collapsed from his gunshot wound, and the rest of the plot unfolded in a world far removed from the violence and brokenness of the detective's world. As he recovered and tried to figure out what to do, the detective became deeply attracted to the life he saw around him. While the boy had been Book's witness to a Philadelphia murder, the boy's Amish family and neighbors became Book's witnesses to another way of living—and thus the film's title turned out to have more than one meaning. The film ends not only with a solved case but also with a tough choice for the detective: to stay with the Amish or to return to Philadelphia a little wiser.

In one scene, Book joined the Amish in an old-fashioned barn-raising. The entire community came together to build a barn for a newlywed couple. To director Peter Weir's credit, he paused the progress of the plot to let the camera linger over the day's work. Old men gave direction, able-bodied men clambered among the framework sharing tools and glasses of lemonade, little boys stood in a row clacking hammers, and women patched together a quilt for the newlyweds. The scene ended with the community walking away from the finished work, silhouetted by the setting sun, singing a hymn.

The scene beautifully symbolized the kind of community John Book witnessed in his days with the Amish Christians. The scene also mirrors the kind of community Jesus forms among those of us who follow his leadership: we are to be a "communion of saints," in the words of our ancient creed. It's the third way the Apostles' Creed defines the church. The church we believe in is "one," "holy," and a "communion."

I think it's significant that, though these three words are ancient, they address the three most common twenty-first century objections against church involvement:

- Some complain that they've seen church groups filled with bickering and divisiveness. But Jesus had a vision for unity among his followers—we are to be "one" with others who believe the biblical teachings.

- Some complain that Christians and their churches can be hypocritical and judgmental. But Jesus expected his people to encourage each other as we learn to leave behind all that used to enslave us—we are to be "holy."

- Some say they've known Christians who were self-centered and they've known churches that were cold and business-like. But Jesus expected his people to support and care for each other—we are to be a "communion."

In the last two chapters we looked at the biblical aim to be "one" and "holy." In this chapter we'll see how Jesus desired those who believe in him to be a *community* of believers—a "communion of saints," in the words of the Creed.

Since the word "saints" is so misunderstood in our culture, believers hesitate to call themselves "saints" today. In fact, people in our culture are more likely to deny the title. "Hey, I'm no saint," we say, and we don't say it as a sad *confession* of our faults but as a proud *defense* of our faults. The biblical writers, however, frequently used the word "saints" as another word for believers. The word is found about forty-five times in the New Testament as a title for God's people, and it shows up another twenty-three times in the Old Testament, primarily in the Psalms. To refer to Christians as "saints" links back to what was said in the last chapter. We are called to be holy—different, set apart. The word "saint" is a translation of the Greek word *hagios*, which means *set apart* or *holy*, and as we saw in the last chapter that is the expectation and hope Jesus has for his followers.

Specifically, though, believers are not merely expected to live set-apart lives, but to live in a *community* of those pursuing the set-apart life. We are *the communion of saints*. It's no accident that the word "communion" sounds so similar to the word "community," which is probably a more familiar term in our culture. Both words capture the same thought of a group of people who have certain things in common—they know each other and they want similar things out of their relationships with each other. They also maintain a certain level of loyalty and appreciation for each other, and they hold each other accountable to agreed-upon standards.

I've seen wonderful models of this kind of community among believers, and maybe you have, too. Still, believers are painfully aware of how we fall short of that vision. Former U.S. Senate chaplain Richard Halverson offered this tongue-in-cheek history of the church: "The church began as a fellowship of men and women centered on Jesus Christ. It went to Greece and became a philosophy. It went to Rome and became an institution. It went to Europe and became a culture. It came to America and became an enterprise."[1] By becoming a believer, you commit your life to working with others toward fulfilling the *original* design for the church: a community of believers.

When I think of God's hopes for my congregation, I know he wants us to be a *fellowship* and a *partnership*. The first word looks inward; the second word looks outward. The first word speaks of sharing life together; the second word speaks of pursuing goals together.

We Are a Fellowship

The first gathering of believers was described with these words: "They devoted themselves . . . to the fellowship" (Acts 2:42). They met regularly together, they prayed for each other, worshipped together, and shared possessions with those who had needs. The warm fellowship impressed and attracted others so much that new people were joining daily.

Take a moment to reflect on all the times the Bible uses the phrase "one another" to describe how believers are to go through life *together*:

> "Love one another" (John 13:34).
>
> "Be devoted to one another in brotherly love. Honor one another above yourselves" (Romans 12:10).
>
> "Live in harmony with one another" (Romans 12:16).
>
> "Agree with one another" (1 Corinthians 1:10).
>
> "Submit to one another out of reverence for Christ" (Ephesians 5:21).
>
> "Accept one another" (Romans 15:7).
>
> "Serve one another in love" (Galatians 5:13).
>
> "Be patient with each other, making allowance for each other's faults because of your love" (Ephesians 4:2 NLT).
>
> "Be kind and compassionate to one another, forgiving each other, just as in Christ God forgave you" (Ephesians 4:32).

"Speak to one another with psalms, hymns and spiritual songs" (Ephesians 5:19).

"Encourage one another and build each other up" (1 Thessalonians 5:11).

"Confess your sins to each other and pray for each other" (James 5:16).

"Offer hospitality to one another" (1 Peter 4:9).

"Have equal concern for each other" (1 Corinthians 12:25).

As these verses are taken together, it is impossible to miss the conviction that life is to be shared. The Christian life was not meant to be a solitary life. The Bible says that our fellowship with God is proven valid by our fellowship with his people: "No one has ever seen God; but if we love one another, God lives in us and his love is made complete in us" (1 John 4:12). Verses like this remind us we cannot really say we're connected to God unless we're also connected to other believers—with all the patience and forgiveness and sensitivity that such a connection requires.

We Are a Partnership

In addition to thinking of our community of believers as a "fellowship" it's also important to remember we are a "partnership." The fact that my congregation is a fellowship reminds me to look *inward* at the life we should share together. The fact that my congregation is a partnership reminds me to look *outward* at the work we should do together.

Without both considerations, our community of believers becomes imbalanced. Without a sense of *fellowship*, all we would do is tackle our projects, complete our assignments, and finish our work. In such settings a person's moral choices would never be challenged, his beliefs would never be refined, and his needs would never be addressed. On the other hand, without a sense of *partnership*, a congregation quickly becomes introverted. Soon, the only factor that is addressed in deciding what to do is simply that which pleases the current participants. So, we are supposed to be a fellowship that meets each other's needs *and* a partnership that mobilizes people for meaningful action.

Paul wrote to one church with deep fondness because they understood the importance of *working* together and not just assembling together. He reminded them: "In all my prayers for all of you, I always pray with joy because of your *partnership* in the gospel" (Philippians 1:4-5). He often expressed by name his appreciation for the men and women who shared the ministry with him. Their names show up in his letters: Timothy, John Mark, Luke, and little-known personalities such as Phoebe, Epaphras, Euodia, and Syntyche (see Romans 16:1, Colossians 1:6-7, Philippians 4:2-3, 1 Thessalonians 3:2, and 2 Timothy 4:11).

As we put our faith in Jesus and start spending time with a congregation of fellow believers, we need to identify the ways we can be useful to that gathering. We partner together through financially supporting the work, through praying for God's blessing on the work, through offering suggestions to improve the work, and through volunteering in the work. The church isn't an institution that does things for us; the church is a community of believers who have partnered together to make a difference in the world. When we say, "I believe in the church, the communion of saints," we are committing to investing in both *fellowship* and *partnership* with others who have drawn the same conclusions that we have about Jesus.

Seeing the Forest for the Trees

Across the last three chapters we've discovered that Jesus expected his church—a collective reference to all believers—to be "one," "holy" and a "communion." When you meet Christians who are divisive, hypocritical, and selfish, ask yourself three questions. These questions may help you in your exploration of Christianity:

First: "Should I be surprised to find sick people in a hospital?" When I've visited hospital patients as a pastor, they were in the hospital because some part of their body wasn't working right. They needed a heart bypass or a hip replacement or a treatment for some disease. I've sympathized with them, grieved for them, and prayed over them—but I've never been surprised to find them there. In fact, since their bodies weren't working right, a hospital room was exactly where they needed to be.

Jesus said, "It is not those who are healthy who need a physician, but those who are sick; I did not come to call the righteous, but sinners" (Mark 2:17). It should come as no surprise, then, that you find lives that are very much "on the mend" when you get involved with other believers. That's good news, though, when you consider that you need a spiritual physician, too. It's unrealistic to expect perfection from the Christians you know and the churches you visit. Together they are under the care of a thorough physician, and they gladly recommend him to others.

Second: "Am I letting my disappointment with some Christians color my perspective of all Christians?" I once talked with a man about joining me at a special event at the church I led. "No," he said. He shook his head firmly and added that worn-out line, "Christians are nothing but hypocrites."

"I suppose that would include your mother, then," I replied. His mother was a devout and loving member of my congregation, one of those ladies who became even more gracious with her advancing years.

"Well . . . of course I'm not referring to her."

"Then you've got to be referring to your boss," I said with a smile. I was referring to another member of our church who had employed him, modeled the Christian life, and even stuck by him through some alcoholic instability. I listed off a few more believers who had made a positive impact on his life and he finally saw how unfair he had been in his cynical view of the church.

If you've been disappointed by a certain Christian or a particular church, especially in a dramatic way, it's easy to end up viewing anything having to do with Christianity through that narrow lens. It would be helpful to balance the negative acts of certain Christians with the many positive ways believers have made a difference in the lives of others—perhaps even in your life.

Third: "Is Christ's vision worth pursuing?" If you give up your examination of Jesus because a certain Christian or a particular church has disappointed you, isn't that like rejecting Beethoven's genius because your kid's Middle School orchestra performed his work so poorly?[2] We've taken three chapters to lay out the intent Jesus had for those who followed him. It's an ideal worth realizing. If your exploration of Jesus concludes with a commitment to him, remember that to love him means loving what he loves—and, according to Scripture, Jesus "loved the church and gave himself up for her" (Ephesians 5:25).

When we put our faith in him, we are accepting his mandate to join with other believers to make one holy church, the communion of saints. The late columnist Mike Royko always had a knack for finding colorful characters and making them come alive in the printed word. In one story he tells, I'm reminded of what we can be together. In a story he tells about Slats Grobnik, a man who sold Christmas trees, I'm reminded of what we can be together:

> Slats remembered one couple on the hunt for a Christmas Tree. The guy was skinny with a big Adam's apple and small chin, and she was kind of pretty. But both wore clothes from the bottom of the bin at the Salvation Army store.
>
> After finding only trees that were too expensive, they found a Scotch pine that was okay on one side, but pretty bare on the other. Then they picked up another tree that was not much better—full on one side, scraggly on the other. She whispered something, and he asked if $3 would be okay. Slats figured both trees would not be sold, so he agreed.

A few days later Slats was walking down the street and saw a beautiful tree in the couple's apartment. It was thick and well rounded.

He knocked on their door and they told him how they worked the two trees close together where the branches were thin. Then they tied the trunks together. The branches overlapped and formed a tree so thick you couldn't see the wire. Slats described it as "a tiny forest of its own."

"So that's the secret," Slats asserts. "You take two trees that aren't perfect, that have flaws, that might even be homely, that maybe nobody else would want. If you put them together just right, you can come up with something really beautiful."[3]

Part Six: "I Believe in Forgiveness"

*I believe
in God the Father Almighty,
Maker of heaven and earth;
And in Jesus Christ his only Son our Lord;
who was conceived by the Holy Spirit,
born of the Virgin Mary,
suffered under Pontius Pilate,
was crucified, dead, and buried.
The third day he rose again from the dead.
He ascended into heaven,
and sits at the right hand of God the Father Almighty.
From there he shall come
to judge the living and the dead.
I believe in the Holy Spirit;
the one holy church;
the communion of saints;
the forgiveness of sins;
the resurrection of the body;
and the life everlasting.
Amen.*

Chapter 17
Beauty and the Beast

Schindler's List won seven Academy Awards in 1993, including Best Picture. It's an account of a German named Oskar Schindler who saved 1200 Jews from Nazi death camps by employing them and bribing Nazi officials to keep them employed.

Who can forget the closing scene of the film as Schindler prepared to leave those he saved? The war was over and, knowing the Allies would try him as a member of the Nazi party and the owner of a munitions factory, he planned to flee. Before he drove away, however, those who owed Schindler their lives surrounded him. They presented him a ring created from the gold fillings extracted out of the teeth of grateful workers. On the ring was a Hebrew inscription from the Talmud: "Whoever saves one life saves the world entire." The gift and its significance caused Schindler to break down in tears.

It's a moving scene, but in reality it wasn't the last of Oskar Schindler and his ring. The film doesn't cover a conversation years later, as one of the "Schindler Jews" talked with the old German rescuer. The survivor pointed to Schindler's naked finger and asked what happened to his gold ring.

"Schnapps," he shrugged. He had sold it for booze.

So, which of those two scenarios best captures the real Oskar Schindler? Would you believe . . . *both*? He was a contradiction: a hero who saved lives, and a dissolute womanizer who abandoned his long-suffering wife. His lack of wisdom and self-discipline caused him to fail in numerous businesses and relationships, and yet a member of the Israeli Supreme Court remembered him as "one of the bravest, finest people."[1]

Oskar Schindler's story is our story, too. Each person is a contradiction: a hero *and* a disappointment; the graceful ballerina *and* the raunchy stripper; Dr. Jekyll *and* Mr. Hyde. The better we understand this, the deeper our gratitude will be when we recite the next line on our Creed: "I believe in the forgiveness of sins."

This is the most personal line in the Apostles' Creed. Certainly there are personal implications from belief in God the Father, in Jesus, in the Holy Spirit, and in the church. However, when we believers say, "I believe in the forgiveness of sins," the line brings to each of us the memory of our own individual failures and regrets.

In Isaiah 53:6, the Hebrew prophet confessed—

> We all, like sheep, have gone astray,
> each of us has turned to his own way.

There's another line to that verse I'll share in a moment, and its incredibly good news. Before we look at the good news, though, we need to let the truth sink in from those first two lines: We have gone astray and turned to our own self-centered way.

The Bible is brutally realistic about this fact. King Solomon said in an aside to his great prayer at the dedication of the Temple, "There is no one who does not sin" (1 Kings 8:46). Much later in life, and after many more experiences, the old king's conviction on this point was even clearer (Ecclesiastes 7:20):

> There is not a righteous man on earth
> who does what is right and never sins.

The Old Testament poet confessed to God, "No one living is righteous before you" (Psalms 143:2). In another Psalm, the poet observed (14:2-3)—

> The Lord looks down from heaven
> on the sons of men
> to see if there are any who understand,
> any who seek God.
> All have turned aside,
> they have together become corrupt;
> there is no one who does good,
> not even one.

You can find the same realistic assessment in the New Testament: "If we claim to be without sin, we deceive ourselves and the truth is not in us" (1 John 1:8).

I was once in a college classroom where we discussed the question, "Are people basically good?" A graduate student said, "Yes. I drive to work every day among people who are obeying the speed limit even though a police officer is rarely seen." I spoke up: "Wouldn't it be more realistic to say that they obey the speed limit because an officer is *occasionally* seen?"

Think about it: Why do we have police officers at all? Why do we have laws to regulate behavior—complete with penalties for the offenders? Why are we given tickets after paying our entrance to a movie—and then the ticket is checked at the door? Why do I have to run my belongings through an X-ray machine—even my shoes—before I can board an airplane? Why do even seminaries and religious colleges have expensive devices at their library doors that set off alarms if a student should walk out the door with a book that hasn't been checked out? Why do we lock our doors at night?

That graduate student had to ignore a lot of obvious data in order to maintain her conviction that humans are basically good. Her response reminded me of the newspaper article about the man who began a publicized walk across America to promote the positive message that people are basically decent. Before he had crossed his own state line, muggers had robbed him and thrown him from a bridge![2]

Don't get me wrong: I've read numerous stories of astonishing love and heroic sacrifice, and I know that you and I could tell each other some accounts to prove our own genuine decency. I am just as reluctant to say that people are *basically* bad anymore as I'd want to say that people are *basically* good. Rather, people are *basically* walking contradictions. I am Oskar Schindler, and so are you.

When we believers say, "I believe in the forgiveness of sins," the line brings to each of us the memory of our own individual failures and regrets

In the first pages of the Bible we read of both the formation and the fall of our first parents. God's creation of Adam and Eve was the apex of all that he had created because they were made in his very image. As their descendants, we are also reflections of God. In our behavior, in the way we treat each other, in our creativity, and in our priorities, we convey to the rest of the created order, "This is what God looks like." To this day, in every story of sacrificial love, uncompromising loyalty, enriching relationships, and delightful creativity, we hear what the philosopher Pascal called "rumors of glory."[3]

But we are not simply descendants of image-bearers, but of *fallen* image-bearers. Adam and Eve doubted God's leadership and wisdom, and they turned away from God. As descendants from that first fallen couple, you and I are fallen image-bearers as well. We see this reality in every story of selfishness, betrayal, rebellion, insensitivity and outright cruelty. In his British wit, G.K. Chesterton complained that those who reject the biblical claim that the human race has been corrupted reject "the only part of Christian theology which can really be proved."[4]

And so we are walking contradictions: we are image-bearers who show a very inconsistent image of God to the rest of the created order. As his little reflections, we say, "This is what God looks like," and then we present a contradictory picture. We paint a brushstroke of love here and selfishness there. We apply the theme of loyalty on one corner of the canvas and the darker shadows of betrayal on another. We splash the discordant colors of kindness and cruelty on the whole display. We all, like sheep, have gone astray.

Even a passing review of our lives against the Ten Commandments (Exodus 20) or Christ's famous "Sermon on the Mount" (Matthew 5-7) will put us face-to-face with our shortcomings: we've been disloyal to our parents, irreverent in our thoughts of God, covetous, hypocritical, bitter in our thoughts toward those who've hurt us, judgmental, inattentive to God, lustful in our lingering looks at others, and so on.

If you're just exploring the Christian faith at this point, of course, you may not consider the Ten Commandments or Christ's Sermon on the Mount as authoritative standards. Whatever guidance we depend on to find direction for life, however, none of us has lived up to it. The English pastor, John Stott, put it this way:

> All men have broken the law they know and fallen short of their own standard. What is our ethical code? It may be the law of Moses or the law of Jesus. It may be the decent thing, or the done thing, or the conventions of society. It may be the Buddhist's noble eightfold path or the Muslim's five pillars of conduct. But whatever it is, we have not succeeded in observing it. We all stand self-condemned.[5]

Through our sin, however, we do more than break the rules; we break a heart. God said, "A son honors his father, and a servant his master. If I am a father, where is the honor due me? If I am a master, where is the respect due me?" (Malachi 1:6.) Sin is failure to give God his proper honor. Fundamentally, it is a *relationship we wound*, not just a line we cross.

As a result, the Bible uses a variety of stern words to describe our condition, such as "lost," "enslaved," and "dead" (see Luke 15, John 8:34, and Romans 6:23). Some of us may be unwilling to use such serious words to describe our moral state, because we feel our decent acts ought to count for something. While we would admit we're not perfect, still we want to describe our lives as "mostly good." However, if a restaurant prepared an omelet for you where a foul, rotten egg was among the ingredients, you would take no comfort from the chef's assurance that the rest of the eggs in the omelet were fresh. A restaurant advertising omelets made of "Mostly Fresh Eggs" simply won't stay in business! God isn't happy with lives of "mostly" good deeds and thoughts, either. The rottenness of our sin spoils these lives of ours.

"Ever Gone a Week Without a Rationalization?"

We have four ways to handle our sin. First, we can respond with *denial*. Consider the life of James Hammond, an antebellum plantation owner who served terms as a congressman and a governor. He was a formidable defender of slavery with an insatiable ambition—and an equally insatiable sexual appetite. In 1839 he purchased an eighteen-year-old slave named Sally and her infant daughter, Louisa. He sired several children by Sally and then when Louisa reached the age of twelve, he began taking her to bed and fathered several more children. In addition, Hammond sexually abused his wife's four nieces, aged thirteen to eighteen.

His wife finally gave up and left him. God must have gotten fed up with him, too, because a series of epidemics beset Hammond's "property" (slaves and livestock), resulting in serious financial setbacks. What's more, his brother-in-law threatened to ruin Hammond's political career by going public with Hammond's sexual molestations of the children. You would have thought the man would have seen the writing on the wall. But read these words, taken from a page out of his diary:

> It crushes me to the earth to see every thing of mine so blasted around me. Negroes, cattle, mules, hogs, every thing that has life around me seems to labour under some fated malediction. . . . Dear God, what have I done? Never was a man so cursed . . . what have I done or omitted to do to deserve this fate?[6]

It's hard to believe that Hammond could be so baffled at God's displeasure. Still, he's not the only one who has failed to connect the dots between ruinous living and a ruined life. While I've never met anyone as clueless about their sins as Hammond, I have met those who deny the *seriousness* of their failings. How could God be offended at our mistakes, they wonder, especially when our actions are no worse than anyone else's? Besides, they say, we can make up for it through sacrificial service or a list of good deeds.

In the 1983 film *The Big Chill*, Jeff Goldblum's character, Michael, hit the nail on the head in his conversation with Sam:

> Michael: I don't know anyone who could get through the day without two or three juicy rationalizations. They're more important than sex.
>
> Sam: Ah, come on. Nothing's more important than sex.
>
> Michael: Oh yeah? Ever gone a week without a rationalization?

The first response to our moral failures, then, is denial. We rationalize away what we've done, or at least the seriousness of what we've done. And, as the corny old saying goes, the definition of "rationalize" is "rational lies."

Excuses, Excuses

The second response to the subject of sin is *blame*. Circumstances and other people are to blame for our failures: we were tired . . . they started it . . . what can you expect from the kind of upbringing we had . . . and on it goes.

Over fifty years ago, novelist William Golding poked holes in these excuses with his widely-read novel, *Lord of the Flies*, which is still on many high school reading lists. The novel describes what happened to some schoolboys marooned on a desert island after a plane crash where all the adults were killed. Written in a time when many believed that the natural goodness of human beings was spoiled by the expectations and pressures of family and society, Golding described what happened to children in a setting without family and society. The boys became shockingly selfish, destructive, and cruel. Golding later said that his book's theme was "an attempt to trace the defects of society back to the defects of human nature."[7] In other words, a corrupt world doesn't make us the way we are; the way we are makes our world corrupt.

Jesus told us the same thing: It is not our education, our upbringing, or our surrounding culture that finally determines what we will become. Instead, Jesus said that the source of sin is found within a person's own heart (Mark 7:21-23).

"Out, Damned Spot!"

There's a third response to sin. When we are unable to deny its reality any longer, and when we can no longer shift the blame for our sins upon others, we may fall into *despair*.

Shakespeare's Lady Macbeth remains a powerful study in the effects of unresolved guilt. In *Hamlet*, Macbeth plots to kill the king to take the crown for himself, and Lady Macbeth supports the plot. In fact, she returns to the scene of the crime to smear the drugged guards with the king's blood and thus incriminate them.

Lady Macbeth begins to sleepwalk. "Out, damned spot!" she says to herself as she walks the night, rubbing her hands roughly in an attempt to remove the bloody stain which seems never to go away. Without relief from the guilt of her crime, she slides into madness and, finally, suicide.

The Cross

There's a fourth response to sin: we can humbly receive divine forgiveness. Earlier I quoted only the first of two lines of Isaiah 53:6. In the last line, the prophet spoke of the cross where Jesus died—

> We all, like sheep, have gone astray,
> each of us has turned to his own way;
> *and the Lord has laid on him the iniquity of us all.*

It is to that astonishing story that we now turn.

Chapter 18
Why the Cross Matters

Lou Johnson was a star player for the Los Angeles Dodgers in the 1965 World Series, but drug and alcohol abuse cost him everything from that magical season. To feed his addiction, he sold his uniform, glove, and the bat he used to hit the winning run in the deciding game. Most painful to him, though, was the loss of his championship ring to a drug dealer in 1971.

When Dodger president, Bob Graziano, learned that Johnson's World Series ring was about to be auctioned on the Internet, he immediately wrote a check for $3,457, bought the ring, and gave it to Johnson. The old outfielder, clean and sober for years, wept, saying, "It felt like a piece of me had been reborn."[1]

We believers know the feeling. Jesus paid a great price to recover what we lost through sin. It's with humble gratitude and astonished reverence that we recite together, "I believe in the forgiveness of sins," because we know that forgiveness came at a great cost to our Forgiver.

In the last chapter, we took a close look at the human condition. Humans were created to reflect the very character of God himself, but we have fallen far away from that intention. In Isaiah 53:6, the prophet said,

> We all, like sheep, have gone astray,
> each of us has turned to his own way.

But the verse doesn't stop at that sad and obvious reality. The prophet went on to say—

and the Lord has laid on him the iniquity of us all.

Isaiah caught a prophetic glimpse of the future when Jesus would suffer and die upon a cross. What does it mean to say God laid our sin upon his own Son, and how does that tie in to his forgiveness of our sin? These are critical questions, because the connection between Christ's cross and our forgiveness dominates the pages of Scripture. Jesus himself made the connection often, and explained it as being consistent with all earlier Scripture. "This is what is written," he said. "The Christ will suffer and rise from the dead on the third day, and repentance and forgiveness of sins will be preached in his name to all nations" (Luke 24:45-47).

Notice the order to the events in Jesus' words: he would suffer, die, rise again, and then forgiveness would be available "to all nations." His death and our forgiveness: the two are connected.

It's hard to miss the centrality of the cross in the Christian message. While many nonbelievers casually respect Jesus as a great moral teacher, his teaching is only a small part of what Christians consider important. As you read through the Gospels, the account of three years of teachings and miracles moves quickly, while the writers slow down to linger over the details of the week leading up to his crucifixion and resurrection. The events of that single week dominate the four New Testament Gospels, taking up two-fifths of Matthew, three-fifths of Mark, a third of Luke and half of John. I recall one of my seminary professors saying that the Gospels were essentially "Passion narratives with extended introductions." The word "passion" traditionally means "suffering," and clearly the four Gospels consider Christ's Passion the most important part of the story.

The other New Testament writers also centered their message on the cross. While the *events* of Christ's Passion dominate the Gospels, the *implications* of Christ's Passion take up much of the other New Testament writings. The apostles insisted that the death and resurrection of Jesus made all the difference in such large-scale issues as rescue from sin, ongoing victory over evil, reunion with God, reconciliation with each other, the ability to live lives of patience and forgiveness, and the chance to attain eternal life.

Even the two Christian rituals of baptism and communion symbolize Christ's Passion. Baptism is a powerful public symbol of union with the death, burial and resurrection of Jesus (see Romans 6:1-4). As believers continue to take the bread and the cup of communion throughout their lives, Jesus said the ritual would continually remind them of his sacrifice, and the "forgiveness of sins" that it achieved (see Matthew 26:26-29).

The Christian writings and rituals rivet our attention upon the cross. While the Star of David or a crescent moon or the Yin-Yang circle identifies other major religions, the cross is the mark of Christianity. If you're exploring Christianity, then, you will have to understand the cross to understand Christ. The meaning of his life will never be grasped apart from the meaning of his death.

> *While the Star of David or a crescent moon or the Yin-Yang circle identifies other major religions, the cross is the mark of Christianity*

Because the cross is so central to the Scriptures, we could turn to numerous passages to gain an understanding of it. However, I want to concentrate on one verse from Simon Peter's writings. Peter was among the first to follow Jesus, he was part of the inner circle during Christ's earthly life, and he was an influential leader of the church following Christ's departure. In short, his interpretation of the sufferings of Jesus carries a lot of weight. In 1 Peter 3:18, he wrote —

> For Christ died for sins
> once for all,
> the righteous for the unrighteous,
> to bring you to God

Like bursts from a machine gun or staccato clips from an orchestra, Simon Peter described the death of Jesus in four brief statements. What happened on the cross was *sacrificial, sufficient, substitutionary,* and *saving.*

Christ's Death Was Sacrificial

Peter wrote, "Christ died for sins." It wasn't the first time Peter expressed this view. A few verses earlier he had already stated (2:24 NLT), "He personally carried away our sins in his own body on the cross. You have been healed by his wounds!" Paul taught the same thing: "Christ loved you and gave himself as a sacrifice to take away your sins" (Ephesians 5:2 NLT). We can find the same conviction in John's writings: "God loved us and sent his Son as an atoning sacrifice for our sins" (1 John 4:10).

This conviction is "of first importance" in the Christian faith. Paul said that as a teacher he was simply passing along what he had been taught as a new believer: "For what I received I passed on to you as of first importance: that Christ died *for our sins*" (1 Corinthians 15:3).

All the earliest believers had come from Jewish households and were familiar with Temple sacrifices. There a family would bring a lamb to the altar, the man would lay his hands on the head of the animal to identify his family's sins with that lamb, and then the animal was sacrificed. As the animal died, the sins of the family died with it. It was a way to teach the people how grievous sin was, how necessary it was for something or someone else to take away their sin, and how costly such a removal was.

The earliest Christ-followers came to understand that the Temple sacrifices had been preparation for understanding the cross. When the prophet Isaiah looked ahead to the cross, he said, "The Lord has laid on him the iniquity of us all."

C.S. Lewis beautifully alluded to this in his 1952 children's book *The Lion, The Witch and the Wardrobe*—recently introduced to a new generation through film. In the story, four English children named Peter, Susan, Edmund, and Lucy, stumble into the world of Narnia through a wardrobe in their uncle's estate. Unfortunately, they enter Narnia at a time when a Witch has taken over the land, but they hear residents whisper the hopeful news that Aslan is on his way. Aslan is a great Lion, the son of the Emperor-Beyond-the-Sea, and the rightful ruler of Narnia. The children eventually meet Aslan, who is clearly a picture of Christ.

When Edmund commits a treacherous act, the Witch claims her right to take his life in keeping with the law of the land. Of course, she's less concerned with honoring the Emperor's law than she is in getting rid of the four English children before they fulfill a Narnian prophecy that will break her control of the land. Whatever her motivation, however, the end result will be the same for Edmund: death.

In a private arrangement, Aslan offers the Witch his life in place of the traitor, which delights the Witch even more. While hidden at the edge of the clearing, Susan and Lucy watch in horror as the great Lion gives himself up to be humiliated by the Witch's minions. They shave off his royal mane, kick him, muzzle him, and finally bind him tight upon a huge Stone Table. The Witch raises her knife over his compliant body, and the girls avert their eyes from the murder (this is a children's book, after all). As the horrible crowd leaves in triumph, the two girls creep up to the Lion's lifeless body and weep inconsolably.

As dawn arrives, however, they hear a deafening crack behind them. They whirl around to see the Stone Table broken in half, with Aslan standing before them alive again. He explains that the Witch didn't look deeply enough into the Emperor's ways. If she had, he says, she would have known a deeper truth—that when a willing, innocent victim is killed in place of a traitor, the Stone Table would crack and death would be reversed.

The entire account re-presents the crucifixion and resurrection of Christ. He died as a sacrifice to protect us from the consequences of our wrongdoing.

Christ's Death Was Sufficient

Simon Peter said that it was "once for all." The Apostles, realizing the Temple sacrificial system was meant to prepare people to understand the death of Christ, taught that there was no need for more sacrifices. A biblical letter specifically written to Hebrew believers says it repeatedly:

> Jesus sacrificed for sins *"once for all* when he offered himself" (Hebrews 7:27).

> Again, we are told that that Jesus "entered the Most Holy Place *once for all* by his own blood" (Hebrews 9:12).

> Driving home the point, the writer says one more time that believers "have been made holy through the sacrifice of the body of Jesus Christ *once for all*" (Hebrews 10:10).

The comment about Jesus entering the Most Holy Place by his own blood would have been deeply meaningful to those familiar with the Jewish Temple. The "Most Holy Place" was a little room at the very center of the Temple compound symbolizing the dwelling place of God himself. Only the High Priest could pass through the veil at the entrance to that room, and only once a year on the Day of Atonement, and only as he carried a bowl containing the blood of a sacrifice. When Jesus died, the veil at the entrance to the Most Holy Place ripped apart as the earth rocked violently (Matthew 27:50-52). It was a powerful demonstration that Christ's death opened the way for a relationship with God.

The last thing Jesus said before dying was, "It is finished" (John 19:30). He was not moaning, "My life is through," or "My mission has failed." Instead, he was saying, "It is accomplished." The death of Jesus is *sufficient* to remove our sins.

Christ's Death Was Substitutionary

Simon Peter said the Lord's sacrifice was "the righteous for the unrighteous." The Apostle Paul wrote, "God made him who had no sin to be sin for us, so that in him we might become the righteousness of God" (2 Corinthians 5:21). Jesus "had no sin"—in other words, he lived in consistent obedience to his Father. He fulfilled the role we were supposed to play as God's reflections. He was the one person able to say about the way he lived, "Look, this is what God is like!" He never failed as the image-bearer that God expected mankind to be. Despite his unblemished moral record, however, he accepted his Father's plan that he would "be sin for us." The darkest moment for Jesus was not when Judas betrayed him or when Peter denied him but when his Father abandoned him upon the cross. The Bible says the sky grew dark over the crucifixion, as if God had removed himself from the spiritual decay Jesus carried. Jesus felt the abandonment, too, because he cried out a line from a familiar Hebrew psalm, "My God, my God, why have you forsaken me?" (Matthew 27:45-46, quoting Psalm 22:1). The garbage of our sin that he was bearing away separated Jesus from the Father.

Mel Gibson's film, *The Passion of the Christ*, opens with a prophecy from the Hebrew Bible (Isaiah 53:5):

> He was wounded for our transgressions,
> crushed for our iniquities;
> by His wounds we are healed.[2]

Like a flower unfurls from a tight bud to reveal the full bloom, the entire film unfurls from those first words the viewer sees. All the pain and suffering that the film depicted was "for our transgressions."

What's more, the director actually inserted himself into the film at a critical point. The viewer never sees the celebrity's famous face, but as Jesus is being nailed to the cross it is Gibson's own hand that holds the first nail driven into Christ.

He's not the first artist to include himself in scenes depicting Christ's suffering. In Rembrandt's 1633 painting, *The Raising of the Cross*, a man in a blue painter's beret is part of the crowd raising Christ upon the cross. That man is Rembrandt himself.[3]

Another believer, Bono of the band, U2, confessed his role in Christ's death in his song, "When Love Comes to Town." He said, "I was there when they crucified my Lord . . . I held the scabbard when the soldier drew his sword. . . ."[4]

Gibson, Rembrandt, and Bono all knew that their own sins required the cross. We, too, have to get to the point where we see that it was our own sins that Christ carried.

Christ's Death Was Saving

Simon Peter said its purpose was "to bring you to God." The Greek word he used was *prosago* (pronounced "proh-SAH-goh"), and it was a word describing a formal introduction such as the announcements used at that time when a visitor was presented in a king's court. Now that he has carried away our sin and has risen in victory over death, Christ can present us to his Father. This access to God impacts our prayers now and our eternal destiny in the future. Maybe it's no accident that we can see in our English word "atone" the words "at one." We are now at one with God, in relationship with him, because of the work of the cross.

Just and Justifier

In his 1908 book, *The Russian Conquest of the Caucasus*, John Baddeley described the fierce leader, Shamil, who led the Caucasian resistance against imperial Russia in the area that is now Chechnya. Even as he led daring guerilla strikes against the Russians, he had to fight the spirit of defeatism among his own countrymen. He once made a proclamation that whoever advocated any capitulation with the Russians would be beaten with a hundred heavy lashes. Shortly after the severe edict, an offender was caught and brought before Shamil. To the warlord's shock and grief, it was his own mother who had called for a treaty with the enemy.

He retreated into solitude for three days to decide what to do. Due to the blatant disregard of his order and its potential impact on morale, he instructed that the penalty should be carried out.

After the fifth stroke ripped into his mother's back, however, he called a halt to the lashing. Then something remarkable took place: He stripped to the waist, knelt down by his mother, and took the remaining ninety-five strokes upon himself.

The story of Shamil's actions wound its way up the mountain passes, carried in astonished whispers from village to village. Impressed by their leader's uncompromising justice and costly compassion, none of his tribesmen ever again mentioned negotiations with the enemy. It's a story that resonates in the region to this day.[5]

God did the same thing for us. He bore the punishment himself, in the person of his own Son, "so as to be *just* and *the one who justifies* those who have faith in Jesus" (Romans 3:26). The cross became that place where God showed both his justice and his love.

As a result, God can *release* us from the penalty of sin, *restore* us to productive living, and *receive* us into his presence in eternity. We'll take a careful look at those three divine actions in the next chapter.

Chapter 19
God Can

"Welcome to Burma," she said, and tossed a pail of water in her guest's face. Laughing, she shouted, "Happy New Year!"

Thus her guest, a writer for *National Geographic* magazine, was introduced to Burma's Water Festival. For three days nearly forty million people in this southeast Asian country get ready for the Buddhist New Year by impishly hurling water at each other to wash away misdeeds of the past year.[1] The practice is mostly a good-natured prank today, but it's based in a fundamental human desire to be cleansed of moral failures.

We have a deep and universal longing to find some way to start fresh—to begin again. We can see it in every culture. In India, pilgrims travel miles, sometimes on their elbows and knees, to bathe in the sacred stream of the Ganges River. On the Indonesian island of Borneo the Dyak people perform an annual ceremony where they release a little boat into the river's flow to carry away the sins of their village.[2] Westerners haven't become too sophisticated for this hope of cleansing, either. A popular American book promoting physical and emotional well-being offers advice for putting your past behind you. The authors suggest that you create a little personal ceremony in your pool or tub where you "baptize yourself" and then "take a new or additional name to signify your new life."[3]

Paul Simon sang of this enduring longing in his song, *Graceland*.[4] As he traveled to Elvis Presley's Memphis home, he reflected on his relationship failures and his need for grace and acceptance. He sang, "Maybe I've a reason to believe we all will be received in Graceland."

The song is ironic and bittersweet; Paul Simon expressed a longing that he knows cannot be met at the mansion of a dead singer.

People *want* the forgiveness of sins and *seek* the forgiveness of sins, but those who follow Christ can say, "I *believe* in the forgiveness of sins!" We can't absolve ourselves of sin, no matter which ritual or ceremony we perform, but God can. Because of the cross, the Bible says God can *release* us, *restore* us, and *receive* us. As we look at these three divine activities in this chapter, our response is simply to yield to God's work in gratitude and loyalty.

God Can Release Us

In the *Peanuts* comic strip, one of the little characters reflected, "I guess it's wrong always to be worrying about tomorrow. Maybe we should think only about today." Charlie Brown replied, "No, that's giving up. I'm still hoping yesterday will get better."[5]

The good news is that yesterday can get better! The Bible says (1 Corinthians 6:9-11 Msg):

> "Unjust people who don't care about God will not be joining in his kingdom. Those who use and abuse each other, use and abuse sex, use and abuse the earth and everything in it, don't qualify as citizens in God's kingdom. A number of you know from experience what I'm talking about, for *not so long ago you were on that list. Since then, you've been cleaned up and given a fresh start by Jesus.*"

In his book, *A Forgiving God in an Unforgiving World*, Ron Lee Davis told of a pastor in the Philippines, a much-loved man of God who carried the burden of a secret sin he had committed many years before. He had repented but still had no peace. In his church was a devout woman who claimed that Christ literally spoke with her in her dreams. To try to open her eyes to what he believed was her deluded superstitions, he said, "The next time you speak with Christ, I want you to ask him what sin your pastor committed while he was in college." The woman agreed.

A few days later the pastor asked, "Well, did Christ visit you in your dreams?"

"Yes, he did," she replied.

"And did you ask him what sin I committed in school?"

"Yes."

"Well, what did he say?"

"He said, 'I don't remember.' "

The story is a beautiful reminder of God's promise in the Bible: "I—yes, I alone—am the one who blots out your sins for my own sake and will never think of them again" (Isaiah 43:25 NLT; see also Jeremiah 31:34). Again and again, the biblical writers celebrated this truth:

> "You have cast all my sins behind Your back" (Isaiah 38:17 NASB)

> "You will cast all our sins into the depths of the sea" (Micah 7:19 HCSB)

> "How far has the Lord
>   taken our sins from us?
> Farther than the distance
>   from east to west!"
> (Psalms 103:12 CEV)

As we visited relatives in Pensacola when my boys were small, our extended family spent a day at the beach. Together we built sand sculptures, and after a few hours we had constructed a number of them. Based on the age and skill of the builders, some sculptures were large and elaborate while some were small and plain. Still, when the tide rolled in at the end of the day, they were all washed away. The waves leveled all of our creations, no matter how elaborate or how simple, and left the beach as we had first found it. That's what God's forgiveness does with our sin, too. Whether our failures are large and dramatic or comparatively small and insignificant, they all give way to the cleansing power of divine forgiveness.

God Can Restore Us

God's forgiveness involves more than *releasing* us from the guilt of what we've done; it also includes *restoring* us to a useful role in life. Some of us may feel that our failures disqualify us from full participation in the life God wants for us. We may be grateful for God's mercy, and yet regard ourselves as second-class members of his family. As those who have put our faith in Christ, we know we're on God's list, so to speak, but always with an asterisk denoting us as those who've screwed up too much to enjoy the blessings and service of life with God.

That's where Simon Peter's story can help us. On the night before Jesus went to the cross, he warned Simon that he would soon abandon the Lord: "Simon, Simon," he said, "Satan has asked to sift you as wheat. But I have prayed for you, Simon, that your faith may not fail. And when you have turned back, strengthen your brothers" (Luke 22:31-32). After Simon vehemently stated his loyalty to Christ, Jesus specified that his impetuous disciple would disown him exactly three times within the span of the next few hours. It happened just as Jesus said it would, and Simon Peter was devastated (Luke 22:61).

That was not the end of Peter's story, however. When the women came to the tomb following Christ's death, they found an empty tomb and an angel who said, "You are looking for Jesus the Nazarene, who was crucified. He has risen! He is not here.

See the place where they laid him. But go, tell his disciples *and Peter*, 'He is going ahead of you into Galilee. There you will see him, just as he told you' " (Mark 16:6-7).

Did you notice that Peter was singled out among the disciples? It was as if Jesus knew the crushed spirit of Peter needed a special invitation: "Go tell the disciples that I want to meet with them. Tell them all, but especially tell Peter."

Simon did meet with his Lord, and an unusual conversation took place (John 21:15-19):

> When they had finished eating, Jesus said to Simon Peter, "Simon son of John, do you truly love me more than these?"
>
> "Yes, Lord," he said, "you know that I love you."
>
> Jesus said, "Feed my lambs."
>
> Again Jesus said, "Simon son of John, do you truly love me?"
>
> He answered, "Yes, Lord, you know that I love you."
>
> Jesus said, "Take care of my sheep."
>
> The third time he said to him, "Simon son of John, do you love me?"
>
> Peter was hurt because Jesus asked him the third time, "Do you love me?" He said, "Lord, you know all things; you know that I love you."
>
> Jesus said, "Feed my sheep." . . . Then he said to him, "Follow me!"

Count how many times Jesus asked Simon Peter of his love. Three times. It was a dramatic way for Christ to cancel each of Peter's denials and restore him to ministry. Before dying on the cross, when Jesus predicted Peter's denial, he also predicted his restoration: "When you have turned back," he said, "Strengthen your brothers." Following the resurrection, he issued the same call to Peter to be the leader among the first disciples: "Feed my sheep."

After a massive forest fire devastated the Rockies a few summers ago, I read an article the next spring about how the forest was returning. The lodgepole pines have seeds in the pine cones that open only after being subjected to the blasting heat of a forest fire. What's true in the natural world is true in the spiritual world: God "will give beauty for ashes" (Isaiah 61:3 NLT). Life and productivity can arise from the ruin of sin.

When a life of compromise and selfishness is turned over to him, God can use these failures in the most astonishing and unexpected ways. Despite regrets for what he called "my all too human tale of weakness and futility," one poet said to God:

> And yet there is a faith in me,
> That Thou wilt find in it
> One word that Thou canst take
> And make
> The centre of a sentence
> In Thy book of poetry.[6]

This is the humble but confident expression of one who believes in the forgiveness of sins. God can *restore* us from the ruin our sins have caused as well as *release* us from the guilt of them.

God Can Receive Us

Years ago, I was idly channel-surfing and landed briefly on the game show, *Family Feud*. Host Ray Combs was getting acquainted with his contestants, and I almost continued my surfing when he pointed to a lapel pin and said, "What do those two question marks stand for?"

I immediately put the clicker down and sat up. I had a lapel pin just like it: a simple brown pin with two gold question marks. I used to wear it to start conversations like the one that had just started on national television.

"Well," the contestant began, "The lapel pin represents the two most important questions anyone could ever ask you."

"I'm almost afraid to ask," Combs joked, "But what are they?"

"The first one is, *If you died today, do you know for certain that you would be welcomed into heaven?*"

Combs laughed and said good-naturedly, "I'm not going to answer that on national TV!"

He continued to introduce the other contestants, but then suddenly returned to the man with the pin and said, "Okay, I'll bite. What's the second question?"

"The second question is, *Suppose you were to die today and stand before God and he asked, 'Why should I let you into my heaven?' What would you say?*"

Combs, a stand-up comedian, said, "Because I'm the host of *Family Feud* and everybody loves me!" The audience laughed, the applause sign came on, and the game began.

I wonder if Ray Combs thought any more about those two questions before his suicide a few years later. They really are two of the most important questions in life, because they center on what it takes to pass our biggest test. The Bible tells us that one day we will stand before God as our life is reviewed. Paul wrote, "Each of us will give an account of himself to God" (Romans 14:12). Another text says, "Nothing in all creation is hidden from God's sight. Everything is uncovered and laid bare before the eyes of him to whom we must give account" (Hebrews 4:13). Simon Peter spoke of the time when everyone "will have to give account to him who is ready to judge the living and the dead" (1 Peter 4:5). Jesus said that this examination will get down to the smallest things: "I tell you that on the day of judgment people will have to account for every careless word they speak" (Matthew 12:36 HCSB).

But those who believe in the forgiveness of sins believe that God will receive them. We have put our faith in Jesus, who has already taken upon himself the punishment we deserved and transferred to us his perfect moral record. (We discussed the concept of Christ's substitution on page 170.)

Earlier I pointed out the biblical assurances that God wants to cast our sins away and "never think of them again." Those who trust in his mercy are comforted by that fact as we prepare to stand before his throne at judgment. The Bible says, "Christ was sacrificed once to *take away* the sins of many people; and he will appear a second time, not to bear sin, but to bring salvation to those who are waiting for him" (Hebrews 9:28).

Not long before she died in 1988, Marghanita Laski joined in a conversation with a believer on British television. In a moment of surprising candor, this well-known secular humanist and novelist said, "What I envy most about you Christians is your forgiveness; I have nobody to forgive me."[7]

We believe in the forgiveness of sins, and so we lift up the poet's relieved praise (Psalms 130:3-4 CEV):

> If you kept record of our sins, no one could last long.
> But you forgive us, and so we will worship you.

We all will be received in Graceland.

Part Seven: "I Believe in Eternal Life"

*I believe
in God the Father Almighty,
Maker of heaven and earth;
And in Jesus Christ his only Son our Lord;
who was conceived by the Holy Spirit,
born of the Virgin Mary,
suffered under Pontius Pilate,
was crucified, dead, and buried.
The third day he rose again from the dead.
He ascended into heaven,
and sits at the right hand of God the Father Almighty.
From there he shall come
to judge the living and the dead.
I believe in the Holy Spirit;
the one holy church;
the communion of saints;
the forgiveness of sins;
the resurrection of the body;
and the life everlasting.
Amen.*

Chapter 20
Waiting for Reveille

A businessman wanted to send a floral arrangement to a colleague who was opening a branch office. The colleague called later in the day to thank him for the considerate gesture, but he expressed his confusion about the attached card that read, "Rest in Peace." The businessman apologized for the mix up and quickly called to chastise the florist. The florist tried to console the executive. "It could be worse," he said. "Somewhere in the cemetery there's a bouquet with a note reading, 'Good luck in your new location.' "

Have you thought much about your new location beyond this life? The Bible teaches that those who are impacted by the saving action of Christ will find personal, conscious experiences beyond this life that will be rich and joyful. Believers do not have the hesitation of François Rabelais, the French writer who lived his life as a religious skeptic and yet died in 1553 with the half-hopeful statement, "I am going to the Great Perhaps." Instead, with confidence and joy we firmly recite together the words of our ancient creed:

> *I believe in the resurrection of the body*
> *and the life everlasting.*

Many people who have never even read a Bible expect some sort of conscious existence beyond death, as we can see in the images of popular culture and the stubborn human belief in the immaterial soul. Scripture confirms the essence of this conviction, and then tells us more. The Bible lets us know that the soul lives on beyond death, but the fullest experiences of the next life will be enjoyed at the resurrection of our bodies.

Let's look closely at the *continuation of your soul* and then the *resurrection of your body*.

Your Soul Will Continue

There will still be a conscious *you* when they pronounce you dead. Few in our culture are willing to embrace the bleak alternative so bluntly described by the famous atheist Bertrand Russell:

> No fire, no heroism, no intensity of thought and feeling, can preserve an individual life beyond the grave; . . . all the labours of the ages, all the devotion, all the inspiration, all the noonday brightness of human genius, are destined to extinction in the vast death of the solar system, and the whole temple of man's achievement must inevitably be buried beneath the debris of a universe in ruins.[1]

Instead of that stark conclusion, what reverberates throughout our culture is the conviction that we live on beyond death. Go to your favorite gift shop to get a sympathy card for someone in grief and you'll find that belief. Go to your favorite bookstore and you'll find it in bestsellers such as *The Five People You Meet in Heaven*. Go to your favorite video store and you'll find it in films like *Ghost, Defending Your Life, What Dreams May Come, The Rapture,* and *The Sixth Sense*. These books and films don't track with the Bible at every point, of course, but they reveal a firm conviction in our culture that the soul survives beyond death.

In a scene from the flawed but hauntingly beautiful film, *City of Angels*, the angel Seth expresses the conviction of the soul's survival to a surgeon named Maggie, who held the naturalistic view.

Troubled at the loss of one of her heart patients, Maggie meets Seth as a human visitor in the hallway:

>Seth: Are you in despair?
>
>Maggie: I lost a patient.
>
>Seth: People die.
>
>Maggie: Not on my table.
>
>Seth: People die when their bodies give out.
>
>Maggie: It's my job to keep their bodies from giving out, or what am I doing here?
>
>Seth: It wasn't your fault, Maggie.
>
>Maggie: I wanted him to live.
>
>Seth: He is living. Just not the way you think.
>
>Maggie: I . . . I don't believe in that.
>
>Seth: Some things are true whether you believe in them or not.

In the world of medical science, researchers and physicians wonder about the survival of the personal soul after hearing the near-death experiences of their patients. In her work with dying children, for example, Elizabeth Kubler-Ross found that the little patients frequently reported seeing loved ones already waiting for them on the other side.

In one instance, a child involved in a family car accident woke up in the hospital. Kubler-Ross asked the boy if he wanted to talk.

"Everything is alright now," he replied. "Mommy and Peter are already waiting for me." With a content little smile, he slipped back into his coma and passed away. The doctor said:

> I was quite aware that his mother had died at the scene of the accident, but Peter had not died. He had been brought to a special burn unit in another hospital, because the car had caught fire before he was extricated from the wreck. Since I was only collecting data, I accepted the boy's information and determined to look in on Peter. It was not necessary, however, because as I passed the nursing station there was a call from the other hospital to inform me that Peter had died a few minutes earlier.[2]

Other researchers have investigated the near-death experiences of hospital patients who flat-lined and then revived. The patients claim to have watched from a few feet above their own bodies as the medical team frantically worked to save them. Researchers have marveled at how detailed and accurate the reports are, from the way the needles worked on the machines, to the color of the oxygen masks, even to the identification of which loved ones were in the waiting room at the time.[3] We shouldn't develop our entire view of the afterlife on reports of those who went no further inside than the foyer, so to speak. Still, it's remarkable to read accounts of those who recall their conscious experiences as their bodies died.

The Bible affirms that conscious experiences beyond death are real. Given the choice between earthly troubles and the next life, the Apostle Paul wrote, "We really want to be away from this body and be at home with the Lord" (2 Corinthians 5:8 NCV). He was confident that to be *away from this body* is to be *at home with the Lord*. Elsewhere, he said the same thing: "The desire to break camp here and be with Christ is powerful. Some days I can think of nothing better" (Philippians 1:22 Msg). He believed that when we *break camp here* (a beautiful image of death), we would then *be with Christ*. This confidence was based in the teaching of Jesus himself. When one of the men hanging on the cross next to Jesus expressed his faith in Jesus, the Lord assured him: "*Today* you will be with me in paradise" (Luke 23:43 NLT).

Those verses emphatically tell us two things: first, that when death separates my soul from my body, I will still be conscious and aware and experiencing things. Second, when the mist that separates this life from the next life clears, the first face I'll see is the face of my Savior. I don't have to be afraid of the next life.

Back in the days when doctors made house calls in horse-drawn carriages, a country doctor was visiting an old man who was dying. As the doctor and the patient sat quietly in the room, suddenly the old man sat up terrified and said, "Tell me, what is it like to die?"

Though the doctor was a Christ-follower, he was momentarily at a loss for words. He was more at ease with healing the living than comforting the dying. He whispered a quick prayer for God to give him the words. Suddenly, there was a scratching and a whimper at the door. The doctor said to his friend, "You know what that sound is? That's the sound of my dog. He followed me here tonight. He doesn't know what's on the other side of this door. But he heard my voice, he's learned to trust my voice, and he wants to be with me." And the doctor continued, "I don't know everything we'll experience at death. But we know that Jesus is on the other side. And we've learned to trust him in this life, so I know we can trust him with what he's got planned for us on the other side." And with those words the doctor's old patient took comfort and died that night in peace.

When believers die they immediately begin to experience the joys of heaven. The operative word in that line, though, is the word "begin." There is more to the story. In the words of the Creed, we Christians believe in *the resurrection of the body*.

Your Body Will Be Resurrected

Some picture death as the soul's release from the prison house of the body, but this idea of the afterlife comes from the Greeks, not from the Bible. The Greeks taught that human life on this earth was a state where the pure and perfect soul was trapped in the body, which was part of this poorly created world. The day of death, then, was a day of freedom for the soul. This notion endures today in the verses of romantic poetry, in the rites of secret lodges, and even in sentimental sympathy cards.

The Bible presents a different picture: God was deeply pleased with the physical world he created. The first chapter of the Bible says he stood back from his creative work and "saw that it was good." As we have already found, it was after this good creation that human sin warped or twisted the physical creation. The deterioration of our bodies, the pain we experience in our bodies, the death that eventually comes to our bodies—all of that came about because of the Fall, not because God made a mistake in creating this place. That means that *God's victory over sin isn't finished until God restores all that sin messed up.* This world isn't a poorly built house we have to abandon but a damaged house that God wants to reform. It's not release *from* our bodies that we wait for, but the release *of* our bodies.

The soul lives on beyond death, but the fullest experiences of the next life will be enjoyed at the resurrection of our bodies

Jesus expected the final reunion of body and soul. "The time is coming when all the dead in their graves will hear the voice of God's Son," he said, "and they will rise again" (John 5:28-29). In fact, some of the strongest language that Jesus used was aimed at people who did not believe in the resurrection of the body. Skeptics once asked him a riddle meant to trap Jesus in what they considered the absurdity of the resurrection. Jesus answered their riddle, but he also cut to the heart of their problem. He said, "Your problem is that you don't know the Scriptures, and you don't know the power of God. . . . You have made a serious error" (Mark 12:24, 27 NLT).

It's true that our personal selves continue beyond death, but that's not the end of the story. Jesus taught that God's eternal plan for us is not complete until God reunites the soul and the body separated at death. It's the resurrection of my body that completes the process!

Theologians use three words to speak of the process of God's saving work: justification, sanctification, and glorification. *Justification* is salvation past; *sanctification* is salvation present; *glorification* is salvation future. Justification is God's decision to count me as righteous through the action of God's Son on the cross. Sanctification is God's way to make me righteous through the action of God's Spirit in daily life. Glorification is God's activity of renovating my body and soul for everlasting life in heaven. The salvation process is not complete until that takes place. It is when "the perishable has been clothed with the imperishable, and the mortal with immortality, then the saying that is written will come true: 'Death has been swallowed up in victory' " (1 Corinthians 15:54).

That's why the line from our Creed is so essential: "I believe in the resurrection of the body." Life with God isn't a matter of abandoning a poorly created world; God plans to return this world to the original condition. Job said (19:25-27 NLT),

> But as for me, I know that my Redeemer lives, and that he will stand upon the earth at last. And *after my body has decayed, yet in my body I will see God!* I will see him for myself. Yes, I will see him with my own eyes. I am overwhelmed at the thought!

Again, Isaiah said (26:19 NLT),

> Yet we have this assurance: Those who belong to God will live; *their bodies will rise again!* Those who sleep in the earth will rise up and sing for joy!

Passages like this were celebrated in Jewish circles, but as the apostles taught the resurrection among the non-Jewish nations, they had to spend time explaining it. As I mentioned earlier, Greeks and the surrounding peoples saw death as the soul's release from this painful and limiting existence we currently know. If Jesus and his followers taught that we would simply return to that kind of existence, who could look forward to it? What Jesus and his followers taught was far more glorious than that, however. Paul compared the burial of the body and the coming resurrection to farming (1 Corinthians 15:37-44):

> When you sow, you do not plant the body that will be, but just a seed, perhaps of wheat or of something else. But God gives it a body as he has determined.... So will it be with the resurrection of the dead. The body that is sown is perishable, it is raised imperishable; it is sown in dishonor, it is raised in glory; it is sown in weakness, it is raised in power; it is sown a natural body, it is raised a spiritual body.

An ugly peach pit is placed in the ground and from that pit comes a leafy tree with bright blossoms and exquisite fruit. The tree is a product of that pit, and yet vastly different. Our new bodies will be like and yet vastly unlike the bodies we now know. Paul wrote, "Christ . . . will transform our lowly bodies so that they will be like his glorious body" (Philippians 3:21).

The Dawn of New Life

When Winston Churchill died, he left behind explicit instructions for his funeral at St. Paul's Cathedral. At the benediction of the service a bugler, high in the cathedral dome, played "Taps"—the universal signal that says the day is over.

But then came the most dramatic part, as Churchill planned it. Another bugler, placed on the other side of the massive dome, played the notes of "Reveille"—the universal signal that a new day has dawned and it is time to rise up. That was Churchill's testimony that at the end of history the last note will not be "Taps" but "Reveille."

Across my years as a pastor, I have watched the physical deterioration of believers I've loved:

> . . . their bodies shaking uncontrollably with Parkinson's

... their bodies panting painfully for one more breath

... their bodies grown thin with chemotherapy

... their bodies supported by machines

Fools say that that's all there is to life. No! It does not all end here! Peach trees spring from peach pits. And something breath-taking will spring from these fallen bodies buried in this fallen world.

Chapter 21
What Is Heaven Like?

Polls show that belief in heaven remains high in our world. Although they may express uncertainty about other points of the Creed, the public has little trouble with the first and the last points—"I believe in God," and "I believe in the life everlasting." Depending on the poll, between eighty-five and ninety-five percent of participants report confidence in an afterlife.

People are less certain, however, when it comes to what heaven will be like. Many think of heaven as populated with people in a state of numb serenity dressed in wings and white robes having nothing to do but flit from one fluffy cloud to another as they pluck harp strings for all eternity. Honestly, if that's heaven, some of us just can't get too excited about it. Not when we set it against some of our fondest experiences of earth:

> . . . a Thanksgiving table, filled with food and surrounded by those we love.

> . . . the feel of a springtime breeze in the morning, gently billowing the curtains from our windows.

> . . . the excitement of feeling a tug on the end of a fishing line.

> . . . the sound of laughter with friends around a table game.

> . . . the warm embrace of the person we most love.

Does heaven mean we have to trade all of that in for wings and robes and an eternity of harp music? In one part of Mark Twain's *The Adventures of Huckleberry Finn*, Huck suffers under Miss Watson's rigid house rules. Described through the eyes of the mischievous boy, Twain writes,

> She went on and told me all about the good place. She said all a body would have to do there was go around all day with a harp and sing, forever and ever. So I didn't think much of it. . . . I asked her if she reckoned Tom Sawyer would go there, and she said, not by a considerable sight. I was glad about that, because I wanted him and I to be together.[1]

Huck had a problem with heaven because Miss Watson had given him the wrong *idea* of heaven. When we replace our mythologies with what the Bible really says about heaven, we can get a lot more excited about it. The Bible unveils seven things about the life everlasting.

Heaven is a Place for Rest

It's probably this image of heaven most familiar to us. The Bible tells us that God has prepared a resting place for us: "Blessed are the dead who die in the Lord. . . . They will rest from their labor, for their deeds will follow them" (Revelation 14:13). Scripture describes life on this earth as a race that we must run well, a battle that we must fight well, a project that we must finish well—and then it's time for a deeply satisfying rest. Think of the feeling you've had after a day of yard work. You sit on the back porch after a shower and supper, enjoying the sweet smell of fresh-cut grass riding on the early evening breeze. You look around at the trimming and weeding and mulching you've done and contentment fills your heart. That's rest! Heaven is a place of rest after a job well done.

Heaven is a Place of Freedom from Life's Pain

No matter how good this life can be, we all experience moments that remind us that we are not home yet. Here our bodies don't always work the way they should, our relationships don't always go the way they should, and we are not always treated the way we should be treated. But when we get home, we can hold up our lives to God like a child holds up a broken toy to his father, and we can say, "Fix it, Daddy."

In the book of Revelation, John was given a glimpse of that moment when time ends and eternity begins, and he heard a voice say (Revelation 21:3),

> "Now the dwelling of God is with men, and he will live with them. They will be his people, and God himself will be with them and be their God. He will wipe every tear from their eyes. There will be no more death or mourning or crying or pain, for the old order of things has passed away."

Paul also assured us, "I consider that our present sufferings are not worth comparing with the glory that will be revealed in us" (Romans 8:18). Heaven is a place of freedom from the pain and injustice of life.

Heaven is a Place of Victory over Sin

In this life, we struggle against a world system at odds with God, against an inner rebelliousness, and against a mighty spiritual opponent in the unseen world. Old-timers used to call this unholy trinity "the world, the flesh, and the devil." When God intervenes at the end of time, everything that makes us ineffective for God will be removed.

I like how Simon Peter spoke of heaven: "We are looking forward to a new heaven and a new earth, *the home of righteousness*" (2 Peter 3:13). Heaven is a place not only where our bodies will work right; our hearts will, too! Anyone who has been frustrated over his moral failures can look forward to a place where we can serve God with pure attitudes and perfect actions.

When Joni Eareckson Tada wrote a book about heaven, she said that this unhindered faithfulness to God was what she anticipated more than anything else. This is especially interesting in light of her condition. When she was seventeen, she was injured in a diving accident and became a quadriplegic. Ever since, she has been confined to a wheelchair, unable to move her arms or legs. You can imagine that the thought of heaven comes easily to her. In her book, she eloquently described how she looked forward to the body she will have at the resurrection—a body that will let her jump and run and dance. Still, it's the unhindered freedom to please God that she wants most:

> Please don't assume that all I ever do is dream about springing out of this chair, stretching glorified fingers and toes, and pole-vaulting over pearly gates. However much I relish the idea of leaving this wheelchair behind, that is still, for me, not the best part of heaven. I can't wait to be clothed in righteousness. Without a trace of sin. True, it will be wonderful to stand, stretch, and reach to the sky, but it will be more wonderful to offer praise that is pure. I won't be crippled by distractions. Disabled by insincerity. I won't be handicapped by ho-hum halfheartedness. For me, this will be the best part of heaven.[2]

Heaven is a Place for Reward

God's acceptance comes by God's grace, not by our efforts. But Scripture lets us know that in the next life, what we've done in *response* to God's acceptance will be recognized. Our efforts at personal righteousness, our faithfulness to an assignment, what we do to improve the world around us— every bit of it counts in the sight of God, and he will reward us accordingly.

I'm sure you remember the closing scene of Steven Spielberg's film, *Saving Private Ryan*. The elderly James Ryan stands shakily in front of his captain's grave on the bluffs above Omaha Beach and remembers the events of fifty years ago. Amid the expanse of manicured lawn and ten thousand white crosses and Stars of David, Ryan reflects on the eight men who risked or gave up their lives to bring him home alive. He recalls how his dying captain, John Miller, had pulled Ryan to himself and gasped, "Earn this! Earn this!" The film closes with the elderly Ryan desperately wanting confirmation that he had indeed lived the kind of life worthy of the death of so many men. "Tell me that I have lived a good life," he begged his wife as he searched her eyes for an answer. "Tell me that I have been a good man." It was Spielberg's way to ask the viewers if we've made the most of the freedoms that others died to protect.

Nothing we do would ever be enough to *earn* the sacrificial death of Jesus, but we must live a life that *honors* his sacrifice. James Ryan spent fifty years in humble appreciation of those who died for him; once we grasp the costly love of God at the cross, it will impact how we live, too. Scripture says that whatever we do in response to God's forgiveness and his abiding presence will be rewarded in heaven. In many places, the Bible refers to "crowns" God wants to give us—a reference to the ancient ritual of giving a crown of laurel leaves to the winning athlete in a contest. It was the equivalent of our gold medal or blue ribbon. Just think of some of the medals that God wants to give us:

- James 1:12 speaks of a crown for *perseverance.* Stand strong in the face of hard times and God will reward you in heaven.

- First Thessalonians 2:19 speaks of a crown for *teaching* people the way of Christ. Lead people to Christ and help others grow in the Lord, and God will reward you in heaven.

- First Corinthians 9:25 speaks of a crown for *purity.* Develop a lifestyle of self-discipline in your thoughts and actions, and God will reward you in heaven.

- First Peter 5:2-4 speaks of a crown for faithful *leadership*. Serve well in a call to the ministry, and God will reward you in heaven.

Nothing you do on this earth goes unnoticed by God. Everything you do has eternal significance to it, and life in heaven will be a place where what we've done here will be recognized and rewarded.

Heaven is a Place for Work

Though we've already described heaven as a place of rest and rewards, that doesn't mean we won't have anything to do in heaven. We'll have work to do—meaningful work, fulfilling work, responsible work.

We sometimes think of work as something to escape. Many of us aren't fulfilled in the work we do. Some of us serve under bosses and conditions that make our days frustrating. The only reason many show up at work is because there are bills to pay and kids to feed. But what if you could work in a place that challenged the best of what you are? A place where your talents and abilities were perfectly matched with the job? A place where you had a great boss? You would probably say, "That would be *heaven!*" In fact, it is!

The myth that some of us have of heaven as a place of leisure and idleness really doesn't match what Jesus said about the afterlife. Jesus once told a story to illustrate the way our faithfulness on earth impacts what we will *do* in eternity (Luke 19:11-27). He told of a man who was about to go to a country far away to be made king, and then he would return. Obviously, he was speaking about himself. Before the man in the story went away, he called ten of his servants to himself and gave them each a gold coin, saying, "See what you can earn with this while I am gone." When the newly-crowned king returned, one servant said, "Sir, I've made a return of ten coins with the one you've given me." And the king said, "Well done, you are a good servant. Since you were faithful in small matters, I will put you in charge of ten cities." Another servant had earned a return of five coins with the one coin his master had given him, and Jesus said, "I will put you in charge of five cities." Jesus was speaking about the *responsibility* he will give us at his return. Our faithfulness in the *past* will be rewarded with greater responsibilities in the *future*.

Heaven is a Place for Fellowship

Someone once described the stars in the night sky in this way: "They were tiny peep-holes in a great black wall with the party lights of heaven streaming through."[3] This is consistent with the way Jesus described heaven; he often described the afterlife as a huge celebration (see Matthew 22).

What is it about the next life that will make it so joyful for us? First, we will be reunited with believers we've lost to death: children reunited to parents, marriage partners reunited one to another, friends with friends. The blockbuster *Titanic* closed with the aged Rose's sweet dream of walking into the presence of all who had died in the icy waters of the north Atlantic, including her beloved Jack. For believers, the hope of reunion with those we love is more than a sentimental wish.

Second, we'll be together in "a new heaven and a new earth" (2 Peter 3:13; Revelation 21:1). There is something about our future forever fellowship with each other that will be like the fellowship we enjoy now. Think about your favorite earthly spot: Colorado mountains in the winter, a New England lakeside cabin in the summer, rock climbing in the Texas hill country. The Bible doesn't say all of that will be *obliterated* but *liberated*: "The creation itself will be liberated from its bondage to decay and brought into the glorious freedom of the children of God" (Romans 8:21). That means, among other things, that you will not have to say good-bye to many of your favorite earthly activities— you will enjoy them in a richer, fuller way than you ever have before.

There's a third reason the next life will be so joyful. As wonderful as it will be to fellowship with each other in a new heaven and upon a new earth, the one with whom we *most* want fellowship is the one who created us and died for us. Imagine your first heavenly meeting with the one who hung on a cross to take away your sin. Imagine being able to say, "Thank you" to him face to face. The joy of heaven is not just from reunions with departed loved ones. We'll be together, but more than that, we'll be "together with the Lord" (1 Thessalonians 4:16-17).

Heaven is a Place for Praise

In the fourth and fifth chapters of the book of Revelation, John reported what he saw when he was caught up into heaven, and everything in his vision centered on the Risen Christ reigning upon the universe's throne. Out from that exalted chair were concentric circles of amazing beings. Closest to the throne were four creatures, then another circle of twenty-four elders, then another circle of innumerable angels, and finally another circle of countless redeemed people. Praise lifted up from one group seemed to stir another group to praise, which stirred yet another group to praise. It's a breathtaking description! In his book, *Edge of Eternity*, Randy Alcorn described the scene as he anticipates seeing it in heaven:

> The army began to sing, perhaps hundreds of thousands, perhaps a million. . . .
>
> We sang together in full voice. . . . Our voices broke into thirty-two distinct parts, and instinctively I knew which of them I was made to sing. "We sing for joy at the work of your hands . . . we stand in awe of you." It felt indescribably wonderful to be lost in something so much greater than myself.
>
> There was no audience, I thought for a moment, for audience and orchestra and choir all blended into one great symphony, one grand cantata of rhapsodic melodies and powerful sustaining harmonies.
>
> No, wait, there *was* an audience. An audience so vast and all-encompassing that for a moment I'd been no more aware of it than a fish is aware of water.

I looked at the great throne, and upon it sat the King ... the Audience of One.

The smile of his approval swept through the choir like fire across dry wheat fields.

When we completed our song, the one on the throne stood and raised his great arms and clapped his scarred hands together in thunderous applause, shaking ground and sky, jarring every corner of the cosmos. His applause went on and on, unstopping and unstoppable.

And in that moment I knew, with unwavering clarity, that the King's approval was all that mattered—and ever would.[4]

I'm Home

Joni Eareckson Tada held a retreat for parents and their handicapped kids. At the end of the week, participants passed a microphone around and spontaneously shared stories and expressed appreciation for what the camp had meant to them. Many of the memories brought tears and laughter. Then one little boy with Down syndrome was given the microphone. Though he had enjoyed the camp with his mother, his father had been unable to come, and he missed his dad. Taking the microphone, he put it right up to his mouth, and his amplified voice reverberated throughout the room as he said, "Let's go home!"

Jesus left us with this promise: "I am going to prepare a place for you.... And after I go and prepare a place for you, I will come back and take you to myself, so that you will be where I am" (John 14:2 TEV). Life on this earth has a lot of joy and beauty, and we probably take the richness of this life for granted much too often. But we anticipate a "life everlasting" with even more astonishing experiences ahead.

Let's go home.

Chapter 22
You Don't Have to Go

As Flora Clark lay dying in 1860, she insisted that the following inscription be engraved upon her tombstone. It was a common one in her time:

> Behold my friends as you pass by
> As you are now so once was I
> As I am now so you will be
> Prepare for death and follow me

Years later, an anonymous visitor to the cemetery added his own message under the inscription:

> To follow you I'm not content
> Until I know which way you went

For believers, reciting the statements of the Apostles' Creed is a celebration—especially the final lines: "I believe in the forgiveness of sins," and therefore "I believe in the resurrection of the body and the life everlasting." While the statements are a celebration of belief, they beg the question of what happens to those who never get interested in life with God.

As we've discussed in earlier chapters, human beings were designed for much more than a few decades of earthly existence, and this means that consciousness continues for us all. The Bible says that at the resurrection, "Some of them will wake up to have life forever, but some will wake up to find shame and disgrace forever" (Daniel 12:2 NCV).

Jesus frequently warned of the fate of those who remain indifferent to God. In one instance, he told the story of a group of kingdom subjects who were callous toward their king and his grand invitation to a banquet (Matthew 22:2-4):

> The kingdom of heaven is like a king who prepared a wedding banquet for his son. He sent his servants to those who had been invited to the banquet to tell them to come, but they refused to come.
>
> Then he sent some more servants and said, "Tell those who have been invited that I have prepared my dinner: My oxen and fattened cattle have been butchered, and everything is ready. Come to the wedding banquet."
>
> But they paid no attention and went off—one to his field, another to his business.

Jesus often used stories like this as a creative way to help people see things from his perspective. In this story, the king's lavish banquet, the king's recalcitrant subjects, and the king's multiple invitations all take us into the way Jesus viewed things. Consider all that life with God means—forgiveness for our sins, guidance for our decisions, comfort for our sorrows, power over our weaknesses, and victory over our death. In his story, Jesus described this kind of life with God as an extravagant party only a king could throw. But Jesus added two surprises into his story: the callous indifference of this king's subjects, and the many chances their patient king gave them. It's hard to know what would have astonished first-century listeners more.

While serving a church in the Cayman Islands, a British overseas territory, my wife and I were invited to attend a reception for Prince Andrew (now His Royal Highness the Duke of York). We were delighted to attend, but mostly out of curiosity and courtesy. In Christ's day, however, a royal invitation would have carried much more weight. All life and livelihood was dependent upon the wisdom and will of the king. So, the people in Christ's story didn't just turn down a chance to rub shoulders with a celebrity; they rebuffed the one who had absolute authority over them.

As astonishing as their behavior was, the king's patience was even more astonishing. He sent out his invitations again and again so that the citizens might share in his joy. His patience came to an end, however, after some of the self-absorbed citizens killed the royal messengers. Jesus said the king sent his armies to destroy the murderers and set fire to the city.

It was one of the many ways Jesus warned about the fate of those who remain indifferent to God. As you read through his teachings in the four Gospels, you find him vivid and relentless in his descriptions. Sometimes he described hell as a tormenting fire (Matthew 13:42) and sometimes he described it as a miserable darkness (Matthew 8:12). Considering that both fire and darkness cannot coexist in the same place, clearly these images were the metaphors of a teacher and not the descriptions of a tour guide. Still, every good metaphor is designed to elicit a reaction. If you told me that the car I wanted to purchase was a "lemon," there would be no need for us to debate whether or not the car was, in fact, sour citrus. Your metaphor would be a vivid warning against a very real disappointment if I insisted on purchasing the car. Likewise, Jesus used many ways to tell us to take spiritual matters seriously because they have serious consequences into eternity.

The topic of hell complicates some seekers' exploration of Christianity. They are attracted to Christ's teaching about things like radical love, a gracious God, and even his call for disciplined purity. They are moved by his gentle acceptance of others, even of society's outcasts. They marvel at his grace and forgiveness of those who mistreated him. Despite all they've learned about the life and lessons of this remarkable man, however, they stumble over his vivid warnings about hell. They shake their heads and ask, "How could a loving God send anyone to hell?"

For some, the thought of hell calls into question God's justice, God's love, and God's grace. Hell does not *eliminate* these things, however. It *illuminates* them.

God's Justice

As we noted a few chapters back, we are God's image-bearers, and so for better or for worse we say to the universe, "This is what God looks like." We have failed at this work—and even the resentment some of us feel at *having* to succeed at this work reveals the depth of our rebellion against the Maker. Every day we move closer to having to account for this failure.

The topic of hell complicates some seekers' exploration of Christianity. They shake their heads and ask, "How could a loving God send anyone to hell?"

Once while making a connection at an airline terminal, I took advantage of the airport's long "moving sidewalks." I stepped on, put down my heavy bag, and let the conveyor do the work of carrying me along. As I approached the end, however, I noticed that a passenger had stepped off the moving sidewalk and had simply stopped. His briefcase was at his feet and he was consulting a terminal map. I could have stubbornly refused to step aside, but the relentless motion of the conveyor would have sent me crashing into him. Instead, I chose to step aside, and the sidewalk deposited me into an open space.

Like an airport conveyor belt, time moves us relentlessly toward judgment, but the cross gives us a way to "step aside" so that we will not run into judgment. Jesus said, "I tell you the truth, whoever hears my word and believes him who sent me has eternal life and will not be condemned; he has *crossed over* from death to life" (John 5:24).

This corrects one of the most widespread misconceptions of the Christian message. I've had people ask, "Why do you believe that God sends someone to hell just because they don't accept the gospel of Christ?" God does not send someone to hell for rejecting the Christian message. No, the basis for God's judgment lies in our sin. We are *rescued* from hell upon receiving the offer of Christ's salvation, but rejecting that offer simply keeps you moving toward the same judgment you've always been moving toward. Hell displays the inevitability of God's justice.

God's Love

If hell is the inevitable consequence of God's perfect justice, then rescue from hell demonstrates God's love. He was under no compulsion to provide us a way out of judgment, and yet he did. In what is probably the most familiar verse in the Bible, Jesus said, "For God so loved the world that he gave his one and only Son, that whoever believes in him shall not perish but have eternal life" (John 3:16). Jesus said it was God's *love* that was behind his act of "giving" his Son. He arranged a way *out of* what this verse said was already our lot: perishing. Paul also spoke of this tender divine motivation when he said that God "wants everyone to be saved and to understand the truth" (1 Timothy 2:4).

In the Bible, men like Jeremiah and Jesus and Paul wept when they thought of those who remained unresponsive to God's love. Those who best represent God's heart today still do. When once asked to answer a dry theological question about hell, the Christian and philosopher Francis Schaeffer instead remained silent and simply wiped tears from his eyes.[1]

If Christ's sacrifice is God's gracious provision for a world in need of rescue, what about those who will never hear of Christ, or those too young or too mentally feeble to grasp what he accomplished? Based on what we've learned about God's love for this world, we can leave these concerns in the hands of God, I believe, and still communicate the need to put one's faith in Christ.

A friend of mine demonstrated this balance between trusting God to do what is right with those *incapable* of responding to Christ, while also communicating with those *capable* of responding to him. As I listened to my friend explain Christ's sacrifice to a man, the man asked, "But what about all those in the Middle East who have never heard this? What happens to them?" My friend gently replied, "I think we can leave that in the hands of a God who knows them all by name and loves them more than we ever could. The big question, however, is what will you do with Christ's story now that *you* have heard it?"

The real test of what we think of God's love isn't found in our answer to the question, "What about those who have never heard about Jesus?" It's found in our answer to the question, "What will I do now that *I* have heard about Jesus?" We have the choice to stay stubbornly on the path to judgment, but that simply calls into question our love for God, not God's love for us.

God's Mercy

If hell is the inevitable consequence of God's perfect justice, and rescue from hell the showcase of God's love, then any delay of judgment is an act of divine mercy.

When hearing the Christian claim that a decision needs to be made now, in this life, some question the fairness of such an arrangement. They wonder why a merciful God wouldn't give a second chance to people who end up regretting their decision in the next life. But would anyone too rebellious to yield to God in this life actually respond to a second chance in the next life? Jesus knew that many *preferred* darkness and would remain in that state. "God-light streamed into the world," he said, "but men and women everywhere ran for the darkness. They went for the darkness because they were not really interested in pleasing God" (John 3:19 Msg). C.S. Lewis said,

> I have heard a story of how certain small monkeys in South Africa put their paw through a small hole to get nuts stored there deliberately for the purpose and how the monkeys are captured and killed because they refuse at all hazards to release the handful of nuts in their grasp. Hell exists because men similarly clutch their private interests at any cost.[2]

As someone once vividly described it, hell is locked from the *inside*. I can conceive of people regretting the *consequences* of their rebellion in the next life; I cannot conceive of anyone doing what is necessary to overcome those consequences if the chance were even offered. Someone who spent this lifetime with little or no regard for what was important to his Maker will not suddenly become interested in these matters in the next.

Besides, to assume that a second chance in the next life would be a fitting display of God's mercy is to assume that God isn't doing enough for people to make this decision in *this* life. God has given us a Bible we can understand, he pursues us with his Spirit, and he patiently extends his invitation. God "is being patient for your sake," Simon Peter wrote. "He does not want anyone to perish, so he is giving more time for everyone to repent" (2 Peter 3:9 NLT). *This* life is the chance to take God seriously, and everything is being done to give people that chance.

Choose Life

The Bible says that "it is appointed for man to die once, and after that comes judgment" (Hebrews 9:27 ESV). There is urgency in these words.

I'm reminded of an old legend of a merchant in Baghdad who one day sent his servant to the market. Before very long the servant came back, white and trembling. In a stutter, he said, "Down in the market place I met Death. She looked at me and made a threatening gesture. Master, please lend me your horse, so I can run away from her! I will ride to Samarra and hide."

The merchant lent him his horse and the servant galloped away in panic. Later the merchant went down to the marketplace and saw Death standing in the crowd. He went over to her and asked, "Why did you threaten my servant this morning?"

"I did not threaten him," Death said, "I was only startled in surprise to see him in Baghdad. You see, I had planned to meet him tonight in Samarra."

Death is an inevitable reality for us all, and after that comes the judgment, where some "will wake up to have life forever" while others "will wake up to find shame and disgrace forever" (Daniel 12:2 NCV).

"Shame and disgrace forever" does not have to be our future. Back in the 1920s in the U.S. Senate, an argument between senators became particularly ugly and one man told a colleague to go to hell. The astonished senator appealed for a sanction from Vice President Calvin Coolidge, who was presiding. Coolidge, who had been idly leafing through a book, looked up and said to the offended senator, "I have been checking the rules manual, and you don't have to go."[3]

Indeed.

The believer celebrates: "I *believe* in the forgiveness of sins" and therefore "I *believe* in the resurrection of the body and life everlasting." It's the truth of the one line that opens us up to the truth of the other line.

"I have set before you life and death," God said. "Now choose life" (Deuteronomy 30:19).

Part Eight: "Amen"

*I believe
in God the Father Almighty,
Maker of heaven and earth;
And in Jesus Christ his only Son our Lord;
who was conceived by the Holy Spirit,
born of the Virgin Mary,
suffered under Pontius Pilate,
was crucified, dead, and buried.
The third day he rose again from the dead.
He ascended into heaven,
and sits at the right hand of God the Father Almighty.
From there he shall come
to judge the living and the dead.
I believe in the Holy Spirit;
the one holy church;
the communion of saints;
the forgiveness of sins;
the resurrection of the body;
and the life everlasting.
Amen.*

Chapter 23
The "Ready Aim-Aim-Aim-Aim Syndrome"

One of the best lines in a university commencement speech came from business tycoon T. Boone Pickens. He told a graduating class, "Be willing to make decisions. Don't fall victim to what I call the 'ready-aim-aim-aim-aim syndrome.' You must be willing to fire."[1]

Many who have become followers of Christ remember the time they were stuck in that syndrome. Just before they stepped into faith, they hesitated. Maybe you can identify. What issues cause the act of *seeking* to turn to *stalling* at the line of commitment?

You Might Be Thinking, "I Need More Answers"

As I mentioned in Chapter 2, one of my favorite Bible verses says, "Test everything that is said to be sure it is true, and if it is, then accept it" (1 Thessalonians 5:21 LB). Some fail the challenge from the first half of that verse: they don't test anything. Others fail the challenge from the second half of that verse: they don't accept what their testing has found trustworthy. You have to come to a point where you act on what you've discovered.

Certainly, if you can't make an informed decision about the Christian faith without further study of the material we've looked at, then by all means keep studying. You might want to read some of the selections I've recommended in the section entitled, "For Further Reading." If you continue to look for answers, however, keep in mind that when you're trying to understand God, you'll never finish asking questions. Although I've been a believer most of my life—and a pastor all of my adult life—I still look for answers to some of my questions. Those questions keep me thinking about God, but they don't keep me from committing to him. As important as it is to collect information, it can become just an elaborate form of procrastination. G.K. Chesterton once wrote to H.G. Wells, "The object of opening the mind, as of opening the mouth, is to shut it again on something solid."[2]

God is not a math formula to ponder or a Rubik's Cube to solve; he is a Person to love. It is a *relationship* we are considering, and that involves more than simply gathering information. When considering a business partnership or a marriage, there's a time when you have to quit weighing the merits and make a commitment. It's no surprise that commitments like this are often described as "taking the leap." While such a leap should never be blind, it will never be tame. Otherwise, why call it a *leap*?

While discussing the difference between blind faith and reasonable faith, the Christian philosopher Francis Schaeffer used an analogy about a group of mountain hikers. In the course of their hike, a fog suddenly descends upon them. They know that the approaching night will expose them to dangerous cold, but the fog shrouds the path back down the mountain. Suddenly they hear a voice from the fog saying, "Just jump from the path you're on and you'll land on a ledge ten feet below which will take you to safety." Perhaps some would jump in blind faith, desperately hopeful that they really would land on a ledge ten feet below and not plummet to their death. But perhaps some would ask questions to the mysterious speaker, discovering that he was the aged mountaineer about whom they had heard so many stories down in the village below, a man who knew the mountain like the back of his hand. Schaeffer said that leaping out into the fog on this mountaineer's advice would still require trust, but it would be the action of a reasonable faith, not a blind faith.[3]

So, take more time to study if you need to. As the verse says, "Test everything that is said to be sure it is true." But know that it all comes down to trusting the Mountaineer. Responding to him is like finding your voice when it comes time to say, "I do," at the altar. It's like watching your hand sign the papers at the lawyer's office with your new business partner. It's like hearing your own shout bursting from your lungs as you follow your crazy, skydiving friend out of the door of the jump plane. No amount of study will ever make your commitment to God anything less than a gutsy leap.

You Might Be Thinking, "I'm Afraid of What I'll Be Asked to Give Up"

As seekers stand at the threshold of faith, some stall because of what they fear they will be giving up. I've found that people fear the loss of *control*, the loss of *fun*, and the loss of *relationships*.

Some fear the loss of *control*. They know that God has certain demands regarding the way life ought to be lived. Most seekers have heard enough Bible lessons to know that God expects things like discipline and generosity in financial matters, loyalty in relationships, and self-control over impulses. A commitment to life with him clearly means yielding to his will on these and other matters, and yielding to him means a certain loss of control.

While true, there are plenty of instances in life where I gladly give up control to others. When I board a plane, for example, I give up control to the pilot. But since I don't know how to fly, I wouldn't want it any other way! Likewise, life only works when we do things God's way. Giving up control to him is a "loss" worth taking!

Some fear the loss of *fun*. Sadly, some Christians provide that impression by the way they live. Although Jesus said, "I have come that they may have life, and have it to the full" (John 10:10), some believers' lives are dull, their attitudes are judgmental, and their priority is safe predictability. I encourage you to spend time with believers who reflect the bold vitality of Jesus.

No doubt, we have to stop doing things that disappoint God. But his commands aren't prison walls that confine but garden walls that protect. As we follow Christ, we gain his perspective on the things people do for fun. We learn to distinguish between the activities that celebrate life and the activities that bring heartbreak and regret. Jesus wants us to develop both sensitivity and resistance to those activities that are harmful to us.

Some fear the loss of *relationships*. By becoming a believer, those closest to you may not understand the path you are taking, and they may feel threatened by the changes you start making to your life. If your family or friends belong to another religion, they may feel hurt at what they perceive as disloyalty on your part. If they have prejudices against Christians, they may apply those same false assumptions to you, at least at first.

Lee Strobel is the author of several popular books that explain the faith, but he was once an atheist who found it difficult to see his wife put her faith in Christ. After ten years of their mutual apathy toward religion, she began to attend a church near their house. When she told him she had become a believer, he felt anything but happy and supportive:

> First, I was feeling hurt. That might sound like an odd reaction, but all of a sudden I felt like I was less in Leslie's eyes. I thought I was losing her respect. . . . And I wondered what would happen if she insisted on raising our children as Christians. Would they think less of me, too? . . . Another emotion I felt was frustration. I was frustrated because, for the first time in our relationship, our values were at odds. . . . And I felt afraid, too. I feared that Leslie was going to turn into a wild-eyed religious fanatic—you know, some sexually repressed prude who would put a damper on all of our fun. Was she going to embarrass me in front of my friends? Was she going to shame me every time I drank too much? Was she going to spill details about our private life in her prayer group?

> Was she going to reject all of our old friends? Were her church buddies going to poke fun at me behind my back? . . . Finally, I was experiencing anger. I'm talking about *serious* anger. If you had asked me back then why I was so mad, I probably couldn't have told you. . . . Now, as I look back, I can pinpoint the root of my rage. Basically, as Leslie pursued a godly lifestyle more and more, her behavior increasingly accentuated the difference between that lifestyle and my own. In other words, the more she sought after purity, integrity, honesty, tolerance, and forgiveness, the more obvious it became that my own life and relationships were corroded with cynicism, bitterness, superficiality, and self-centeredness.[4]

Maybe you're expecting these reactions from your own family or friends, and it's causing you to hesitate at the line of faith. In Strobel's case, his initial offense at Leslie's conversion gave way to an examination of the faith she had embraced, which eventually led to his own conversion. It may be that your decision for Christ will jump-start a spiritual search among those close to you. Regardless, you must ask whether the momentary difficulties and tensions in your relationships are worth it. Jesus thought so, even promising that "everyone who has left houses or brothers or sisters or father or mother or children or fields for my sake will receive a hundred times as much and will inherit eternal life" (Matthew 19:29).

You Might Be Thinking, "I Can't Keep Up"

I talked with someone recently who said, "Well, I believe in Christ but I'm not a Christian." This seemed odd to me, but as we continued to talk I discovered that she loved Jesus but she didn't want to say she was a follower until she could do it all perfectly. Maybe that's what you're thinking. You're saying, "I can't live up to it. What if I start following Christ and I can't keep up with him?" It's important to remember the provision of *grace* and *strength* that Christ provides those who follow him. As we understand the promise of these two provisions, we lose the fear of failure.

Christ provides *grace*. Understand that a relationship with Christ doesn't result *from* living a good life; a relationship with Christ results *in* living a good life. As you follow Christ, you're going to fail from time to time. In those instances, it's good to know that we *continue* in the Christian life the same way that we *begin* the Christian life: through God's decision to save us. The Bible says, "I am sure that God, who began the good work within you, will continue his work until it is finally finished on that day when Christ Jesus comes back again" (Philippians 1:6 NLT). Therefore, we can proceed in confidence, knowing that mistakes do not cancel our relationship with Christ. I like what Benjamin Franklin said. He wasn't speaking about following Christ, but the words apply. He said, "The man who does things makes many mistakes, but he never makes the biggest mistake of all—doing nothing."

Christ provides *strength*. During the Second World War, the British Army enlisted the help of the Gurkha Indians of Nepal. However, when the Gurkhas were told they would have to jump from airplanes, they promptly refused. The next day, the leader of the Gurkhas approached his British counterpart. He said that his men had been discussing the matter all evening and had agreed to jump on two conditions: the plane must fly slowly and no higher than fifty feet off the ground. The British officer explained that the planes always flew slowly on jumps, but pointed out that flying too low to the ground would not give their parachutes enough time to open.

At this the Gurkha leader looked confused and asked, "What's a parachute?"[5]

I'm impressed at the bravery and commitment behind their decision to jump from an airplane with no knowledge of how a parachute could aid them. Still, imagine all the unnecessary hesitations they had to overcome as they spent the night wrestling with the decision. In the same way, seekers sometimes wrestle with unnecessary hesitations about their ability to follow Christ. According to Scripture, God will "strengthen you with power through his Spirit in your inner being" (Ephesians 3:16). In Chapter 12 we discussed how the Holy Spirit helps believers, and as a believer you can trust God to give you the resources you need to follow him.

You Might Be Thinking, "I Have Time"

Standing at the threshold of Christian commitment, many people will put their decision on an indefinite hold on the assumption that the decision can always be made another day. Jesus saw that presumption among people in his own day, and told a story about it (Luke 12:16-20):

> The ground of a certain rich man produced a good crop. He thought to himself, "What shall I do? I have no place to store my crops."
>
> Then he said, "This is what I'll do. I will tear down my barns and build bigger ones, and there I will store all my grain and my goods. And I'll say to myself, 'You have plenty of good things laid up for many years. Take life easy; eat, drink and be merry.'"
>
> But God said to him, "You fool! This very night your life will be demanded from you. Then who will get what you have prepared for yourself?"

Jesus wasn't trying to frighten people into a decision. What he said can't be called a "scare tactic" if the scenario he describes is true. We really have no control over when we'll die and enter judgment. I recently talked with a man who kissed his wife good-bye as she ran off to work—and he never saw her again. She died of a heart attack at the office, and she was only forty-two. He said it was such a sobering thing to thumb through his wife's calendar and see plans she had made for work and family months into the future. We really have no control over when those plans end for us.

Furthermore, we really have no control over how often God invites us to make a commitment to him. Why do we think that God's invitation is like a constantly transmitted radio broadcast that can we can tune to whenever we want? Understand that anytime you're stirred to explore spiritual things, that stirring is the activity of God, calling on you to consider him. Note carefully what the prophet Isaiah said about these unique times (55:6)—

> Seek the Lord *while he may be found*;
> call on him *while he is near*.

Let those words marinate in your brain cells a moment:

> "... while he may be found"
> "... while he is near"

God is a merciful Sovereign, but he is still the Sovereign, and it is his prerogative to do the inviting. He chooses when and how often he will invite us. We must not think we have all the time in the world to accept the offer of a King. The blind nineteenth-century hymn-writer who wrote the following words had the right attitude:

> Pass me not, O gentle Savior,
> Hear my humble cry;
> While on others Thou art calling,
> Do not pass me by.[6]

The words come from someone who recognized that an invitation from God is a precious thing to be treasured. We should consider ourselves fortunate to be called into life with him, and we should respond gladly.

Where the Fruit Is

I once read about a young man on his first voyage in the days of the great sailing ships. He was ordered to take his watch up in the crow's nest, but after climbing halfway up the mast, he made the mistake of looking down. The great swells of the sea rocked him back and forth and far down below, he saw the tiny figures of his mates at work on the deck, and he froze in fear. For a long time, he wavered. He was too fearful to climb any higher and too ashamed to climb back down to his mates. He was in the "ready-aim-aim-aim-aim syndrome."

Maybe you're at that point in your search. You've come too far to climb back down to where life used to be, but something is keeping you from finishing. I can sympathize with the hesitations, but we have to get out on the limb. That's where all the fruit is!

For decades, Billy Graham's crusades ended the same way all around the world. As people streamed down stadium aisles in response to the beloved evangelist's invitation to receive Christ, the crowd in the stadium would sing the same song, "Just As I Am." One line in the 125-year-old lyrics gives voice to the hesitations that we overcome as we yield to Christ's call:

> Just as I am, though tossed about
> With many a conflict, many a doubt,
> Fightings and fears within, without,
> O Lamb of God, I come, I come.[7]

If you're ready to step across the line of faith, how is it done? It's to that matter we now turn.

Chapter 24
Alrightokuhuhamen

The Apostles' Creed ends with the word, "Amen," a Hebrew word that means, "This is true." To say "Amen" means, "I agree with this, I'm committing myself to this." When we sign at the bottom of a contract, it's a way of formally saying, "I've read this, I agree with it, and I will live by its terms." The word, "Amen," serves the same purpose at the end of the Creed.

If you're ready to cross into faith, what should you do? You have to *Admit, Believe,* and *Commit.* These are the "A-B-Cs" of beginning a life with Christ.

Admit That Your Sins Have Separated You From God

Did you read about the teenager in New York who set fire to his exam papers in the privacy of his bedroom? It seems he wanted to hide the poor grades from his parents. The fire quickly grew out of control, though, and ended up gutting the entire second floor of his home.

It began as a way to keep his parents from discovering his poor grades, but his effort at hiding his failures resulted in disaster. Far from hiding his failures, eight fire trucks and sixty firefighters responded to the blaze, and newspapers around the world ran the story as an offbeat news item.[1]

The police said there were no injuries. Yeah, right. Anyone who can remember being fifteen knows *that's* not true! The boy felt "the price of admission" was too high, but the price of denial turned out to be higher. In the same way, we get in trouble—and *stay* in trouble—when we ignore the impact of our sins.

So, the first step into a life with God is to admit the truth about yourself. Acknowledge what you've done in times of anger, or where your lack of self-control has taken you, or how often you've put your desires ahead of everyone else's, or the way you abandoned a friend—or a family. Recognize how often you've ignored chances to do the right thing, and how often you fantasize about bitter retaliations or sexual adventures that you would never have the courage to act out. Some of these sins have hurt our relationship with others while some of these things have only hurt us. *All* of these things, however, have hurt our relationship with God, both now and into the next life. The Bible says, "Your sins have cut you off from God" (Isaiah 59:2 NLT).

We may be tempted to hold up evidences of our goodness as a defense—our sacrifices, for example, or our acts of kindness, or our moments of tolerance and forgiveness. In doing so, however, we may end up looking like Sydney Pollack's character in the 2002 film, *Changing Lanes*. The film starred Ben Affleck as Gavin Banek, a morally conflicted junior partner in a big Manhattan law firm. Pollack played Stephen Delano, Banek's father-in-law and senior partner in the same law firm.

In one of the most important scenes in the film, Banek confronted Delano with the ethical compromises he had found in the firm. The partners stood to make millions from a fraudulent document that gave them control of a deceased client's charitable foundation. In turn, Delano tried to reassure Banek that he shouldn't struggle over it. Instead, Delano said, Banek should spend a few months in Texas defending a death row inmate, and return to New York feeling better about himself. After all, he told Banek, the man behind the charitable foundation they were bilking wasn't so noble himself—

Delano: C'mon. How do you think Simon Dunn got his money? Huh? Do you think those factories in Malaysia have day care centers in them? Want to check the pollution levels of his chemical plants in Mexico or look at the tax benefits he got from this foundation? [*He pauses at Banek's disillusionment with this news.*] This is all a *tightrope*. You gotta learn to balance.

Banek: How can you live like that?

Delano: I can live with myself because at the end of the day I think I do more good than harm. [*Pauses.*] What other standard have I got to judge by?

What a contrast Stephen Delano makes to King David in the Old Testament! When confronted by actions that revealed his dark side, he admitted the truth about himself. The poet-king wrote this prayer to God (Psalms 51:3-4 NLT):

> For I recognize my shameful deeds—
> they haunt me day and night.
> Against you, and you alone, have I sinned;
> I have done what is evil in your sight.
> You will be proved right in what you say,
> and your judgment against me is just.

What's remarkable is how honest David was in regard to his darkness, because he could have pointed to a lot of virtuous acts if he hoped that his good deeds could cancel out his bad deeds. He was the most popular and admired king of Old Testament history, and I've found that those who enjoy the admiration of their peers—or at least the acceptance of their peers—have difficulty admitting the darker stuff of the soul. C.S. Lewis was right when he said:

> A world of nice people, content in their own niceness, looking no further, turned away from God, would be just as desperately in need of salvation as a miserable world—and might even be more difficult to save.[2]

Jesus encountered people who were reluctant to admit their need of God's mercy (Luke 18:9-14):

> To some *who were confident of their own righteousness and looked down on everybody else,* Jesus told this parable: "Two men went up to the temple to pray, one a Pharisee and the other a tax collector. The Pharisee stood up and prayed about himself: 'God, I thank you that I am not like other men—robbers, evildoers, adulterers—or even like this tax collector. I fast twice a week and give a tenth of all I get.'
>
> "But the tax collector stood at a distance. He would not even look up to heaven, but beat his breast and said, 'God, have mercy on me, a sinner.'
>
> "I tell you that *this man, rather than the other, went home justified before God.* For everyone who exalts himself will be humbled, and he who humbles himself will be exalted."

Tax collection was a very corrupt and corrupting business in Christ's day. It often involved extortion of the community as well as collaboration with the hated Roman occupiers. The tax collector in Christ's story, however, admitted the truth about himself and asked for divine forgiveness. The other listed off his merits and said, "God, you're lucky to have me around."

Jesus wanted us to see ourselves in this story, and he gave us only two roles to choose between: we can be like the man who denied his need for God's forgiveness, or we can be like the man who cried out for it. So, the first step is to admit the truth about our dark side. Jesus said, "Healthy people don't need a doctor—sick people do. I have come to call sinners, not those who think they are already good enough" (Mark 2:17 NLT).

Believe in the Forgiveness of Jesus

Here's an interesting story from the history of Supreme Court rulings. While Andrew Jackson was President of the United States, he pardoned a man named George Wilson who was convicted of a capital crime. To everyone's surprise, the condemned man actually refused the pardon.

Prison authorities, the Attorney General of the United States, and others tried to convince the man to accept the pardon. They tried to impress upon him that it would not only spare his life, but that if he did not accept the pardon, it would be an insult to the President. The man remained obstinate. The Attorney General even consulted the Supreme Court, asking legal authorities to force the man to receive the pardon. The court ruled that the pardon was merely a printed statement until the man accepted it. The Chief Justice wrote, "A pardon is a slip of paper, the value of which is determined by the acceptance of the person to be pardoned. If it is refused, it is no pardon."[3]

We may wonder why Jackson pardoned the man, or why Wilson refused it, or why the Attorney General worked so hard to get Wilson to accept it. I also wonder: Why would people turn down a pardon offered by God, even after friends or family tried so hard to get them to accept it?

We've got to respond to the offer of new life in Christ. Jesus said, "I stand at the door. I knock. If you hear me call and open the door, I'll come right in and sit down to supper with you" (Revelation 3:20 Msg). Many great friendships form around the supper table, and Jesus used this image to speak of the close friendship he wants to build with us. In order for this friendship to take place, it requires mutual action: he calls and knocks, and then we have to open the door. That's what it means to believe: to open the door to Jesus.

The Apostle John wrote, "To all who receive Him, He gives the right to become children of God. All we need to do is trust Him to save us. All those who believe this are reborn!" (John 1:12-13 LB.) I'm reminded of the story of John Paton, the missionary to the New Hebrides Islands who worked hard to translate the New Testament into the language of the islanders. When he got to the word "faith," however, he was at a loss for how to communicate the concept. One day, a friend came to his house. The friend had walked a long way, and as he settled wearily into the missionary's comfortable chair, he said (in his language), "It is so good to rest my whole weight on this chair." With that, the missionary immediately had the word he needed to capture the concept of faith. Throughout the translation, he spoke of faith in Jesus as "resting one's whole weight" on Jesus.

When Paul wanted to tell people how to begin a life with Christ, he emphasized the importance of belief. He said (Romans 10:9-10 Msg),

> Say the welcoming word to God—"Jesus is my Master"—embracing, body and soul, God's work of doing in us what he did in raising Jesus from the dead. That's it. You're not "doing" anything; you're simply calling out to God, trusting him to do it for you. That's salvation. With your whole being you embrace God setting things right, and then you say it, right out loud: "God has set everything right between him and me!"[4]

To make things right with God, it's not about doing one hundred hard things for God but rather trusting in the one great thing he did for us at the cross

So, once we *admit* the truth about ourselves, we must *believe* the truth about Jesus: he died on the cross to take away our sin and he rose again in victory. To make things right with God, it's not about doing one hundred hard things for God but rather trusting in the one great thing he did for us at the cross.

Commit Yourself to Jesus Publicly

Do you know what it means to "stake a claim"? It comes from the days when the American West was being settled. In the late 1800s, the United States government opened the "Unassigned Lands" in territory that is now Oklahoma. The land was granted to settlers on a first-come, first-served basis in an event called the "Land Run" or "Harrison's Hoss Race." Between 50,000 and

75,000 people participated in the Land Run. Once the event began, people dashed to the plot of land they wanted and then they planted a stake into the ground. Today, we use the phrase "to stake a claim" when speaking of making a decisive and public commitment to something. That's what we need to do with Jesus. We need to make a decisive and public commitment to him—to "stake our claim" in him. According to Scripture, we do this through baptism, worship, and witness.

We stake a claim in Jesus through *baptism*. Jesus expected that those who became his followers would become baptized after they put their faith in him. In his last "marching orders" to the church, he said, "Go to the people of all nations and make them my disciples. Baptize them in the name of the Father, the Son, and the Holy Spirit, and teach them to do everything I have told you" (Matthew 28:19-20 CEV).

His earliest followers took this command seriously. In the stories of the early church, found in *The Acts of the Apostles*, baptism was a prominent feature:

- When three thousand people committed themselves to Christ on the Day of Pentecost (about two months after Christ's death and resurrection), they were immediately baptized (2:41).

- When an Ethiopian leader converted to Christ in a conversation with a church leader who traveled with him, he stopped along a body of water and asked the church leader to baptize him (8:36-38).

- During the time Paul and Silas were imprisoned for preaching the gospel, they led their jailer and his household to Christ, and baptized them all that very evening (16:16-34).

Like my wedding ring is a visible symbol of the commitment I have to my wife, my baptism was a visible symbol of my union with Christ. We commit publicly to Christ through baptism. Although the routine of baptism varies from church to church, in many churches like mine, we follow a common procedure. In waist-deep water, I stand with the person being baptized and introduce him or her to those witnessing the baptism. Just like I ask some questions of a bride and groom in a wedding ceremony, I ask a question of the candidate for baptism: "Have you asked Jesus into your life as your Forgiver and Leader?" When the person replies, "I have," I lead them to lean back into the water, like a body being lowered into the ground at a funeral. As I bring them under the water and back up again, I say, "Buried with Christ in baptism, and raised to walk in a new way of life"—a reference to Paul's comment on baptism in Romans 6:4. While this is a solemn time in some churches, in churches like ours baptisms are met with joyful applause.

We stake a claim in Jesus through public *worship*. While worship opportunities give us a chance to grow through the teaching that is shared, more is happening when we worship together. It becomes a way to serve notice to those around us that we unapologetically honor Jesus. The simple act of arranging our schedules in order to consistently gather with others for worship becomes a powerful signal to co-workers, friends, and family that our priorities have changed.

We stake a claim in Jesus through *witness*. We believers often find that our conversations with others lead to natural opportunities to express what we believe about Jesus. While we should always listen to others' opinions and respect their convictions, we should find our voice in expressing our own convictions as well. It's one way we stake our claim in Christ.

Stake Your Claim

The late Rich Mullins had a way with song lyrics, and he wasn't afraid to express his Christian faith in unexpected, rugged terms. One of his more popular songs called on people to respond to God's call with, "Alrightokuhuhamen."[5]

That's the right reaction to Christ's offer of forgiveness and leadership: "Alright . . . Okay . . . Uh-huh . . . Amen."

If you're ready to take that step, let God know. You could pray a prayer like this:

> Jesus, I open the door to you, and I ask you to come into my life. I'm sorry for my sins. Thank you for dying on the cross to take them away. Forgive me and be my Leader from now on. Make me a new person inside. Amen.

If you've prayed that prayer, let a believing friend or relative know right away. Talk with a church about scheduling your baptism, and start growing in your knowledge and experience of Christ. In the next chapter, we'll look at some new habits and routines to form in your new walk with Christ.

Chapter 25
Your Mount Everest

Pressed against the sheer face of the cliff, the rock climber looks up for the next place to grip. Seeing one, he clamps his fingers upon it and lifts himself a few feet higher. Methodically, he repeats the exercise—finding handholds, finding footholds, bracing against the winds that would unbalance him, locking safety anchors into minute cracks in the wall. Finally, he reaches the top and sits on the summit with a quiet contentment from his successful climb.

Believers can identify with a rock climber's passion, because we're climbers, too. And the goal of any climber, whether he or she takes a hike up an inclining trail or scuttles spider-like up a cliff, is to reach the top. It's the same in a life with Christ! It's work, but there are vistas that can only be seen at higher elevations. So, let me introduce you to the H.I.L.L. before you. Those letters stand for *Honor, Invite, Love,* and *Live.* These aren't listed in order of priority: we have to practice all four actions in order to climb the Everest of spiritual maturity.

Honor
"Those who honor me I will honor"
1 Samuel 2:30

Do you live a God-oriented life? Many people live a God-mindful life, but a God-oriented life is different. Almost everyone I've met thinks about God from time to time. They wonder what he's like, they wonder what he expects, they wonder if he's happy with their lives, they wonder how to get him to meet their needs. Almost everyone I've met does this—at least occasionally. Someone who lives a God-oriented life operates differently. That person...

> ... is stirred by the greatness of God
>   ... is moved by the grace of God
>   ... expects the activity of God
>   ... hungers for the word of God
>   ... longs for the glory of God.

The commitment to live in this manner isn't a one-time event but a life-long process. We have to constantly challenge each other to orient our lives to God like a compass needle drawn to the North.

God promises us, "Those who honor me I will honor." We've been toasted at weddings and roasted at anniversaries and we've been asked to stand while people applauded. We've been the focus of parties that took a lot of other people's time and travel and we couldn't believe people would do all that for us. The Hebrew word that we translate *honor* means "to heap, to make heavy." To honor someone means to heap our appreciation and commitment and gifts upon him until he is heavy with it all. God says he wants to do that for us. That amazes me. Praise and loyalty is really a one-way street: God deserves it from me; I don't deserve it from him. Yet he promises what he doesn't have to promise: He says if I will honor him, he will honor me.

According to Scripture, you honor God in four commitments.

We honor God with our worship. In public services and in private times, we should praise God and thank him. God said, "Giving thanks is a sacrifice that truly *honors* me" (Psalms 50:23 NLT).

We honor God with our giving. The Bible says, "*Honor* the Lord with your wealth; then your barns will be filled to overflowing, and your vats will brim over with new wine" (Proverbs 3:9-10). Get involved in a church that does the kind of work that excites you and regularly give a portion of your income to that church. This kind of giving isn't like paying dues to a local club; it's the way we honor God.

We honor God with our prayer. The poet of the Old Testament said to God, "I will *honor* you as long as I live, lifting up my hands to you *in prayer*" (Psalms 63:4 NLT). When we're faced with problems, pains and decisions, asking for God's help needs to be a "first response" rather than a "last resort." When we depend on God, we honor him.

We honor God with our lifestyle. The Apostle Paul wrote, "God bought you with a high price. So you must *honor* God with your body" (1 Corinthians 6:20 NLT). From what we access on the Internet to how we react in traffic to the choices we make in entertainment to the promise we keep in a marriage—believers should aim to honor God with a life well-lived.

Invite
"Let us invite them to come and join us"
1 Chronicles 13:2 (NLT)

Another aspect of following Christ involves communicating your faith to others. "Come, be my disciples," Jesus said, "and I will show you how to fish for people!" (Matthew 4:19 NLT.) Notice how Jesus defined what it means to be his disciple: it involves influencing those in our world with his life-changing message. Across the *street* and across the *sea*, we need to let others in on this good news we've found.

It's understandable that some people see this as nothing more than sanctified solicitation. Business reps sell their products, military recruiters enlist personnel, and lobbyists persuade people to join their cause. Surrounded by those appeals, some naturally think that sharing the Christian faith is just another sales pitch. However, we need to understand that helping others in their spiritual search is part of our own spiritual development.

Those in Alcoholics Anonymous know this. Recovering alcoholics understand that one of the most effective means of staying sober is to help other alcoholics recover. In fact, the entire idea of AA was formed when Bill Wilson, only a few months sober, was gripped with a powerful urge to drink. The thought came to him, "You need another alcoholic to talk to. You need another alcoholic just as much as he needs you!" He found a physician who had been trying desperately and unsuccessfully to stop drinking. And by helping the physician stay sober, he helped himself stay sober. Later, the two men codified what has become known as the Twelve Steps, and the last step is to carry the message of sobriety to other alcoholics. In what is affectionately nicknamed "the Big Book," Bill Wilson wrote: "Practical experience shows that nothing will so much insure immunity from drinking as intense work with other alcoholics. It works when other activities fail. This is our *twelfth suggestion:* Carry this message to other alcoholics!"

That suggestion is not only found in the Big Book, it's found in the Good Book! We believers communicate our faith not only to share what we've found but also to develop our own spiritual growth. I remember what my English professor once said. As she tried to convince the class of freshman university students to grasp the importance of good writing, she said, "You do not understand a subject fully until you can lead someone else to understand it." I think she's right. We often have trouble putting a thought into words because the idea is vague and hazy in our minds. As we Christians struggle to make the gospel clear enough and relevant enough for another person to understand, the gospel becomes more clear and relevant to us.

Helping others in their spiritual search, then, will help you, too. So look to communicate your faith in a way that is natural to your personality. Also, support others who are sharing the faith: a faith-based prison aftercare program in the inner city, for example, or a crisis pregnancy center in the suburbs, or a training college for church leaders in another country. Support this kind of work as a volunteer or a donor.

If what has been discussed in this book is true—and we believers are convinced it is—then we can't keep it to ourselves. Our world needs the good news of the gospel, so we need to "invite them to come and join us." It's one way we climb the H.I.L.L. of spiritual maturity.

Love
"We love each other as a result of his loving us first"
1 John 4:19 (NLT)

While the work of inviting others into life with Christ involves spending time with those still on the spiritual search, we also need to spend time with those who have made the same commitment to Christ that we have made. The Bible tells us to "have fellowship with each other" (1 John 1:7) and *"love* your Christian brothers and sisters" (1 Peter 2:17 NLT).

In earlier chapters of the book, we reviewed what it means to say, "I believe in the church." Jesus expected his church to be "one," "holy," and a "communion." Once you cross into faith, you will want to make Christ's vision of his church a reality. This will be impossible until you identify a gathering of believers as your own "church home." While we can—and should—enjoy the special opportunities for inspiration that various churches provide, we cannot grow spiritually if we merely flit from one church to another like patrons enjoying the fare of different restaurants. We have to find a spiritual home and say, "*This* is where I will work to make Christ's vision for his church a reality." How can we love our chosen Christian fellowship? Here are some suggestions:

Find your place of service. Those who row the boat don't have time to rock it! Scripture tells us that, "A spiritual gift is given to each of us as a means of helping the entire church" (1 Corinthians 12:7 NLT). Find out how you can be useful to the work your church is trying to accomplish.

Get connected, especially to a small group. Paul wrote, "And since we are all one body in Christ, we belong to each other, and each of us needs all the others" (Romans 12:5 NLT). We are not to be spectators who slip in for the church's "show" on Sundays and then slip out. Find a way to attach yourself to other believers in your chosen church.

Respect each other, especially the leadership. The sweet movie, *My Big Fat Greek Wedding*, can teach you a lot about getting along in your chosen church. Gus Portokalos was the proud Greek-American father who found himself in a crisis when his beloved Toula wanted to marry Ian Miller, who was tall and handsome, but definitely *not* Greek. Most of the comedy in the movie revolved around the cultural differences as the courtship proceeded—serving lamb to a vegetarian, playfully tricking Ian into saying something embarrassing in a language he didn't know, learning how serve a Bundt cake. But Gus came to terms with his struggles in the end. At the wedding reception, he launched into his infamous habit of tracing back the origin of all words to their foundation in the Greek language. He reminded the audience that "Portokalos" comes from the Greek word meaning "orange" (the fruit, not the color). And the family name "Miller"— he claimed—comes from the Greek word for "apple."

"So here we have 'apples' and 'oranges,'" he said, to some scattered laughter from those who knew that the two families were as different as, well, apples and oranges. Then he looked sweetly at his daughter and said, "But in the end, we're all fruit." It was Gus's way of coming to terms with his daughter's choice.

No matter what church you connect with, you will probably find some people who are as different from you as apples from oranges. Like Gus discovered in his family, it's mutual respect that gets us through. James wrote, "You can develop a healthy, robust community that lives right with God and enjoy its results only if you do the hard work of getting along with each other, treating each other with dignity and honor" (James 3:18 Msg).

It's especially important that we respect a certain segment of the church fellowship: those who lead. "Now we ask you, brothers," Paul wrote, "to respect those who work hard among you, who are over you in the Lord and who admonish you. Hold them in the highest regard in love because of their work. Live in peace with each other" (1 Thessalonians 5:12-13). Notice how that verse makes *respect for the leaders* a foundation for *living in peace*. When you get involved in a church, you'll find that the leaders are human just like you are. They're not perfect, but they deserve your appreciation as persons whom God is using to lead his people.

Be an encourager. Motivate those in your fellowship to make the right choices in their lives—and stay open to the encouragement others give you. "Let's see how inventive we can be in encouraging love and helping out," the Bible says, "not avoiding worshiping together as some do but spurring each other on, especially as we see the big Day approaching" (Hebrews 10:24-25 Msg).

Share your stories. Talk with other believers about what you're experiencing with God, and encourage them to share their stories. I love how Paul put it (Romans 1:12 NCV): "I want us to help each other with the faith we have. Your faith will help me, and my faith will help you." When Paul wrote that he had been a believer for perhaps thirty years and a church leader for twenty-five, yet he acknowledged how he needed to hear about the experiences others were having with God. We never get too old or too experienced in following Jesus that we outgrow the need to learn from others.

Minister to each other. Through prayer and caring, heal the hurts of other believers. "My children, John tenderly wrote, "Our love should not be just words and talk; it must be true love, which shows itself in action" (1 John 3:18 TEV).

As you climb higher in your spiritual maturity, aim for this kind of love between the members of your chosen fellowship.

Live
"I live by your Word"
Psalm 119:49 (Msg)

In Chapter 4, I suggested three steps to benefit from the Bible during your spiritual search. These three steps will also help you find value in the Bible during your spiritual *growth* as a believer.

Read it. Set aside time for this every day. Read it when there's nothing worthwhile on TV. Read it while you're waiting in an airport terminal. Listen to recordings of scripture readings while you're driving.

Now, maybe you doubt you'll get anything out of Bible reading because you tried it before and concluded, "I'm never going to understand it!" You will if you keep at it. A few years ago, I bought an internal CD drive for my computer, and when I opened the instruction manual to install the thing, I saw all kinds of language I had never seen before. The instruction manual told me to locate the primary IDE channel, secondary IDE channel, 40-pin IDE cable, and a shunt. I said to myself, "Uh-oh." Then when I opened the computer case, I saw all these wires running everywhere and I thought, "What have I gotten myself in to?" But I kept working with it and in about fifteen minutes I had the thing installed and working perfectly.

Keep working with your Bible and what is currently strange and foreign will eventually become rich and beautiful to you. That's the way it has become for other believers. When reading a book that was written several thousand years ago in a Near Eastern culture very different from yours, it takes time to understand the ancient customs and idioms and theological concepts. But as you consistently read Scripture your understanding will grow.

Think about it. Take time to reflect on what you're reading. Get in Bible study groups that will help you understand your Bible. Read books that will answer the questions that come up during your reading times. As you study the Bible, keep a journal of your reactions and questions.

Live it. James Emery White described believers who do not grow in spiritual maturity as "saved but not seized."[1] It's not enough to simply read the Bible and think about it. We need to let ourselves be seized with conviction by the scriptural challenges. When we discover changes that need to be made or habits that need to be started, we need to take action, depending on the power of the Spirit and the encouragement of other believers.

Putting it Together

When Jesus was asked what the greatest commandment was, he said we should love God and love others (Matthew 22:36-40). That's your H.I.L.L. to climb. We love God as we *HONOR* him and as we *LIVE* the principles of his Word. And, as we relate to God, we're also to relate to others. We must *INVITE* others to cross the line into faith, and we must *LOVE* our fellow believers. All four actions are equally important, because they fulfill what Jesus said was the greatest commandment: loving God and loving others.

Don't worry that you're a novice to this climb—you'll catch on quickly! It's like a beginner to rock climbing, who wrote:

> Each step up the rock was a little *yes!* as I searched for another small crack or corner to grab on to. Every time I came to a "stuck" place, where I thought, how can I get anywhere from here—there's nothing to grab on to!—I would methodically study the rock face, and the next move would be there.[2]

Let me challenge you to put everything you've got into making this climb. There's no excuse good enough for failing to make it up this H.I.L.L. A few years ago, Gary Guller made it to the top of the tallest "hill" in the world: Mount Everest. If that weren't impressive enough, he did it without a left arm. He had lost his arm in a climbing accident years earlier, but it didn't keep him from pursuing a dream that first stirred in him upon seeing Everest at the age of twelve—he wanted to reach the top. When he finally did make it, though, he took some people with him. Others with disabilities of various severity climbed with him fifteen thousand feet above sea level to the Everest base camp, and then he himself went on to the top. His philosophy is, "Be great, but make others great."

What's keeping you from climbing your hill? What's keeping you from putting everything you've got into it? Some of us feel, "I can't do this. I'm too old, I'm too young, I'm too broken. My marriage is handicapped; my bad decisions have sidelined me from this climb. I can't do it." Think about Gary and then take whatever excuse you've used to keep you from climbing your hill and turn it over to God. The climb up the hill of spiritual maturity is hard, because we're all handicapped in some way. Whatever your handicap is, though, don't let it stop you from climbing!

Tell me about your experience with The Anchor Course!
Write me at tom@anchorcourse.org

www.anchorcourse.org

Find additional articles and links for further study of the topics covered in The Anchor Course

Learn how to lead a small-group study of The Anchor Course

Order more books and other resources

Discussion Questions

This book was designed to generate conversations between those who are curious about Christ and those who are committed to him. Feel free to use these questions as you discuss the material together.

Part One: "I Believe"
After reading chapters 1-4, discuss the following:

In the first chapter, Tom listed four advantages to faith. What are they and which one seemed most attractive to you?

The Bible describes a believer's hope in forgiveness and eternal life as "an anchor for the soul" (Hebrews 6:19). Ask the believers in your group to describe the ways their faith has been like an "anchor" for them.

The Apostle John wrote, "What we have heard, what we have seen with our eyes, what we have looked at and touched with our hands, concerning the Word of Life [Jesus] . . . we proclaim to you also, *so that you too may have fellowship with us.*" (1 John 1:1-3 NASB). The purpose of our Bibles, then, is that we might have a share in the experiences of those who were eyewitnesses of Jesus. However, it is fashionable in some circles to say that the Bible was written long after the events took place. As discussed in Chapter 3, the evidence shows that the Bible was actually written within the generation that would have seen these events.

How can that strengthen our confidence in the Bible as a reliable guide to the actions and words of Jesus?

Were you surprised to read in Chapter 3 that archaeological discoveries verify the stories of the Bible and that no archaeological discovery has refuted a biblical claim?

Have you ever tried to read the Bible? Did you find it frustrating? If so, why? What is your favorite book of the Bible and why?

The Bible encourages us be "constantly nourished on the words of the faith" (1 Timothy 4:6 NASB). For the next two months, what can you change in your schedule so that you can be "nourished" from reading and discussing the material in *The Anchor Course*?

Part Two: "I Believe in God"
After reading chapters 5-6, discuss the following:

The words of Isaiah 40:21-31 describe the practical benefits of knowing God as "Father," "Almighty," and "Maker of heaven and earth." Have someone read these verses for the group.

What comes to mind when you think of God as Father? How can our relationship with an earthly father impact our view of God? If you know someone with negative memories of their father, how could you help them appreciate the fatherhood of God?

How can the thought of God as "Father" help you when you pray? How can the thought of God as "Almighty" help you when you pray? When your prayers aren't answered the way you wanted, how can the thought of God as both "Father" and "Almighty" help you?

Since God is "Maker of heaven and earth," is there a particular place in creation that you find yourself aware of God's presence?

How do you think God feels about our care of his creation? What steps could you take to take better care of his creation?

If you could ask God one question, what would it be?

Part Three: "I Believe in Jesus"
After reading chapters 7-10, discuss the following questions:

Tom compared Jesus to a pearl diver who (1) left the heights of heaven, (2) descended to the depths of human experience, and (3) returned to heaven with treasure in his hand. Have someone read Philippians 2:5-11 for the group. Identify the words that describe (1) Christ's divinity and heavenly existence, (2) Christ's humanity and earthly experience, and (3) Christ's triumphant return to heaven.

What did you think of C.S. Lewis's comments that are quoted on page 65? He said you don't have the option of calling Jesus a great moral teacher and ignoring his claims of being the God who made us and the God who deserves our worship. Lewis said that as we considered Jesus claims, we only had two options: he was insane (and therefore no great moral teacher) or he was who he claimed to be. What is your reaction to Lewis' options?

God the Son suffered pain, encountered temptation and did not give in to it, experienced rejection, and even endured torture and death. Does this awareness help you deal with the trials in your own life? If so, how?

Have someone read 1 Corinthians 15:12-20 to the group. Paul said that if we take away Christ's resurrection, we take away the very foundation of Christianity. Why is Christ's resurrection so important to faith?

Have someone read Hebrews 7:25 and Romans 8:34 to the group. The Bible reveals that Jesus is now at "the right hand" of the Father where he prays for us. What do you think Jesus is asking the Father on *your* behalf at this period in your life?

Part Four: "I Believe in the Holy Spirit"
After reading chapters 11-13, discuss the following questions:

Have someone read John 16:5-8 to the group. Jesus said the Spirit would convict "the world" regarding three things. In this context, Jesus uses the phrase "the world" to describe anyone who has not committed to him. What were the three "convictions" Jesus said the Spirit would bring to the world? Review and summarize Tom's explanation of those three things from Chapter 11.

From Chapter 12, review and summarize the four things Tom said the Spirit does with those who have put their faith in Christ.

Have someone read 2 Corinthians 3:17 to the group. Notice that the Bible says, "The Lord is the Spirit." Now that your group has reviewed what the Spirit does with nonbelievers and believers, how does it make you feel to know that these things are the actions of the Lord himself? Do you feel *valued* that God would take such a personal interest in your life, or do you feel *uneasy* that God is so close to everything you experience?

Have someone read Galatians 5:25 to the group. This verse urges us to "keep in step with the Spirit" (NIV). What can you do in your daily life to follow the Spirit's leading throughout your day?

Have someone read Galatians 5:22-23 to the group. This passage lists "fruit" (or "results") of giving control of your life to God's Spirit. Of the nine traits, which one is your strongest at this point in your life? Which one is your weakest? Would you be willing for the group to pray that your life would bear more of the fruit that is listed in this passage?

Part Five: "I Believe in the Church"
After reading chapters 14-16, discuss the following questions:

Why is it so hard for some people to say, "I *believe* in the church?" If you've had personal experiences with Christians or churches that have disillusioned you, feel free to share them.

Christ's vision for his church is captured in the three words of the Creed: "one," "holy," and "communion." In other words, we are to be a united righteous community. The truth is, when it comes to this vision, we can tell plenty of stories of *exemplary*

Christians and *embarrassing* Christians. Why do you think that is so and what should be done about it?

In Chapter 15, Tom wrote:

> Once you become a believer, Jesus expects you to join other disciples in pursuit of an inspiring vision of what "church" is supposed to be. I talked with a man once who was active in a church until he saw behavior in the leadership that disillusioned him. When I asked him what he did about it he shrugged his shoulders and said, "I left." It never occurred to him that he was expected to work with others to find a remedy for the situation. For him, the church was merely an institution under someone else's responsibility, not his. He drew benefit from it until the institution no longer pleased him. The man did not understand that Christ expects his followers to actually pursue Christ's vision for a church that is "one," "holy," and "a communion."

What would you say to this man? What could he have done differently at that church?

Have someone read Ephesians 5:25-27 to the group. What earthly relationship does Paul use to compare Christ's relationship to his church? When we read that Christ "gave himself up" for the church (NIV), that's a reference to his death on the cross. We will discuss the meaning of Christ's death in the next section. For now, compare Christ's love for the church to your love for the church. Discuss the following questions:

> So many people who say they believe in Christ have no meaningful involvement in a specific church. Can you love Christ and yet have no love for what he loves?

> Just as Christ's love led to sacrifice, what might we have to "give up" out of love for the church?

Discuss what you think a person should look for when choosing a church. Although Christ's followers "believe in the church," is it ever right to leave a specific church?

Part Six: "I Believe in Forgiveness"
After reading chapters 17-19, discuss the following questions:

Make a list of the different symbols for the world's major religions: Judaism, Islam, Hinduism, Buddhism/Taoism, and so on. Why is the cross the symbol that most associate with Christianity?

Though most people are willing to say, "I'm not perfect," few are willing to accept that such imperfections separate them from God. Why?

In our modern world, what has taken the place of "sin" in our vocabulary and thinking? What is the result?

Designate someone in the group as a reader and have him or her find Isaiah 53:6 in the Bible. Have everyone else in the group extend their left hand, palm up, and have them place an object in the open palm. Explain that the left hand in this exercise represents our life and the object represents the sin that we carry. Have the members of the group extend their right hand, palm up, and explain that the right hand will represent Jesus in this exercise. Have the designated reader read Isaiah 53:6. When the reader gets to the line, "and the Lord has laid on him the iniquity of us all," have everyone transfer the "sin" from their left hand to their right hand. When the object is in their right hand, they should return their left hand to the original position, palm open and empty.

In Chapter 19, Tom wrote that, because Christ carried away the sin of those who belong to him, God can *release* us, *restore* us, and *receive* us. Review that chapter and answer these questions: From what can God release us? To what can God restore us? Where can God receive us?

Most believers have a story of the life-events that led them to place their trust in Christ. Ask the believers in the group if they are willing to tell their story.

Part Seven: "I Believe in the Life Everlasting"
After reading chapters 20-22, discuss the following questions:

Have someone read 1 Peter 3:15 to the group. Do your attitudes about death make people want to ask you about the *hope* you have?

Have someone read Philippians 3:20-21 to the group. In Chapter 20, Tom explained why the Bible teaches that eternal life is more than merely continuing to exist after death. The Bible teaches that body and soul will be reunited at the resurrection. While most of our world believes in some sort of life beyond this life, the resurrection is a teaching unique to the Bible. From what you read in Chapter 20, recall why the resurrection is an important part of God's plan.

Have someone read Jesus' words in John 14:2-3 to the group. Tom described seven characteristics about heaven in Chapter 21. Were any of the characteristics surprising? Which characteristic most makes you look forward to heaven?

Have someone read Jesus' words in John 3:16 to the group. In Chapter 22, Tom wrote, "For some, the thought of hell calls into question God's justice, God's love, and God's grace. Hell does not *eliminate* these things, however. It *illuminates* them." Briefly describe how hell illuminates these three things, using Tom's comments from Chapter 22.

Part Eight: "Amen"
After reading chapters 23-25, discuss the following questions:

Have someone read Luke 12:16-21 to the group. In this story, Jesus described a man who enjoyed the benefits of this life as if it would go on forever. He gave no thought of his accountability to God. Have the group suggest a one-sentence "moral of the story" from this passage.

Jesus expected us to *commit* to him, not just *study* him. In Chapter 23, Tom pointed out four reasons people will study Jesus but then hesitate when it comes to committing to him. If you are a Christ-follower, share with the group which of these four reasons caused you to hesitate before committing to Christ. If you are examining the claims of Christ, share with the group which of these four reasons may be behind your own hesitation to put your faith in him.

Have someone read Luke 18:9-14 to the group. Based on this story, would Jesus agree with the popular notion that "God accepts all people"? What disappointed Jesus about the Pharisee: the man's good works or the man's attitude toward his good works? Why? How can this story help us in our own relationship with God?

Summarize the "A-B-C's" of a commitment to Christ that Tom described in Chapter 24. If you have made a commitment to Christ during this study, share your decision with the group if you feel comfortable in doing so.

In Chapter 25, Tom pointed out that a commitment to Christ is the beginning of a lifelong climb toward spiritual maturity. Summarize the "H.I.L.L." acronym Tom used in Chapter 25 to explain way a believer follows Christ.

1 Thessalonians 5:21 in the Living Bible says, "Test everything that is said to be sure it is true, and if it is, then accept it." If you are still considering a commitment to Christ, what remains to be tested? In other words, what questions or issues remain unresolved? What books in the section entitled "For Further Reading" interest you in your continuing test?

What has been the most helpful thing you have learned or experienced in this eight-week study?

Who else should be part of a study like this? Would some members of your study group be willing to form a new study group with these new people? You can order additional books and learn how to lead your own study at www.anchorcourse.org.

For Further Reading

You will find additional articles and links for further study of the topics covered in the Anchor Course at:

www.anchorcourse.org

If you are interested in further study regarding the Bible's reliability, I suggest *The Authority of the Bible*, by John R.W. Stott (Downers Grove, Ill: InterVarsity Press, 1974). It is one of the most accessible overviews of Jesus' view of Scripture. Also, F.F. Bruce has written *The Canon of Scripture* (Downers Grove, Ill: InterVarsity Press, 1988), a popular book on the historical formation of the Bible. A briefer treatment can be found in his book, *The New Testament Documents: Are They Reliable?* (Grand Rapids: Eerdmans, 1984). Also, check out Carsten Peter Thiede and Matthew D'Ancona's book, *Eyewitness to Jesus: Amazing New Manuscript Evidence About the Origin of the Gospels* (New York: Doubleday, 1996). I enjoyed the perspective of a journalist in Jeffery L. Sheler's book, *Is the Bible True? How Modern Debates and Discoveries Affirm the Essence of the Scriptures* (San Francisco, HarperSanFrancisco, 1999). You may be familiar with Sheler through his work with *U.S. News and World Report* or PBS's *Religion and Ethics Newsweekly*. Craig Bloomberg's work has been helpful, including *The Historical Reliability of the Gospels* (Downers Grove, Ill.: InterVarsity Press, 1987), and his chapter, "The Historical Reliability of the New Testament" in the book *Reasonable Faith* (Westchester, Ill.:

Crossway, 1994, pages 193-231). Lee Strobel's book, *The Case for Christ* (Grand Rapids: Zondervan, 1998), remains one of the most popular modern defenses of the Christian faith. The first six chapters of the book are helpful for those investigating whether the Bible is a reliable source for information about Jesus.

The historic and biblical understanding of Jesus has been challenged by the work of the Jesus Seminar. The "findings" of the Jesus Seminar have been widely reported in the media, leaving some seekers wondering if the biblical portrayal of Jesus can be trusted. I recommend *Jesus Under Fire: Modern Scholarship Reinvents the Historical Jesus* (Michael J. Wilkins and J.P. Moreland, General Editors. Grand Rapids: Zondervan, 1995). It was written by various scholars with the aim of pointing out the flaws of the Jesus Seminar methodology.

If you are trying to gain a better understanding of the Bible, I suggest the *Holman Bible Handbook* (Nashville: Holman Bible Publishers, 1992), a helpful guide to the people, places, and cultural setting of the Bible. Also, *The Journey* (Grand Rapids: Zondervan, 1996) is an edition of the Bible designed for seekers, with helpful explanations provided along with the scripture text.

For those who want to dig deeper into Christian truth, I recommend Millard Erickson's *Christian Theology* (Grand Rapids: Baker, 1983). If you are looking for more information on the defense of God's existence, check out *God: The Evidence: The Reconciliation of Faith and Reason in a Postsecular World* by Patrick Glynn (Roseville, California: Prima Publishing, 1997). Lee Strobel also discusses the evidence for God in the natural world in *The Case for a Creator* (Grand Rapids: Zondervan, 2004).

Since the triune nature of God is so difficult to understand, you may want to read *Understanding the Trinity* by Alister McGrath (Grand Rapids: Academie Books, 1988) and *Is the Father of Jesus the God of Muhammad?* By Timothy George (Grand Rapids: Zondervan, 2002). While George's book is primarily a study of the differences between Christianity and Islam, he does an excellent job explaining why the biblical concept of the Trinity is essential to understanding God.

The resurrection of the crucified Christ is the central story of our faith, so for those who need further study on this event (as well as other miracles described in the Bible), I suggest *Miracles* by C.S. Lewis, *The Case for Christ* by Lee Strobel (already mentioned), and Colin Brown's *Miracles and the Critical Mind* (Grand Rapids: Paternoster Press, 1984).

For those who need further encouragement in their spiritual search, I recommend *Epic: The Story God is Telling and the Role that is Yours to Play* by John Eldredge (Nashville: Thomas Nelson, 2004). Also, check out *The Unknown God: Searching for Spiritual Fulfillment* by Alister McGrath (Grand Rapids: Eerdmans, 1999). James Emery White has a helpful book called *A Search for the Spiritual: Exploring Real Christianity* (Grand Rapids: Baker, 1998). Os Guinness nudges the seeker along with his book, *Long Journey Home: A Guide to Your Search for the Meaning of Life* (Colorado Springs: WaterBrook Press, 2001). Finally, *Mere Christianity* by C.S. Lewis remains a classic explanation of Christian basics.

Appreciation

This book is the product of a lot of great relationships. I am so grateful for those wonderful participants of my first "seeker classes," and especially for those who hosted those studies in their homes. I learned so much from the honest questions and remarkable insights of those who allowed me to be a partner in their spiritual search. Special thanks to those who hosted those first seeker classes while I served as pastor of the First Baptist Church of Grand Cayman: Peter and Claire, Jackie and Rod, Julie—and especially Terry and Susan, who hosted my first group and asked me to baptize them in the beautiful Caribbean Sea when they put their faith in Christ. Thank you all!

I'm also grateful to those members of the Hillcrest Baptist Church in Austin, Texas, who met with me each Wednesday evening for nine months to read the chapters as I completed them. Your encouragement and suggestions were invaluable!

I can't say enough about my editor, Heidi Finch. Despite her busy life, she committed to a months-long process of reviewing this material. She corrected many a grammatical mistake and also helped me re-evaluate my thought progression in many chapters.

I'm grateful for my graphic designer, Elishea Smith, who took a personal interest in this project and worked through many revisions for the book cover.

Throughout the years, Judi Hayes has constantly encouraged me as a writer and she has been an advocate for this project from the beginning.

I'm also thankful to a new friend, Richard Dereus, who took an interest in the project after attending a class I was teaching. Richard introduced me to Lulu.com and drew from his experience in the publishing world to offer many helpful pointers.

During the editing process, I realized I had someone else to thank, though I was only two years old when he died. I'm speaking about C.S. Lewis, who passed away on the same day of the Kennedy assassination, November 22, 1963. Lewis was an Oxford English professor whose explanations of the Christian faith have been enjoyed by millions. His writing has recently received fresh attention with the release of the film series, *The Chronicles of Narnia*, which is based on his children's novels of the same name. During the long process of writing this book, I had no idea how often I was quoting from Lewis. Apparently, his explanations of the Christian faith found their way into my bloodstream from the moment I first began to read his books in college. These many years later, as I groped for the words to explain the faith while writing this book, his words and images came back to me from my college days. When I began to review my material for publication, I considered thinning out my frequent references to him. My decision to leave them in the book, as you can see, is an expression of my appreciation for him.

Finally, I thank my wife, Diane, for her companionship and her constant prayers and encouragement regarding all I do. I cannot imagine my life, or my life's work, without you. I love you!

Tom Goodman
Austin, Texas

Notes

Introduction

[1] You may be more familiar with the version of the Apostles' Creed using the line, "I believe in the holy catholic church." The word translated "catholic" (Latin, *catholicam*; Greek, *katholikos*), means "universal," and refers to the universal oneness of all believers. Today, though, most people understand the word "catholic" to refer to a specific branch of Christianity: the Roman Catholic Church. Since a word that once referred to the oneness of *all* Christians is now identified with only a segment of the Christian body, I prefer to simply speak of the church as *one* instead of as *catholic*. We will discuss this in Chapter 14.

[2] Rich Mullins, "Creed," on *A Liturgy, A Legacy, and a Ragamuffin Band* Audio CD (Nashville: Reunion, 1993). Listeners may be more familiar with this song as covered by Third Day on their 2003 Audio CD, *Offerings*.

Chapter 1: The Benefits of Believing

[1] Jann S. Wenner, "Bono: The Rolling Stone Interview," *Rolling Stone* Online, http://www.rollingstone.com/news/story/_/id/8091949/u2?rnd=1129829251135&has-player=false/, accessed October 29, 2005.

[2] In Thomas G. Long, *Preaching and the Literary Forms of the Bible* (Philadelphia: Fortress, 1989), 52.

[3] The Yorke comment is found in the *New Musical Express*, quoted in Rico Tice and Barry Cooper, *Christianity Explored* (London: Authentic Media, 2002). The Geldof comment is found in *The London Times*, September 1998, also quoted in *Christianity Explored*. The Iacoca comment comes from his book, *Straight Talk*, quoted in Ravi Zacharias, *Can Man Live Without God* (Dallas: Word, 1994), 58.

[4] Quoted in Charles Colson and Nancy Pearcey, *How Now Shall We Live?* (Wheaton, Ill.: Tyndale, 1999), 91-92.

[5] Steven Weinberg, *The First Three Minutes: A Modern View of the Origin of the Universe*, quoted in Carl F.H. Henry, *The Christian Mindset in a Secular Society* (Portland, OR: Multnomah, 1984), 12.

[6] Jacques Monod, *Chance and Necessity*, quoted in Vincent Cronin, *The View from Planet Earth* (New York: William Morrow, 1981), 297.

[7] Quoted in "New study shows students are commonly spiritual," Tanner Kroger, posted 6-1-05, technicianonline.com/06.01.2005/news/, accessed 6-6-05. The student who was quoted was defending her decision to embrace Wicca, illustrating how people are looking for a way to fulfill their need for meaning and purpose in life, even through nontraditional avenues.

Chapter 2: The Barriers to Believing

[1] Chuck Swindoll attributed this poem to Wilbur Rees in *Improving Your Serve: The Art of Unselfish Living* (Waco: Word, 1981), 29.

[2] A recent incarnation of this persistent myth appeared in Bill Moyers' comments upon receiving Harvard Medical School's Global Environment Citizen Award on December 1, 2004. See, "On Receiving Harvard Medical School's Global Environment Citizen Award," by Bill Moyers at http://www.commondreams.org/views04/1206-10.htm/, accessed August 17, 2005. Moyers later apologized for passing along the false claim that James Watt, President Reagan's first Secretary of the Interior, told the U.S. Congress that protecting natural resources was unimportant in light of the imminent return of Jesus Christ.

[3] These cases are numerous, but a typical instance of a capital sentence for Christian conversion can be found in the news piece, "Yemen Court Sentences Somali Convert To Death:

Former Muslim given one week to recant Christianity or face execution," at http://www.christianitytoday.com/ct/2000/127/55.0.html/, accessed August 17, 2005.

[4] For example, *Sports Illustrated*'s Hank Hersch asked if the Twins' failure to win the 1987 World Series had something to do with Gary Gaetti, an All-Star third baseman who had become "a born-again Christian." Hersch wondered if Gaetti had "lost the fire so vital to his success as a ballplayer." In response to Hersch's article, Watson Spoelstra, founder and president emeritus of Baseball Chapel, said that the notion that Christian athletes care less about success is "the biggest lie in sports," but a persistent one. *Christianity Today*, Vol. 33, No. 15, Oct. 20, 1989, p. 56.

Chapter 3: Trust the Bible

[1] The apostles reminded people that they were "eyewitnesses of his [Christ's] majesty" (2 Peter 1:16), and so they spoke about "what we have seen and heard" (Acts 4:20) and they proclaimed "that which was from the beginning, which we have heard, which we have seen with our eyes, which we have looked at and our hands have touched" (1 John 1:1). Furthermore, Jesus chose them to accurately communicate his word to others (see Luke 10:16; 1 Thessalonians 2:13).

[2] Karen Armstrong, for example, promotes this theory in her popular and highly accessible book, *A History of God* (New York: Ballantine/Epiphany, 1993).

[3] The website for the Jesus Seminar is http://www.westarinstitute.org/. Several helpful books refute the claims of the Jesus Seminar panelists and confirm the historical validity of the biblical presentation of Jesus' words and actions. See Ben Witherington III, *The Jesus Quest: The Third Search for the Jew of Nazareth* (Downers Grove, Ill: Intervarsity Press, 1995); Michel J. Wilkins and J.P. Moreland, eds., *Jesus Under Fire: Modern Scholarship Reinvents the Historical Jesus* (Grand Rapids: Zondervan, 1995); and Douglas Groothuis, *Searching for the Real Jesus in an Age of Controversy* (Eugene, Oreg: Harvest House, 1996).

[4] While the characters and plot of Brown's book are fictional, he continues to insist that he has based his book upon certain historical facts that most art historians and biblical scholars do not support. For more information about the inaccuracies of Brown's claims, see Collin Hansen, "Breaking the Da Vinci Code" at the website for *Christian History and Biography* located at http://www.christianitytoday.com/history/newsletter/2003/nov7.html/, accessed October 6, 2005.

[5] Elaine Pagels, for example, dismisses the New Testament as a reliable record of Jesus' claims, advocating late Gnostic documents as valid alternatives to the story of Jesus. See Elaine Pagels, *The Gnostic Gospels* (1979, 1989), and *Beyond Belief: The Secret Gospel of Thomas* (Random House, 2003). Also, *A Course in Miracles* is one popular study that re-invents Jesus as one of many New Age ascended masters—a way-shower whose function is to awaken humanity and illuminate the path. This is pantheism, which will be discussed on page 52. "In his 1906 book, *The Quest of the Historical Jesus*, no less than Albert Schweitzer concluded that all his major predecessors tended to find a Jesus who suited their own personal and ideological needs." Jay Tolson, "The Kingdom of Christ," *U.S. News and World Report*, 17 April 2006, http://www.usnews.com/usnews/news/articles/060417/17christ.htm, accessed 17 April 2006.

[6] "There is little doubt that the earliest texts in what eventually would become known as the New Testament were letters from the apostle Paul written around 50 CE. It is known from second-century sources that Paul's letters were being copied and widely circulated among the churches of Asia Minor by no later than the early decades of the second century, along with what were described as 'memoirs' of the apostles, which later would become known as the 'gospels.'" Jeffery L. Sheler, *Is the Bible True? How Modern Debates and Discoveries Affirm the Essence of the Scriptures* (San Francisco, HarperSanFrancisco, 1999).

[7] "The most widely held dating of the first Epistle [to the Corinthians] is in the spring of AD 57, although some have proposed an earlier dating." Donald Guthrie, *New Testament Introduction* (Downers Grove, Ill: InterVarsity, 1970), 441.

[8] Gerald F. Hawthorne says that the belief that Philippians 2:6-11 "constitute a beautiful example of a very early hymn of the Christian church," has "almost universal agreement." Gerald F. Hawthorn, *Philippians*, Word Biblical Commentary, Volume 43 (Waco: Word, 1983), 76.
[9] Sheler, 35. His review of the debate can be found on pages 30-35.
[10] On this, see Carsten Peter Thiede and Matthew D'Ancona, *Eyewitness to Jesus: Amazing New Manuscript Evidence About the Origin of the Gospels* (New York: Doubleday, 1996).
[11] Bruce M. Metzger, *Manuscripts of the Greek Bible* (New York: Oxford University Press, 1981), 54.
[12] Metzger discusses this fragment in an interview with Lee Strobel in *The Case for Christ: A Journalist's Personal Investigation of the Evidence for Jesus* (Grand Rapids: Zondervan, 1998), 61-62.
[13] Metzger, quoted in Strobel, *The Case for Christ*, 60.
[14] Strobel discusses the issue of textual variants with Metzger in *The Case for Christ*, 64-65.
[15] See Lee Strobel's interview with John McRay, a professor and author of *Archaeology and the New Testament* (Grand Rapids: Baker, 1991). McRay's discussion of the Bethesda excavations is found on page 99 of the interview in *The Case for Christ*.
[16] Renowned Jewish archaeologist, Nelson Glueck, observed, "It may be stated categorically that no archaeological discovery has ever controverted a biblical reference." *Rivers in the Desert: History of the Negev* (Philadelphia: Jewish Publications Society of America, 1969), 31, quoted in James Emery White, *A Search for the Spiritual: Exploring Real Christianity* (Grand Rapids: Baker, 1998), 71. The statement continues to be true, despite countless archaeological discoveries since 1969.
[17] Simon Greenleaf, *The Testimony of the Evangelists* (Grand Rapids: Baker, 1984), vii. Quoted in Strobel, *The Case for Christ*, 46.
[18] Strobel discusses the Gospel of Thomas with Metzger in *The Case for Christ*, 67-68.

Chapter 4: Use the Bible

[1] Quoted in "To Illustrate," *Leadership* 22, no. 1 (Winter 2001): 69.
[2] Peggy Noonan, *Simply Speaking* (San Francisco: HarperCollins, 1998), 22.
[3] With thanks to Doug Jackson, pastor of the Second Baptist Church of Corpus Christi, Texas.

Chapter 5: Don't Ignore the Evidence for God

[1] For Hubble's research in the early 1900s and the COBE satellite of the late 1900s, see Patrick Glynn, *God: The Evidence: The Reconciliation of Faith and Reason in a Postsecular World* (Roseville, CA: Prima, 1997), 21-55, and White, *A Search for the Spiritual*, 26-28.
[2] Freeman Dyson, *Disturbing the Universe* (New York: Harper and Row, 1979), 250.
[3] John Leslie, *Universes* (New York: Routledge, 1989).
[4] Glynn, *God: The Evidence*, 26.
[5] Michael Behe, *Darwin's Black Box: The Biochemical Challenge to Evolution* (New York: Touchstone, 1996).
[6] Interview with Leon Kass in Bill Moyers, *A World of Ideas* (New York: Doubleday, 1989), 362.
[7] Attributed to Marvin Minsky in Lee Strobel, *The Case for a Creator* (Grand Rapids: Zondervan, 2004), 250.
[8] See Wilder Penfield, *The Mystery of the Mind* (Princeton: Princeton Univ. Press, 1975), 76-77, and Penfield's article, "Control of the Mind" Symposium at the University of California Medical Center, San Francisco, 1961).
[9] See Kenneth L. Woodward, "Faith is More Than a Feeling," *Newsweek* (May 7, 2001).
[10] Sam Parnia, "Near Death Experiences in Cardiac Arrest and the Mystery of Consciousness," available at www.datadiwan.de/SciMedNet/library/articlesN75+/N76Parnia_nde.htm (accessed September 21, 2004), quoted in *The Case for a Creator* by Lee Strobel, 251.

[11] This analogy was first made by Phillip Bishop in "Evidence of God in Human Physiology—Fearfully and Wonderfully Made," http://www.leaderu.com/science/bishop.html/, accessed September 7, 2004. Material for this chapter came from reading the following books: Kenneth D. Boa and Robert M. Bowman, Jr., *Twenty Compelling Evidences That God Exists* (Tulsa, Oklahoma: RiverOak Publishing, 2002); Patrick Glynn, *God: The Evidence: The Reconciliation of Faith and Reason in a Postsecular World* (Roseville, California: Prima Publishing, 1997); Lee Strobel, *The Case for a Creator* (Grand Rapids: Zondervan, 2004).

Chapter 6: Clear Up Your Misunderstandings of God

[1] This verse says God made all things "by" and "for" his Son. We'll look at that teaching in a later chapter.
[2] Barbara Curtis, "Soul Food," *World*, 13 June 1998, 45.
[3] A.W. Tozer, *The Pursuit of God*, available at http://scott.shanebweb.com/christian/pursuit/tozer3.htm/, accessed September 30, 2004.

Chapter 7: Jesus is Everything It Means to Be God

[1] Amy Reynolds, "Freediver Tanya Streeter," *AustinWoman* August 2004, 30-55.
[2] C.S. Lewis, *Mere Christianity* (New York: Macmillan, 1952), 40-41.
[3] John Stott, *The Cross of Christ* (Downers Grove: Intervarsity, 1986), 25.
[4] John Stott, *I Believe in God*. Quoted in "The Quotable Stott: Reflections on the occasion of John R.W. Stott's 80th birthday," *Christianity Today* online at http://www.christianitytoday.com/ct/2001/005/27.64.html/. Accessed October 13, 2004.

Chapter 8: What if God Was One of Us?

[1] Eric Bazilian wrote "One of Us," a song made famous by Joan Osborne on *Relish* Audio CD (Nashville: Mercury/Universal, 1995).
[2] Bob Greene, *He Was a Midwestern Boy on His Own* (New York: Athenaeum, 1991), pp. 17-19. Quoted in *Dynamic Preaching* 7, no. 11 (November 1992): 12.

Chapter 9: What Does the Resurrection Prove?

[1] Richard N. Ostling, "Who Was Jesus?" *Time*, 15 August 1988, cover story.
[2] J.B. Cheaney, "But Can It Save? Even the Best 'Good Advice' Only Goes So Far," *World*, 20 September 1997, 34. http://worldmag.com/displayarticle.cfm?id=1180, accessed October 26, 2004.
[3] See Josh McDowell, "If I Had Faked the Resurrection," *Focus on the Family*, April 2000, 2-4. http://www.family.org/fofmag/cl/a0023957.cfm/, accessed October 26, 2004.
[4] For a helpful resource on some of the discrepancies in the Easter stories, see John Wenham, *The Easter Enigma: Are the Resurrection Accounts in Conflict?* (Grand Rapids: Academie/Zondervan, 1984).
[5] Charles Colson, *Loving God* (Grand Rapids: Zondervan, 1983), 61ff.
[6] Eakin, Emily, "So God's Really in the Details?" *New York Times*, 11 May 2002. www.nytimes.com/2002/05/11/arts/11GOD.html
[7] This concept of Christ at the "right hand" of God was an essential and regular element in the apostles' teaching. See Acts 2:33-35; 5:31; 7:55-56; Romans 8:34; Ephesians 1:20; Hebrews 1:3, 13; 8:1; 10:12; 12:2; 1 Peter 3:22; Revelation 3:21. The concept goes back to the teaching of Jesus himself, who claimed that Psalms 110:1 applied to himself: "The Lord says to my Lord: 'Sit at my right hand, till I make your enemies your footstool'" (Mark 12:36).

Chapter 10: The Return of the King

[1] Quoted in a sermon found at http://www.sermoncentral.com/print_friendly.asp?ContributorID=&SermonID=67199/, accessed October 6, 2005.
[2] C.S. Lewis, "The Christian Hope," *Eternity* March 1954.
[3] Quoted in, "To Illustrate," 13, no. 3 (Summer 1992): 47.

Chapter 11: The Hound of Heaven

[1] The Leffler story is from John Kramp, *Out of Their Faces and Into Their Shoes* (Nashville: Broadman and Holman, 1995), 167-68.
[2] Francis Thompson's poem, "The Hound of Heaven," can be read in its entirety at http://eir.library.utoronto.ca/rpo/display/poem2204.html, accessed November 14, 2004.

Chapter 12: You Can Live Strong

[1] http://www.bcheights.com/news/2004/09/28/Features/live-Strong.Campaign.Becomes.Fad-732478.shtml/, accessed November 30, 2004.
[2] Genesis 41:38; Numbers 27:18; Judges 3:10; 6:34; 11:29; 1 Samuel 16:13.
[3] 2 Samuel 23:2; Acts 4:8f., 31; 6:10.

Chapter 13: Great Is the Mystery of Our Faith

[1] The song, "From a Distance," was written by Julie Gold. It's been recorded by Nanci Griffith and Cliff Richard, but most people know the rendition by Bette Midler from *Some People's Lives* Audio CD (New York: Atlantic/WEA, 1990).
[2] C.S. Lewis, *Mere Christianity* (New York: Macmillan, Paperback Edition 1960), 152.
[3] James Weldon Johnson, "The Creation," http://www.nku.edu/-diesmanj/johnson.html#creation/, accessed December 8, 2004.
[4] "Easy-Going Ecumenism," by Chuck Colson at http://www.boundless.org/2001/departments/head_and_heart/a0000504.html/, accessed December 8, 2004.
[5] cf. Deut. 6:4. This declaration is known as the *Shema* because of the first word in the declaration, "Hear"—which in Hebrew is *shema*.
[6] Timothy George, *Is the Father of Jesus the God of Muhammad?* (Grand Rapids: Zondervan, 2002), 55.
[7] quoted in George, *Is the Father of Jesus the God of Muhammad?*, 67.

Chapter 14: Don't Go It Alone

[1] As told by John Drakeford, *People to People Therapy* (New York: Harper and Row, 1978), 5.
[2] Quoted in Cathy Lynn Grossman, "Deciding on the church of your choice," *USA Today*, http://www.usatoday.com/news/religion/2003-06-01-church-usat_x.htm/.
[3] Randy Frazee, *The Connecting Church: Beyond Small Groups to Authentic Community* (Grand Rapids: Zondervan, 2001), 242.

Chapter 15: Lost in Translation

[1] Charles Goldsmith, "Look See! Anyone Do read this and it will make you laughable," *The Wall Street Journal*, 19 November 1992.
[2] "Watch This!" article from *This is True* for 5 August 2001, newsletter via e-mail.
[3] As told by Zacharias in *Can Man Live Without God*, 101-102.

Chapter 16: Life Together

[1] Quoted in Marshall Shelley, "Heart and Soul," *Leadership* 17, no. 3 (Summer 1996): 130.
[2] James Emery White used this analogy in his book *A Search for the Spiritual: Exploring Real Christianity* (Grand Rapids: Baker, 1998).
[3] Mike Royko, *One More Time* (Chicago: University of Chicago Press, 1999).

Chapter 17: Beauty and the Beast

[1] "Oskar Schindler's Sad Decline," *U.S. News and World Report*, March 21, 1994, 63.
[2] "Man on hike to prove people are good is robbed and pushed from bridge," Associated Press, The Baton Rouge *Advocate*, 16 May 1992, A1.
[3] Russell Chandler attributed this to Blaise Pascal in *Understanding The New Age* (Dallas: Word, 1988), 304.
[4] G.K. Chesterton, *Orthodoxy* (Garden City, N.Y.: Image/Doubleday, 1959, repr. ed.), 15.
[5] John R.W. Stott, *Basic Christianity* (Downers Grove, Ill: InterVarsity Press, 1982), 64.
[6] John Ortberg, *The Life You've Always Wanted* (Grand Rapids: Zondervan, 1997), 124-125.
[7] Editorial, "The Evil in Us," *Christianity Today*, http://www.christianitytoday.com/ct/2004/007/2.22.html/, accessed February 2, 2005.

Chapter 18: Why the Cross Matters

[1] In "To Illustrate," *Leadership* (Summer 2001), 81.
[2] Isaiah 53:5, as quoted from the film.
[3] Francis Schaeffer pointed this out in his book, *How Should We Then Live?* (Westchester, Ill.: Crossway, 1976), 98.
[4] U2, "When Love Comes to Town," from *Rattle and Hum* Audio CD (New York: Island, 1998).
[5] John Baddeley, *The Russian Conquest of the Caucasus* (London: Longmans, Green, and Co., 1908).

Chapter 19: God Can

[1] Byan Hodgson, 'Time and Again in Burma,' *National Geographic* (July 1984), 90-121. The nation's name was changed to Myanmar in 1989.
[2] Don Richardson, *Eternity in Their Hearts* (Ventura, CA: Regal Books, 1981), 114ff.
[3] Regina Sara Ryan and John W. Travis, *Wellness Workbook* (Berkeley, Calif.: Ten Speed Press, 1981), 69. Cited in Chandler, *Understanding the New Age*, 254.
[4] Paul Simon, "Graceland," from the LP *Graceland* (New York: Rhino,1986). Lyrics online at http://www.paulsimon.com/index_main.html/, accessed February 23, 2005.
[5] In *Reader's Digest*, February 1984, 152.
[6] G. A. Studdert Kennedy, "It Is Not Finished," in *The Unutterable Beauty: The Collected Poetry of G. A. Studdert Kennedy*, 1927. Online at http://www.mun.ca/rels/restmov/texts/dasc/TUB.HTM#Page92, accessed February 23, 2005.
[7] As found in John R.W. Stott, *The Contemporary Christian: Applying God's Word to Today's World* (Downers Grove, Ill.: InterVarsity Press, 1992), 48.

Chapter 20: Waiting for Reveille

[1] Quoted in Stott, *The Contemporary Christian*, 83.
[2] Elizabeth Kubler-Ross, *On Children and Death* (New York: Collier, 1983), 210-11, quoted in Glynn, *God: The Evidence*, 117-18.

[3] Patrick Glynn explored this research and the inadequacy of merely physical explanations for the phenomenon in pages 99-137 of his book, *God: The Evidence*.

Chapter 21: What Is Heaven Like?

[1] Mark Twain, *The Adventures of Huckleberry Finn*.
[2] Joni Eareckson Tada, *Heaven: Your Real Home* (Grand Rapids: Zondervan, 1995), 40-41.
[3] poem quoted in Tada, *Heaven*, 118.
[4] Randy Alcorn, *Edge of Eternity* (Colorado Springs: WaterBrook Press, 1998), 261-63.

Chapter 22: You Don't Have to Go

[1] John Blanchard, *Whatever Happened to Hell?* (Darlington: Evangelical Press, 1993), 114-15, quoted in *The Nature of Hell: A Report by the Evangelical Alliance Commission on Unity and Truth Among Evangelicals* (2000), 112.
[2] C.S. Lewis, *The Problem of Pain*, quoted in Clyde S. Kilby, *The Christian World of C.S. Lewis* (Grand Rapids: Eerdmans, 1964), 69-70.
[3] In an Ann Landers column dated Jan. 10, 1993 in the St. Louis Post-Dispatch. Quoted in Edward William Fudge and Robert A. Peterson, *Two Views of Hell: A Biblical and Theological Dialogue* (Downers Grove, Ill.: InterVarsity, 2000), 11.

Chapter 23: The Ready Aim- Aim- Aim- Aim Syndrome

[1] Quoted in "Commencement 1988," *Time*, 13 June 1988, 74.
[2] Quoted by James Emery White, *Serious Times: A Life That Matters in an Urgent Day* (Downers Grove, Ill.: InterVarsity, 2004), 111.
[3] Francis Schaeffer, *He Is There And He Is Not Silent* (1972), Book Three in *The Francis A. Schaeffer Trilogy* (Westchester, Illinois: Crossway, 1990), 349-50.
[4] Lee Strobel, *Inside the Mind of Unchurched Harry and Mary* (Grand Rapids: Zondervan, 1993), 143-146.
[5] The stories of Gurkha heroism have been passed around in so many forms that it is difficult to know which ones are true. This story was found in the Spring 1990 edition of *Leadership* journal on page 48.
[6] Fanny Crosby, 1868; first appeared in *Songs of Devotion*, by Howard Doane (New York: 1870).
[7] Words by Charlotte Elliott, 1835.

Chapter 24: Alrightokuhuhamen

[1] January 22, 2003 http://www.mostnewyork.com/front/breaking_news/story/53698p-50336c.html/.
[2] Quoted in Charles Colson, *Against the Night* (Ann Arbor, MI: Servant Books, 1989), 139.
[3] http://www.anecdotage.com/index.php?aid=9236/, accessed April 19, 2005.
[4] Romans 10:9-10 (Msg).
[5] Rich Mullins, "Alrightokuhuhamen," *Never Picture Perfect* Audio CD (Nashville: Reunion, 1989).

Chapter 25: Your Mount Everest

[1] White, *Serious Times*, 12.
[2] Susan Devitt, "Rock Climbing: A First Timer's Story," Southeastern Outdoor Recreation Magazine Online, Monday, May 12, 2003, story found at http://www.sormagazine.com/pages/climbing/suefirstrockclimbing.html/.